Contents

🐎 - Horses OK 🚲 - Bicycles OK 🐕 - Dogs on leash 🚫 - No pets
🌼 - Wildflowers (count petals for peak month) *NW Forest Pass site **Other parking fee
C - Crowded or restricted backpacking area 🥾 - Pacific Crest Trail 🚗 - Rough access road

5

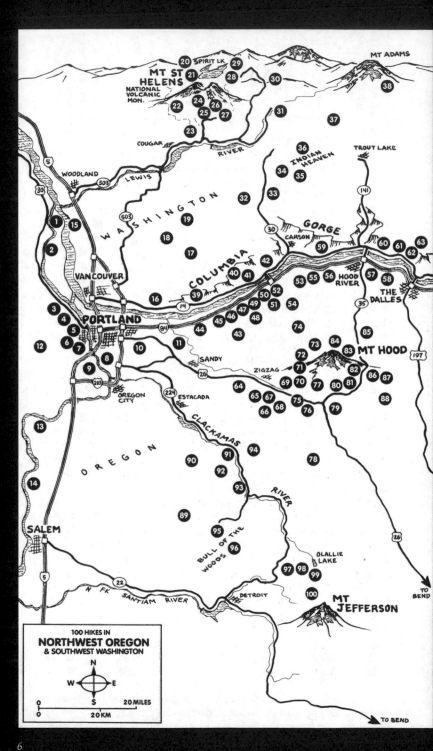

100 HIKES IN
NORTHWEST OREGON
& SOUTHWEST WASHINGTON

0   20 MILES
0   20 KM

🐴 - Horses OK   🚲 - Bicycles OK   🐕 - Dogs on leash   🚫 - No pets
🌸 - Wildflowers (count petals for peak month)   *NW Forest Pass site   **Other parking fee
C - Crowded or restricted backpacking area   (PCT) - Pacific Crest Trail   🚗 - Rough access road

🐴 - Horses OK   🚲 - Bicycles OK   🦮 - Dogs on leash   🐾 - No pets
🌼 - Wildflowers (count petals for peak month)   *NW Forest Pass site   **Other parking fee
C - Crowded or restricted backpacking area   (PCT) - Pacific Crest Trail   🚙 - Rough access road

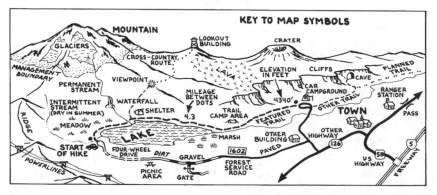

KEY TO MAP SYMBOLS

MOUNTAIN, GLACIERS, LOOKOUT BUILDING, CRATER, CROSS-COUNTRY ROUTE, MANAGEMENT BOUNDARY, VIEWPOINT, LAVA, ELEVATION IN FEET, CLIFFS, CAVE, PLANNED TRAIL, PERMANENT STREAM, INTERMITTENT STREAM (DRY IN SUMMER), WATERFALL, SHELTER, MILEAGE BETWEEN DOTS 4.3, TRAIL CAMP AREA, 4340', CAR CAMPGROUND, OTHER TRAIL, RANGER STATION, TOWN, PASS, RIDGE, MEADOW, LAKE, MARSH, OTHER BUILDING, OTHER HIGHWAY 126, START OF HIKE, FOUR-WHEEL DRIVE, DIRT, GRAVEL, 1602, PAVED, US HIGHWAY 58, FREEWAY 5, POWERLINES, PICNIC AREA, GATE, FOREST SERVICE ROAD, FEATURED TRAIL

Introduction

Where else but in the Portland/Vancouver area could hikers have so many great options within a two-hour drive? This guide covers more than just the well-known trails of Portland, the Columbia Gorge, and Mount Hood. You'll discover a chocolate-colored waterfall at Mt. St. Helens, a Vancouver-area bird refuge with an Indian lodge, and an alpine wildflower meadow at Mount Adams. Forty-seven of the trips are open even in winter.

This book features several difficulty levels. Hikers with children will find 55 hikes carefully chosen for them. On the other hand, a quarter of the hikes included are unabashedly difficult. Thirty-nine of the trails are rated as suitable for backpackers as well as day hikers. At the back of the book you'll find a list of 36 barrier-free trails suitable for strollers and wheelchairs. And if you really want to get away from it all, there's an appendix describing 103 more hikes in Northwest Oregon and Southwest Washington, little-known but interesting trails for adventurous spirits.

HOW TO USE THIS BOOK

It's Easy to Choose a Trip

The featured hikes are divided into six regions, from the Clackamas Foothills to Southwest Washington. To choose a trip, simply turn to the area that interests you and look for the following symbols in the upper right-hand corner of each hike's heading. Whether you're hiking with children, backpacking, or looking for a snow-free winter trail, you'll quickly find an outing to match your tastes.

 Children's favorites — walks popular with the 4- to 12-year-old crowd, but fun for hikers of all ages.

 All-year trails, hikable most or all of winter.

 Hikes suitable for backpackers as well as day hikers. Crowds unlikely.

 Crowded or restricted backpacking areas. Expect competition for campsites, especially on summer weekends.

The Information Blocks

Each hike is rated by difficulty. **Easy** hikes are between 2 and 7 miles round trip and gain less than 1000 feet in elevation. Never very steep nor particularly remote, they make good warm-up trips for experienced hikers or first-time trips for novices.

Trips rated as **Moderate** range from 4 to 11 miles round trip. The longer hikes in this category are not steep, but shorter trails may gain up to 2000 feet of elevation — or they may require some pathfinding skills. Hikers must be in good condition and will need to take several rest stops.

Difficult trails demand top physical condition, with a strong heart and strong knees. These challenging hikes are 8 to 15 miles round trip and may gain 4000 feet or more.

Distances are given in round-trip mileage, except for those trails where a car or bicycle shuttle is so convenient that the suggested hike is one way only, and is listed as such.

Elevation gains tell much about the difficulty of a hike. Those who puff climbing a few flights of stairs may consider even 500 feet of elevation gain a strenuous climb, and should watch this listing carefully. Note that the figures are for each hike's *cumulative* elevation gain, adding all the uphill portions, even those on the return trip.

The **hiking season** of any trail varies with the weather. In a cold year, a trail described as "Open May through October" may not yet be clear of snow by May 1, and may be socked in by a blizzard before October 31. Similarly, a trail that is "Open all year" may close due to storms.

The **allowed use** of some featured trails specifically includes horses and bicycle riders. Note that many of the hikes do not have a *use* listing at all. These are open to *hikers only*. For a quick overview of paths recommended for equestrians and mountain bikers, refer to the table of contents. The additional trails listed at the back of the book also include symbols identifying their allowed use.

Dogs are allowed on 88 of the 100 featured hikes, and leashes are required on 15 trails. Restrictions are noted both in the text and in the table of contents.

TOPOGRAPHIC MAPS

All hikers in wilderness and other remote areas should carry a **topographic map,** with contour lines to show elevation. Topographic maps can be downloaded for free at *www.digital-topo-maps.com* and many other Internet sites. Maps of Wilderness Areas can be purchased at outdoor stores or from Nature of the Northwest at *www.naturenw.org*. In addition, it pays to pick up a Mt. Hood National Forest Visitor Map (for the south side of the Columbia) or a Gifford Pinchot National Forest Map (for the north) at a ranger station.

TRAILHEAD PARKING PERMITS

You'll need a **Northwest Forest Pass** to park within ¼ mile of many trailheads described in this book. This permit costs $5 per car per day or $30 per year and can be purchased at ranger stations, outdoor stores, and some trailheads. The pass is valid in National Forests in the Northwest and also in the Columbia Gorge National Scenic Area and Mount St. Helens National Volcanic Monument.

Permit systems are subject to change, but the featured hikes in this book currently requiring some kind of parking fee are marked with an asterisk in the table of contents. Note that certain state parks, visitor centers, and recreation areas have their own fees, described in the entries for the affected hikes.

WILDERNESS RESTRICTIONS

Certain restrictions apply to designated Wilderness Areas, and affect many of the hikes featured in this guide:

- Groups must be no larger than 12.
- Campfires are banned within 100 feet of water or maintained trails.
- No one may enter areas posted as closed for rehabilitation.
- Bicycles and other wheeled vehicles (except wheelchairs) are banned.
- Horses and pack stock cannot be tethered for more than a short break within 200 feet of any water source or trail.
- Motorized equipment and fireworks are banned.
- Live trees and shrubs must not be cut or damaged.

Mt. St. Helens from the Johnston Ridge Observatory (Hike #21).

In addition, some rules apply to all federal lands:

- Collecting arrowheads or other cultural artifacts is a federal crime.
- Permits are required to dig up plants.

SAFETY ON THE TRAIL

Wild Animals

Part of the fun of hiking is watching for wildlife. Lovers of wildness rue the demise of our most impressive species. Grizzly bears are extinct in Oregon. The little black bears that remain are so profoundly shy you probably won't see one in 1000 miles of hiking. In this portion of the Cascades, the main reason for backpackers to hang their food from a tree at night is to protect it from chipmunks. Likewise, our rattlesnakes are genuinely rare and shy—and they never were as venomous as the Southwest's famous rattlers.

Mosquitoes can be a nuisance on hikes in the High Cascades, particularly in the Olallie Lake and Indian Heaven areas. To avoid these insects, remember that they hatch about ten days after the snow melts from the trails and that they remain in force three or four weeks. Thus, if a given trail in the High Cascades is listed as "Open mid-June," expect mosquitoes there most of July.

Drinking Water

Day hikers should bring all the water they will need—roughly a quart per person. A microscopic parasite, *Giardia,* has forever changed the old custom of dipping a drink from every brook. The symptoms of "beaver fever," debilitating nausea and diarrhea, commence a week or two after ingesting *Giardia*. If you're backpacking, bring an approved water filter or boil water 5 minutes.

Car Clouting

Parked cars at trailheads are sometimes the targets of *car clouters*, thieves who smash windows or jimmy doors. This is particularly a problem at the trailheads for Eagle Creek and Bagby Hot Springs (Hikes #51 and #95). The simplest solution is to leave no valuables in your car when you set out on a trail.

Proper Equipment

Even on the tamest hike a surprise storm or a wrong turn can suddenly make the gear you carry very important. Always bring a pack with the ten essentials: a warm, water-repellent coat, drinking water, extra food, a knife, matches in a waterproof container, a fire starter (butane lighter or candle), a first aid kit, a flashlight, a map (topographic, if possible), and a compass.

Before leaving on a hike, tell someone where you are going so they can alert the county sheriff to begin a search if you do not return on time. If you're lost, stay put and keep warm. The number one killer in the woods is *hypothermia* – being cold and wet too long.

Global Positioning System (GPS) Devices
Some of the hikes in this book include GPS notations, such as *N43°45.554' W122°37.147'*. This optional information may be used to pinpoint your location using a handheld, battery-operated GPS device that tracks satellite signals. Though handy, GPS devices are no substitute for a map and compass, because the devices do not always work in dense forest and because their batteries can fail.

THE PACIFIC CREST TRAIL

The 2650-mile Pacific Crest Trail (PCT) from Mexico to Canada is one of the world's great athletic challenges. To follow it through this book's section of the Cascades, look for PCT symbols beside hikes in the table of contents. Then flip to the specific hike descriptions, where you'll find PCT symbols in the margin highlighting each section of the trail. Although the maps do not always overlap, arrows at the edge of one map indicate the distance to PCT destinations on the next. For an overview of the entire route (without mileages), pick up a *PCT Northern Oregon* map at an outdoor store or online at *www.nationalforeststore.com*.

COURTESY ON THE TRAIL

As trails become more heavily used, rules of etiquette become stricter. Please:

- Pick no flowers.
- Leave no litter. Eggshells and orange peels can last for decades.
- Step off the trail on the downhill side to let horses pass.
- Do not shortcut switchbacks.

For backpackers, "leave-no-trace" camping is essential to protect the landscape and to preserve a sense of solitude for others. The most important rules:

- Camp out of sight of lakes and trails.
- Build no campfire. Cook on a backpacking stove.
- Wash 200 feet from any lake or stream.
- Camp on duff, rock, or sand – never on meadow vegetation.
- Do not move rocks, dig trenches, or build camp furniture.
- Pack out garbage and toilet paper – don't burn or bury it.

GROUPS TO HIKE WITH

If you enjoy the camaraderie of hiking with a group, contact one of the organizations that leads trips to the trails in this book. None of the groups requires that you be a member to join scheduled hikes. Hikers generally carpool from a preset meeting place. If you have no car, expect to chip in a few cents per mile.

Chemeketans. Based in Salem, this group was founded in 1927 and now hosts about three to ten hikes a week. Cabin near Mt. Jefferson. Meetings at 360½ State

St., Salem. Write P.O. Box 864, Salem, OR 97308 or check *www.chemeketans.org*.

Lake Oswego Recreation Department. Thursday hikes carpool from Lake Oswego. Call 503-675-2549.

Mazamas. The state's oldest and largest outdoors group, with about three to ten hikes a week. Cabin at Mt. Hood, office and meetings at the Mazama Mountaineering Center, 527 SE 43rd Avenue (at Stark Street), Portland, OR 97215. Founded 1894. Call 503-227-2345 or check *www.mazamas.org*.

Portland Parks & Recreation. Guided family walks in Portland parks for a $3 fee. Call 503-823-7529.

Sierra Club Columbia Group. Weekly hikes except in winter. Meetings at 1821 SE Ankeny, Portland, OR 97214. Call 503-238-0442.

Trails Club of Oregon. Hikes on Wednesdays, Saturdays, and Sundays. Cabins at Mt. Hood and Columbia Gorge. Founded 1915. Meetings in Milwaukie. Call 503-233-2740 or check *www.trailsclub.org*.

Tryon Creek Daytrippers. Weekly hikes except in winter. Carpool from City of Lake Oswego West End Building, 4101 Kruse Way. Call 503-636-4398.

FOR MORE INFORMATION

This book is updated each spring. If you'd like to check for news about snow levels, trail maintenance, and new construction, call directly to the trails' administrative agencies. The offices are listed below, along with the hikes in this book for which they manage trails. News updates for trails and roads on National Forest land are also available online at *www.fs.fed.us/r6*.

Hike	Managing Agency
86-88	Barlow Ranger District — 541-467-2291
64, 89	BLM Salem District — 503-375-5646
13	Champoeg State Heritage Area — 503-678-1251
39, 42-57, 59-61	Columbia R. Gorge Nat'l. Scenic Area — 541-308-1700
78, 90-100	Clackamas River Ranger District — 503-630-6861
62	Friends of the Columbia Gorge — 541-386-5268
72-74, 79-85	Hood River Ranger District — 541-352-6002
63	Klickitat County Public Works — 509-773-4616
32-38	Mt. Adams Ranger District — 509-395-3400
17-31	Mt. St. Helens Nat'l. Vol. Mon. — 360-449-7800
11	Oxbow Regional Park — 503-663-4708
58	The Nature Conservancy — 503-802-8100
44, 45, 48-50, 56, 57	Oregon State Parks (Col. Gorge) — 800-551-6949
3-8, 10	Portland Parks and Recreation — 503-823-7529
15	Ridgefield Nat'l. Wildlife Refuge — 360-887-4106
1, 2	Sauvie Island Wildlife Area — 503-621-3488
9	Tryon Creek State Park — 800-551-6949
12	Tualatin Hills Parks & Rec. District — 503-629-6313
16, 18	Vancouver-Clark Parks & Rec. — 360-487-8311
17, 42	Wash. Dept. of Natural Resources — 360-902-1000
40, 41	Washington Parks (Beacon Rock) — 509-427-8265
14	Willamette Mission State Park — 800-551-6949
65-72, 75-77	Zigzag Ranger District — 503-622-3191

Portland Area

Campgrounds

	Campsites	Water	Flush toilet	Open (mos.)	Rate range
1 OXBOW REGIONAL PARK. On the Sandy River at the edge of the Portland metro area, this campground in an old-growth forest has showers, a beach, and trails (see Hike #11). Entry fee of $5 per vehicle.	67	●	●	●	$22
2 MILO McIVER STATE PARK. On the Clackamas River, with large wooded sites, a boat ramp, showers, and a visitable fish hatchery. Reservations: 800-452-5687.	54	●	●	III-X	$14-21
3 CHAMPOEG STATE PARK. This historic camp on the Willamette River has a museum and showers (Hike #13). Res: 800-452-5687.	85	●	●	●	$15-24

◁ *McMenamin's Edgefield in Troutdale.*

Cabins, Lookouts & Inns

	Rental units	Private bath	Breakfast	Open (mos.)	Rate range
1 PORTLAND INTERNATIONAL HOSTEL. Near downtown Portland at 425 NW 18th at Glisan. Res: 503-241-2783 (*www.nwportlandhostel.com*).	96	1		●	$20-88
2 HEATHMAN HOTEL. 1927 art deco hotel in downtown Portland at 1001 SW Broadway. Pets OK. Res: 800-551-0011 (*www.heathmanhotel.com*).	150	●		●	$160-325
3 CRYSTAL HOTEL. Historic downtown inn with brewpub, live music, soaking pool at 303 SW 12th. Res: 503-972-2670 (*www.mcmenamins.com*).	51	9		●	$85-165
4 GEORGIAN HOUSE. Stately brick bed & breakfast with a rose garden at 1828 NE Siskiyou. Res: 888-282-2250 (*www.thegeorgianhouse.com*).	4	2	●	●	$113-142
5 THE LION & THE ROSE. Bed & breakfast inn in 1906 mansion near Lloyd Center at 1810 NE 15th Ave. Res: 800-955-1647 (*www.lionrose.com*).	8	●	●	●	$125-225
6 A PAINTED LADY. Comfy bed & breakfast in an 1894 Victorian house at 1927 NE 16th Ave. Res: 503-335-0070 (*www.apaintedladyinn.com*).	5	2	●	●	$109-179
7 PORTLAND'S WHITE HOUSE. Bed & breakfast uses replica White House at 1914 NE 22nd Ave. Res: 800-272-7131 (*www.portlandswhitehouse.com*).	8	●	●	●	$125-235
8 McMENAMIN'S KENNEDY SCHOOL. This Northeast Portland elementary school from 1915 has been converted to a pub, theater, and hotel at 5736 NE 33rd Ave., Portland. Res: 888-249-3983 (*www.mcmenamins.com*).	35	●		●	$115-145
9 72nd AVENUE STUDIOS. Affordable rooms near Portland airport at 3415 NE 72nd Ave. Res: 503-288-8501 (*www.72ndavenuestudios.com*).	2	●		●	$70-75
10 HOSTELLING INTERNATIONAL - HAWTHORNE. In SE Portland at 3031 SE Hawthorne Blvd. Res: 866-447-3031 (*www.portlandhostel.org*).	34			●	$20-58
11 McMENAMIN'S EDGEFIELD. 1911 poor farm converted to hotel with artworks, 5 pubs, theater, winery, and a golf course at 2126 SW Halsey St., Troutdale. Reservations: 800-669-8610 (*www.mcmenamins.com*).	114	90		●	$30-175
12 CHAMPOEG STATE PARK. Historic campground (Hike #13) has 6 yurts and 6 rustic cabins. Res: 800-452-5687 (*www.oregonstateparks.org*).	12			●	$36-39

Above right: Portlandia statue downtown.

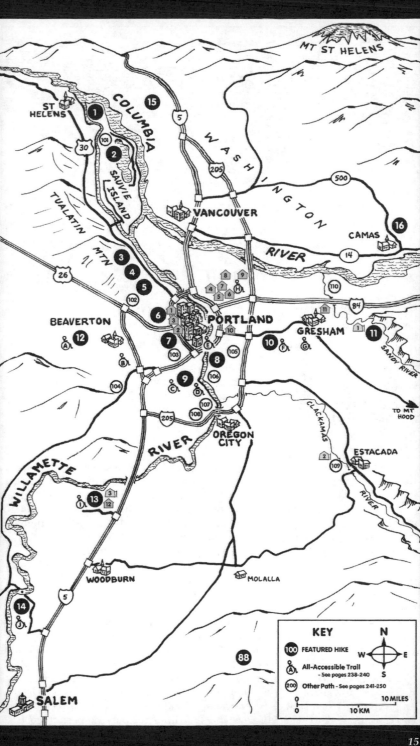

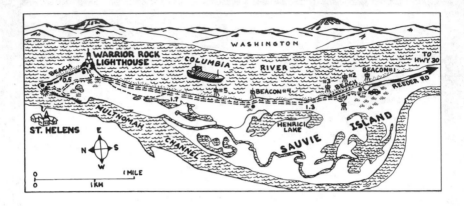

1   Warrior Rock

Moderate
7 miles round trip
No elevation gain
Open except during floods

At the tip of Oregon's largest island, this woodsy hike along the Columbia River leads to a miniature lighthouse and a secluded, sandy beach. Because the route is within the Sauvie Island Wildlife Area, you can expect to spot great blue herons, geese, or even a bald eagle—particularly in winter. It's also fun to watch ocean-going freighters steam past, and at the end of the island there's a view across to the picturesque old town of St. Helens. High water sometimes closes the trail here in May—and can hatch mosquitoes in June.

Sauvie Island was once the winter home of the Multnomah Indians, who subsisted mainly on fish and on the potato-like roots of the water-loving wapato (arrowhead plant)—a staple they shared with Lewis and Clark in 1805. In the 1830s a French-Canadian named Laurent Sauve converted much of the island to a dairy farm to supply Fort Vancouver. The southern end of the island was diked against floods in 1941 and now produces an enormous variety of vegetable and berry crops. The northern half of Sauvie Island is managed for wildlife and recreation. Overnight camping and unleashed dogs are prohibited.

To reach the starting point of the hike, drive north of downtown Portland on Highway 30 toward St. Helens. After 11 miles, turn right across the Sauvie Island Bridge and then head left on Sauvie Island Road to the Cracker Barrel Grocery. You can stop here to get a Sauvie Island Wildlife Area parking permit (cost: $7 a day or $22 a year). Permits are also available at stores that sell hunting and fishing licenses, or online at *www.dfw.state.or.us*. Equipped with a permit, drive 1.8 miles past the store on Sauvie Island Road, turn right onto Reeder Road, and follow this road for 12.8 miles to its end at a turnaround with a parking area and an outhouse. The final 2.2 miles of Reeder Road are gravel.

Walk through a fence opening at the far right end of the parking area to the beach and walk left. Sharp eyes will already be able to spot the lighthouse 3 miles ahead. Walk along the beach for half a mile or so, watching sailboats and ducks on the river. Note the stick nests of osprey atop beacon towers. When the sand narrows near the third beacon, climb up to the left and continue on an old road that parallels the beach.

It's a good idea to wear boots because this road can be muddy after winter floods and for about a month after the Columbia River's usual high water from mountain snowmelt in May. Tall cottonwood trees and August-ripening wild blackberries line the route. Farther on, the forest shifts to ash trees with licorice ferns sprouting from the mossy branches.

After 2.8 miles the road fades in a meadow and forks. Keep right to find the road leading 0.2 mile through the woods to the lighthouse's small rocky headland. A white-sand beach beside the little lighthouse makes an ideal lunch spot. To find the hidden viewpoint of the town of St. Helens, hike to the end of the beach and follow an overgrown trail 200 yards across the tip of Sauvie Island.

Other Options

Hikers who wish to return on a slightly different route can follow a branch of the dirt road back from the viewpoint. Unmarked side trails veer off to the right. Off limits in winter, these cow paths lead to lakes replete with geese, ducks, and many other birds — but beware of stinging nettles along the way.

Columbia River beach on Sauvie Island.   Opposite: The Warrior Rock lighthouse.

2   Oak Island on Sauvie Island

Easy
2.9-mile loop
No elevation gain
Open April 16 to September 30

This walk explores an island on an island: an unusually wildlife-rich oak grassland in the middle of Sauvie Island's Sturgeon Lake. Over 250 species of birds visit this portion of the Sauvie Island Wildlife Area, including huge flocks of geese, ducks, and sandhill cranes during the spring and fall migrations. At any time of year it's pleasant to stroll beneath the huge, gnarled white oaks and look across the lake to the pale outlines of Mt. St. Helens and Mt. Adams.

From downtown Portland take Highway 30 toward the town of St. Helens, but after 10 miles turn right across the Sauvie Island Bridge. Head north along Sauvie Island Road past a small grocery store. If you don't have a Sauvie Island Wildlife Area parking permit, stop at the store to get one. Permits are $7 a day or $22 a year; they're also available at stores that sell hunting and fishing licenses. Continue driving 1.8 miles past the store on Sauvie Island Road, turn right onto Reeder Road for 1.2 miles, and turn left onto Oak Island Road. After 3.1 miles the road turns to gravel. In another 0.7 mile, after crossing a dike, go straight at a 4-way junction for 0.4 mile to a parking area where the road is closed by a yellow gate. Overnight camping and unleashed dogs are prohibited.

Walk past the gate 50 feet to a crossing and go straight, following an abandoned road through oak woods. Wild roses bloom here in early summer. Expect inedible white snowberries and yummy ripe blackberries in summer. Look for squirrels and listen for pheasants' squawks. After 0.3 mile the road-like path forks at a broad meadow with a view of the Tualatin Mountains. Go straight across the field.

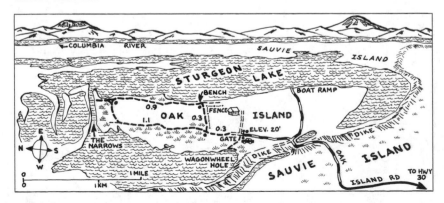

Oak Island and Sturgeon Lake.   Opposite: Edible wild blackberries.

In another 1.1 miles the trail forks again at the beachless, somewhat brushy edge of Sturgeon Lake, with Mt. St. Helens seemingly just across the water. The left-hand fork (blocked by high water in rainy months) leads 200 yards to The Narrows, a neck of Sturgeon Lake edged with picnickably grassy banks. Expect to spot a stilt-legged great blue heron patrolling these shores for frogs and fish.

To continue the loop hike, return to the junction and take the path paralleling the lakeshore. After 0.9 mile watch for a faint fork in a small, grassy opening. Turn right here and head uphill past a bench, a memorial plaque, and a fenceline for 0.3 mile to return to the path leading to your car.

Other Options

Children will enjoy spotting wildlife on Oak Island, but they might be disappointed by the shortage of good places to get right down by the lake. If so, point them to the little gate at the parking area; a trail here leads 300 yards to Wagonwheel Hole and an accessible, grassy lakeshore ideal for exploring.

Northern Forest Park

Easy (Newberry to BPA Rd)
5.7-mile loop
450 feet elevation gain
Open all year

Moderate (Germantown to Fire Lane 7a)
8.3-mile loop
400 feet elevation gain

Forest Park is Portland's wilderness secret, where the 30.2-mile Wildwood Trail contours through 5000 acres of soothing woodlands along a scenic ridge above the Willamette River. When development threatened a 73-acre private inholding in the park's northern corner in 1999, a "Fix the Hole" campaign rallied donors to buy the property for the city. Today the Wildwood Trail extends through this addition, a place so tranquil that the noisiest characters are squirrels scolding you from trees as you hike by.

The first loop recommended here follows the Wildwood Trail south from Newberry Road to a "Fix the Hole" monument. A second option explores the Wildwood Trail south from Germantown Road, returning on a loop along Leif Erikson Drive, an old road closed to motor vehicles.

From the Interstate 405 freeway at the west end of the Fremont Bridge, turn north onto Highway 30 toward St. Helens for 10 miles. Opposite milepost 10, turn left on NW Newberry Road for 1.5 miles. (If you reach Skyline Road, you've gone 0.5 mile too far). Near mailbox 14207, look closely for a "Hikers Only" symbol sign on a tree to the left. Park on the narrow gravel shoulder near the sign. If there's no room here, drive back 0.3 mile to the Leif Erickson trailhead to park.

From Newberry Road the Wildwood Trail switchbacks down into mossy bigleaf maple woods with big sword ferns and delicate maidenhair ferns. Douglas

The Wildwood Trail in northern Forest Park.   *Above: Milepost marker near trailhead.*

firs along the trail have grown to three feet in diameter; larger blackened snags tell of an old fire. April in these woods brings yellow violets and white, three-petaled trilliums. May adds stalks of fringecups and paired, white fairy bells. Pink salmonberries, red thimbleberries, and blue Oregon grape ripen as the summer progresses. The dense woods block far-ranging views.

After 2.7 miles the Wildwood Trail appears to end at the gravel BPA Road. The trail actually jogs left 100 feet before continuing, but for the easy loop hike, simply follow the road downhill to the left 0.3 mile to the "Fix the Hole" plaques at a junction in a powerline clearing. Turn left here, following grassy Firelane 12 down into the woods. This track descends steeply for half a mile to a canyon bottom. Then turn sharply left on Firelane 15 to climb 0.4 mile back up to the Wildwood Trail and the route to your car.

If you'd like more loop options, try the trail network near Germantown Road instead. To find this trailhead, take Highway 30 from downtown Portland toward St. Helens for 7.4 miles. After driving underneath the St. Johns Bridge turn left at a stoplight, following a pointer for NW Germantown Road. After another 0.2 mile, turn sharply right up this road for 1.6 miles to a gravel parking lot on the left.

This section of the Wildwood Trail likewise lacks wide-ranging views, but then you won't see any buildings or automobiles either. The only clues that you're in a metropolis are occasional clangs and toots from the river docks far below.

Your return route is Leif Erikson Drive, a woodsy old road closed to motor vehicles. Because it runs parallel to the Wildwood Trail but about a quarter mile downhill, you can cut over to it on a number of different cross-trails to make the loop hike as short or long as you wish. Your first option comes after just 0.6 mile, when you cross the Water Line Trail. Turning left here makes a 2.3-mile loop. If you continue on the Wildwood Trail to Springville Road, you can turn left to make a 4.6-mile loop. If you go as far as the Hardesty Trail you can make a 5.6-mile loop. For the full 8.3-mile loop, however, wait to turn off the Wildwood Trail until you reach the Fire Lane 7a (Gas Line Road), a marked trail on a ridge. Follow this grassy roadbed 200 yards downhill. Just before it gets steep, look for a small path to the left that switchbacks through the woods to Leif Erikson Drive. Then head left on this rustic forest lane 2.4 miles and walk up Germantown Road 0.3 mile to your car.

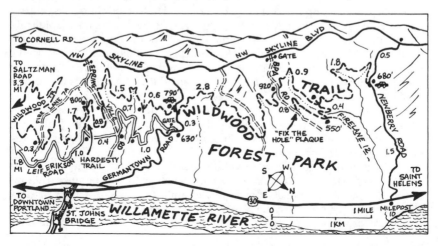

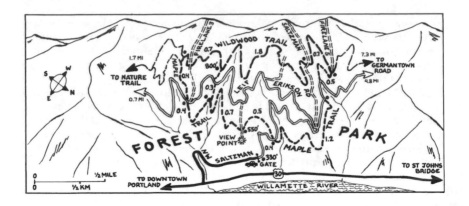

4   Maple Trail

Easy (to Leif Erikson)
4 miles round trip
350 feet elevation gain
Open all year

Moderate (to Wildwood Trail)
7.7-mile loop
600 feet elevation gain

In the middle of Portland's vast Forest Park, the surprisingly quiet Maple Trail passes a viewpoint of Cascade peaks and explores grotto-like canyons where mossy bigleaf maples arch above delicate woodland wildflowers. For an easy hike, turn back where the Maple Trail crosses Leif Erikson Drive. For a longer loop hike, continue up to the Wildwood Trail and follow this almost level path as it contours around densely forested ridges back to the start of the Maple Trail.

From the Interstate 405 freeway at the west end of the Fremont Bridge, turn north onto Highway 30 toward St. Helens. After 2.7 miles you'll pass a traffic light for Kittridge Avenue. Continue straight another 0.9 mile. Then turn left at a small, easily overlooked sign for "NW Saltzman Rd." Follow this tiny paved road 0.7 mile through an industrial area and up steeply through the woods to a gate closing the road. Parking space is tight, but don't block the gate.

Start the hike by walking 0.4 mile up the road to a small "Maple Trail" sign on the left. Turn left onto this path, climbing through a forest of bigleaf maples, sword ferns, and western hemlock.

Two kinds of triple-leaved, white wildflowers thrive here: trilliums and vanilla leaf. It's easy to tell the difference in spring when they bloom, because trilliums have a dramatic, three-petaled flower while vanilla leaf puts up a modest, fuzzy stalk. By summer, however, the plants are best distinguished by their three big leaves: teardrop-shaped for trilliums but butterfly-wing-shaped for vanilla leaf.

Ferns and alders along the Maple Trail.   Opposite: Trail sign.

Forest Park's ban on flower picking is particularly important for trilliums, as they require seven years to bloom again once cut.

After half a mile, the trail crosses under powerlines on an open ridgetop. At this point, sidetrack left 150 yards to a somewhat overgrown viewpoint on the powerline's service road. The view, through powerlines, extends across the Willamette River to the Columbia River, Mt. Adams, and Mt. St. Helens.

Returning to the Maple Trail, the path now zigs and zags into mossy canyons with footbridges over little creeks. After 1.1 mile, reach Leif Erikson Drive—an old road closed to motor vehicles. Turn back here if you're tired. If you're interested in a longer loop, however, cross Leif Erikson and continue up the Maple Trail, avoiding the road marked "Firelane 3." After 0.4 mile turn right at a junction, and 150 yards later turn right again onto the Wildwood Trail. Follow this nearly level trail a total of 3.2 miles, crossing a couple of abandoned roads, several small creeks, and a few sets of powerlines. Mile markers on trailside trees measure the distance from the start of the Wildwood Trail in Washington Park. A quarter mile before reaching the "17" marker, you'll come to a ridge end with a crossing of Firelane 5.

Turn downhill to the right on Firelane 5 for 0.3 mile to Leif Erikson Drive. Head right on Leif Erikson for 300 yards. At the road's first curve, cross a grassy flat on the left to a sign marking the Maple Trail. Follow the Maple Trail 1.2 miles back to Saltzman Road and turn left for 0.4 mile to your car.

Other Options

The Wildwood Trail continues in either direction from the Maple Trail, so you can hike one way to a different trailhead by arranging a shuttle. The hike north to the trailhead at Germantown Road is 10 miles (see Hike #3), while it's 8.9 miles south to Thurman Street (see Hike #5) and 15.9 miles south to the Vietnam Memorial by the zoo (see Hike #6).

23

Stone ruin of 1930s rest station.   Below: Balch Creek.

5   Balch Creek

Easy (Balch Creek)
3-mile loop
400 feet elevation gain
Open all year

Moderate (to Nature Trail)
8.8-mile loop
700 feet elevation gain
Use: hikers, bicycles

This convenient portion of Portland's 5000-acre wilderness park is just a few minutes from skyscrapers, but a world apart. The hiking loops suggested here visit the park's two year-round creeks. The first hike is a short circuit of Balch Creek's beautiful canyon. The second, longer trek follows the Wildwood Trail to Rockingchair Creek. If you're bicycling, you'll have to stick to Leif Erikson Drive and Firelane 1, the only routes open to bikes in this area. Dogs must be on leash.

Forest Park was originally proposed by the Olmsteads, a visionary New York landscape architect team hired to help Portland prepare for the Lewis and Clark Exposition of 1905. But most Portlanders of that day had seen more than their fill of forests. The city opened a woodcutting camp in the area to help the unemployed, and developers built the 11-mile Leif Erikson Drive in 1915 as part of a plan to subdivide and conquer the wilds. Fires, landslides, and the Depression finally defeated the developers' schemes. In 1946 the Mazamas outdoor club began planting trees and building trails in a campaign to revive the Olmsteads' plan. Forest Park was dedicated in 1948—not merely as another manicured garden, but as a refreshing swath of wilderness in the city.

To find the Balch Creek trailhead from downtown Portland, take the Everett Street exit of Interstate 405, go straight to either Glisan or Burnside, turn west to the first stoplight, turn right on 18th for half a mile, and turn left on Lovejoy. This street curves right after 0.7 mile, becomes Cornell Road, and then ducks through two tunnels. Half a mile beyond the second tunnel, pull into the Upper Macleay parking lot on the right. Donald Macleay donated the parkland here in 1897 after he complained about paying property tax and a cagey tax assessor suggested a philanthropic alternative.

Step over the parking area's log bumpers and walk left on the Wildwood Trail.

This wide path descends 0.2 mile to a bridge over Balch Creek. Danford Balch was a father of nine who homesteaded along the stream in 1850. In 1859 Balch became the first Oregonian hanged for murder after he shot the man who ran off with his 15-year-old daughter. Below this park the creek has been buried in a culvert for a century, so biologists in 1987 were astonished to discover that native cutthroat trout still survive up here. The city's largest Douglas fir trees are here too.

Follow the splashing, mossy creek downstream 0.3 mile to the scenic stone ruin of an elaborate restroom built by the Civilian Conservation Corps in the 1930s. It's been derelict since a 1962 windstorm. For the loop, fork left at the ruin, continuing on the Wildwood Trail. After another half mile you'll reach a junction by a small meadow, the former site of a dairy and then a Girl Scout day camp. Turn right on Holman Lane to a gate marking the start of city streets. At this point you have to follow quiet sidewalks for 0.6 mile. Zigzag downhill, turning left on Aspen, right on Franklin, left on 32nd across Thurman Street, and right on Vaughn to its end. Then continue on a footpath to the right under the Thurman Street bridge and follow a paved path up Balch Creek on the route back to your car.

For the other hike it's better to park at a different trailhead. To find it from downtown, turn off I-405 at the west end of the Fremont Bridge (following Highway 30 toward St. Helens) and immediately take the Vaughn Street exit. Next turn left on 25th Avenue for two blocks, and then turn right on Thurman Street for 1.1 miles. At a switchback to the left, go straight 100 yards to a small parking area and a gate blocking the start of Leif Erikson Drive. Originally called Hillside Drive, this forest lane was renamed by petition of the Sons of Norway in 1933. Now it's a paved hiker/biker path.

Walk along Leif Erikson 0.3 mile, turn uphill to the left on the Wild Cherry Trail for 0.6 mile, and turn right on the Wildwood Trail. Then simply follow the Wildwood Trail as far as you like. When you start to wear down, turn right on a side trail and return on a loop via Leif Erikson. To see Rockingchair Creek, follow the Wildwood Trail 3.4 miles, turn right on Firelane 1 for 150 yards and then fork left onto the Nature Trail. After half a mile, the Nature Trail turns right at a trail junction and descends along the creek. At trail's end turn right onto Leif Erikson Drive—a 3.4-mile promenade with occasional views across the Willamette River to the shipyards, the University of Portland campus, Mt. St. Helens, Mt. Adams, and Mt. Hood.

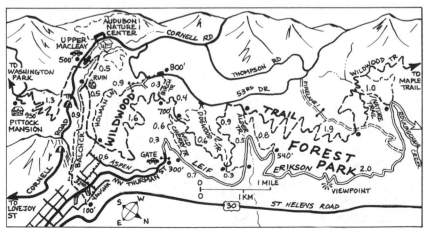

Washington Park

Easy (to Hoyt Arboretum)
3.6-mile loop
500 feet elevation gain
Open all year

Moderate (to Pittock Mansion)
6-mile loop
800 feet elevation gain

The walk through Washington Park is a reminder of what's so wonderful about Portland. What other city would have a forest path leading from a world-class zoo, past a Japanese garden, to a mansion with a mountain view?

This first portion of the famous, 30.2-mile Wildwood Trail begins beside the Vietnam Veteran Memorial. To get there, take the MAX light-rail train to the underground Washington Park station and ride the elevator up. If you're driving, head west from Portland on Highway 26 toward Beaverton, take the zoo exit, and park at the far end of the zoo's huge parking lot beside the MAX station, opposite the World Forestry Center. Expect to pay $4 to $6.40 for parking. Dogs must be on leash.

Walk up the road from the MAX station 100 yards to a sign marking the start of the Wildwood Trail on the left. But along the way you'll pass the steps for the entrance to the Vietnam Veteran Memorial—and it's actually more dramatic to start your hike here, going under the memorial's bridge and following its spiral path up to the Wildwood Trail. From there on, expect trail junctions every few hundred yards. Just keep an eye out for the Wildwood Trail signs. Within 0.4 mile you'll cross a paved road and pass a huge green water tank to a viewpoint of Mt. St. Helens and Mt. Rainier. Even if the weather hides these distant peaks, you'll still be able to spot a potential goal of your hike: the Pittock Mansion, atop a forested ridge.

After 1.7 miles on the Wildwood Trail you'll get a glimpse down through the

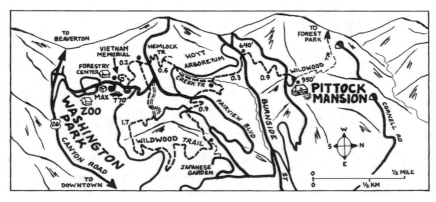

The Wildwood Trail in the Hoyt Arboretum.   Opposite: The Pittock Mansion.

forest to the Oriental bridges and manicured greenery of the Japanese Garden. Shortly afterward, a side trail switchbacks down to the right. If you have time, it's tempting to detour here to visit this acclaimed, 6.5-acre garden, complete with Japanese pavilion and a Portland panorama. Otherwise continue on the Wildwood Trail, which now climbs, crossing several paved roads and a ridgecrest before descending into the Hoyt Arboretum.

Arboretum means "tree museum," and in fact this entire valley is filled with native and exotic trees. You'll switchback down through ponderosa pines reminiscent of Central Oregon and then traverse an impressive grove of coastal redwoods and giant sequoias. Finally you'll reach a footbridge over a creek. If you're tired or if you're hiking with children, turn left onto the Creek Trail here to complete the shorter, 3.6-mile loop. In this case, follow the Creek Trail across a paved road, turn left onto the Hemlock Trail, and take that path over the ridge (crossing Fairview Boulevard) back to the Vietnam Veteran Memorial.

If, however, you've got enough energy for a 6-mile hike, continue on the Wildwood Trail through the Hoyt Arboretum. Soon the path crosses Burnside Street—a busy, fairly frightening highway you'll have to cross at a run. Then the trail climbs 0.9 mile through a Douglas fir forest, crosses a paved road, and reaches the Pittock Mansion parking lot. Walk through the portico on the left side of the mansion to the spacious front lawn where there's a magnificent view of downtown Portland and the mountains.

The 16,000-square-foot palace was built in 1909-14 by banker, real estate magnate, and *Oregonian* editor Henry L. Pittock. For its day, the mansion was astonishingly modern, with an elevator, intercom, and central vacuum cleaning. Tours are available in summer between 10am and 5pm (adults $9.50, children $6.50).

To complete your hike, return on the Wildwood Trail to the Hoyt Arboretum footbridge, turn right onto the Creek Trail until it hits the Hemlock Trail, and then follow this path left, over the ridge to the Vietnam Veteran Memorial.

Aerial Tram & Council Crest

Easy (to Marquam shelter)
1.8-mile loop
450 feet elevation gain
Open all year (except when tram is closed)

Easy (to Council Crest)
4.2-mile loop
480 feet elevation gain

Include a ride on the Portland Aerial Tram as part of a loop hike into Portland's wooded hills. You ride the tram for free if you take the longer "Four Ts" loop—named because it uses a trail, a tram, a trolley (the Portland Streetcar), and a train (the MAX light rail). The tram runs 9am to 5pm on Saturdays and 5:30am to 9:30pm on weekdays. Don't plan this trip when the tram is closed on holidays! Sundays from June to September the tram runs only from 1-5pm.

For a quick, kid-friendly hike, take a 1.8-mile loop through Marquam Nature Park. To start this stroll, it's easiest to take the Portland Streetcar from 11th Avenue downtown and simply ride south to the tram station. If you're driving, take Corbett Street exit 298 of Interstate 5 and turn left on Macadam Avenue half a dozen blocks—but be forewarned that parking is spendy and scarce near the tram station. Pets are not allowed on the tram, and must be on leash elsewhere.

Bring a credit card to buy a $4 tram ticket at a machine. The two 78-passenger, Swiss-made gondolas depart every 5 minutes and complete the 3-minute trip at 22 miles per hour, jiggling stomachs as they pass the central support tower. Views en route extend from the skyscrapers of downtown to Mt. Hood.

At the top station, walk straight ahead through the hospital, go out a door, and continue straight along what becomes Gibbs Street. Pass under two pedestrian bridges and turn right on 9th Avenue for a block to a sign for the Connor Trail. This path switchbacks down through the woods half a mile to a larger trail. Here you can detour 200 yards to the right to see the Marquam shelter's historic photos, or simply continue the loop by turning left. After another 0.2 mile, turn left again to follow a switchbacking trail 0.2 mile up to Gibbs Street. Turn left and follow

Portland's Aerial Tram.   Above: Council Crest's viewpoint patio.

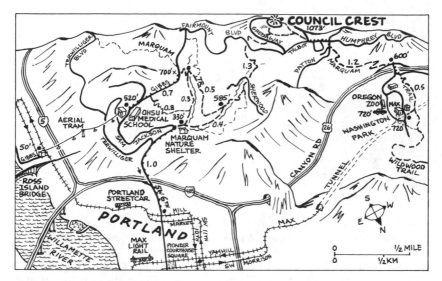

Gibbs 7 blocks downhill back to the tram station to complete the loop.

If you have time for a longer hike, start instead at the Oregon Zoo, hike to Portland's highest point (1073-foot Council Crest), ride the tram downhill (for free!), and return to your starting point via the Portland Streetcar and the MAX light rail.

Begin this tour at the Washington Park MAX station next to the Oregon Zoo. If you're driving, take Highway 26 from downtown Portland toward Beaverton, pull off at the zoo exit, and park by the MAX station's elevator building, between the zoo entrance and the World Forestry Center. Expect to pay $4 to $6.40.

Walk across the street from the MAX station to the World Forestry Building and take the sidewalk uphill. Just before the official paved entrance to the Vietnam Veterans Memorial, turn left on an unmarked gravel path into the woods. Behind the World Forestry Building this path joins the Marquam Trail. Turn left, following the Marquam Trail down behind the Children's Museum to a paved street. Jog briefly left, cross Highway 26 on a freeway bridge, and walk left 150 feet along an on-ramp to the poorly marked continuation of the Marquam Trail, a path angling up into the woods to the right.

The forest here is a mix of cedars, bigleaf maples, and vine maples, with an understory of frilly lady ferns, stern sword ferns, and delicate fringecup. Big white trilliums bloom best around April Fools Day, but that's also a season when you can expect a few patches of mud, so boots are better than sneakers.

When the path ends at Patton Road, turn right on the sidewalk 200 feet and then turn left on Talbot Road for two blocks to find a wide paved path up to Council Crest's summit patio, with views from Mt. Rainier to Mt. Jefferson. From there, head east toward Mt. Hood to find the Marquam Trail into the woods. Follow signs downhill 1.7 miles to the Marquam Shelter, go up a wide gravel trail to the right 200 feet and turn left on the smaller Connor Trail up to Gibbs Street near the hospital. Turn left on this street, continue under two pedestrian overpasses, and go straight up a covered stairway into the hospital to find the upper tram station. The ride down is free, but then you'll need to buy a ticket to take the Portland Streetcar to Morrison Street, where you can catch a MAX train back to the zoo at Washington Park.

8   Oaks Bottom

Easy
2.8-mile loop
100 feet elevation gain
Open all year
Use: hikers, bicycles

In the midst of the city but shielded by a 100-foot cliff, the animals in this riverside wildlife refuge don't seem to realize they're in a metropolis. As you hike the trail around these wetlands you're almost certain to see ducks, beaver-gnawed trees, and great blue herons calmly fishing for frogs. But wildlife watching isn't the only reason this trip is a hit with families. At the far end of the loop you can visit Oaks Park, an old-timey carnival midway complete with kiddy rides and refreshment stands.

To find the trailhead, drive south from the Ross Island Bridge on McLoughlin Boulevard (US Highway 99E). After 1 mile take the Milwaukie Avenue exit and immediately pull into a paved parking area on the right, at a sign for the Oaks Bottom Wildlife Refuge. You can get here easily by bus, too, since the #19 Woodstock/Glisan bus stops by the trailhead.

The broad, paved trail starts beside a sign reminding visitors that camping, fishing, hunting, and motorized vehicles are banned in the wildlife refuge and that dogs must be leashed. After 0.3 mile the trail forks. Veer left on a smaller path (closed to bicycles) through shady bigleaf maples. Keep left, and soon cross a footbridge with your first view across the refuge's extensive swamplands. Waterfowl thrive in this Everglades-like sea of reeds and willows.

After another half mile pass beneath the seven-story fortress of the Portland Memorial Funeral Home and reach a couple of small gravelly beaches — the trail's only access to the refuge's large central lake. Look here for freshly-gnawed beaver wood in the swampy forest ringing the shore.

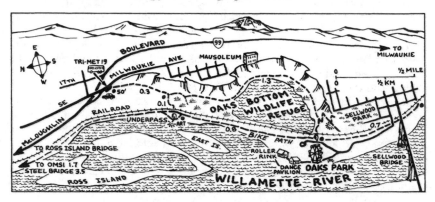

Downtown Portland from Oaks Park picnic area.   Opposite: Antique sign on building.

At the end of the lake keep right to an underpass beneath a set of railroad tracks by the main entrance of Oaks Park. This entire railroad track was moved a few feet east in 1999 to make room for a bike path that extends 5 miles along the Willamette River's bank, from the Sellwood Bridge through Oaks Bottom and OMSI to the Steel Bridge. If you like, you can go straight across the bike path to tour the amusement park before completing the loop hike.

Oaks Park opened in 1905 just two days before tourists descended on Portland for the city's grand Lewis and Clark Exposition. The following year Portland had a second amusement park at Council Crest (see Hike #7), also located at the end of a trolley line to entice excursionists. The Great Depression and the decline of trolleys killed the Council Crest carnival and nearly bankrupted Oaks Park. In 1985 the owner donated the park to a non-profit group dedicated to restoring the amusement park to its former splendor. Today admission is free and tickets to the 28 rides are inexpensive. From mid-June to early October the park is open Tuesday through Sunday, noon to 10pm. From spring vacation to June it's only open weekends.

When you continue on the loop, take the paved bike path alongside the railroad toward downtown Portland. You'll gain some nice views across the Willamette River to East Island and Ross Island. Stick nests in the tall cottonwood trees of these islands are home to the great blue heron, Portland's symbol. The railroad embankment itself has Scotch broom that blooms yellow in spring and black-berries that ripen in late summer. After a mile, you'll reach another underpass beneath the railroad. Detour briefly left here to see an installation of riverbank artwork, sliced stones layered with glass. Then duck through the underpass and keep left to return to the parking area.

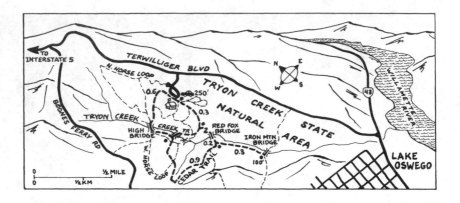

9   Tryon Creek Natural Area

Easy
2-mile loop
200 feet elevation gain
Open all year
Use: hikers, horses, bicycles

Quiet paths and scenic footbridges highlight this densely forested canyon, a pocket wilderness tucked between Portland and Lake Oswego. The woods here are particularly beckoning in spring when the trilliums bloom, but any season is fine for a morning stroll or an afternoon outing with the kids.

Take Terwilliger exit 297 of Interstate 5 and drive south on Terwilliger Boulevard through numerous twists and intersections, following "Tryon Creek State Park" signs. After 2.2 miles, turn right onto the entrance road and park at the end of the loop. Dogs are allowed only on 6-foot or shorter leashes.

Start with a visit to Nature Center, an interpretive center with exhibits and a staff naturalist to help identify plants and explain forest ecology. Pick up a map brochure here, too. The trail route described below is open only to hikers, but the park brochure describes similar loops designed for horses and bicycles.

Now walk back out the front door of the Nature Center and turn right at the signboard. In 100 feet the paved Trillium Trail veers off to the left. Detour briefly to visit this pair of short, barrier-free nature loops if you like, or else simply continue straight, following the Old Main Trail and then the Red Fox Trail 0.3 mile to Red Fox Bridge. Along the way, look for big white trilliums, yellow wood violets, stalks of white fringecups, and stands of stinging nettles. Also notice the little licorice ferns sprouting from the mossy branches of bigleaf maple trees.

After crossing the Red Fox Bridge it's worth detouring 0.3 mile downstream along the South Creek Trail to the Iron Mountain Bridge, just to see Tryon Creek grow wider and lazier in this lower end of the park. Then return to a trail junction near the Red Fox Bridge and turn left.

If the weather's dry enough that the paths aren't slick, follow the Cedar Trail on a tour of a side canyon. The forest floor here is carpeted with waterleaf — a wildflower with large, dramatically lobed leaves. After 0.7 mile the Cedar Trail twice crosses a confusing horse trail, but simply head for Tryon Creek and follow it upstream to reach High Bridge. (In wet weather this portion of the Cedar Trail is so slippery it's safer to shortcut on the Middle Creek Trail from Red Fox Bridge to High Bridge.) Then cross High Bridge, turn right, and follow "Nature Center" pointers back to your car.

A non-profit group, the Friends of Tryon Creek State Park, sponsors a number of activities at the park, including school class tours, a "Sunday at Two" lecture series, a photography club, a library of nature-oriented books, and organized hikes in the Portland area. In addition, the Trillium Festival on the first weekend in April brings wildflower exhibits, house plant sales, and a photo contest to the park. Call 503-636-4398 for more information about these programs or about the Friends of Tryon Creek.

Volunteer naturalist at Tryon Creek.   Opposite: Trillium Festival poster.

10   Powell Butte

Easy
3.5-mile loop
400 feet elevation gain
Open all year
Use: hikers, horses, bicycles

Perfect for a spring picnic or a quick winter walk, this convenient loop explores Powell Butte's broad summit meadow — with views across East Portland to three snowpeaks — and then winds through a quiet woodland glen. The route described here is for hikers only, but maps at the trailhead describe alternate, similar tours for mountain bikers and equestrians.

Powell Butte is a volcanic cone less than 10 million years old. The butte earned its name when three pioneers by the name of J. Powell, all of them unrelated, took up homesteads near its base in 1852-53. The orchard of walnut, apple, and pear trees on the butte's top was planted in the late 1800s. Today the delightfully wild 608-acre Powell Butte Nature Park coexists peacefully with a 50-million-gallon reservoir buried beneath the summit meadow. The unseen tank is the hub of Portland's water supply, receiving 152,000 gallons a minute from the

Trail signs at Powell Butte.   *Above: Reservoir construction continues in 2013.*

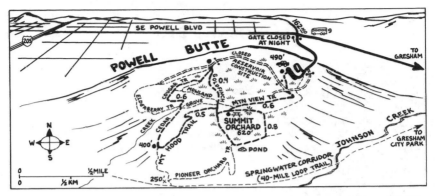

Bull Run Watershed. Construction on a second giant reservoir began in 2009, and will cause occasional trail closures or detours until 2014.

To reach the park, take exit 19 of Interstate 205, follow SE Powell Boulevard eastward 3.5 miles, turn right at 162nd Avenue, and drive up to the main parking area. This parking lot reopened in May 2013 after reconstruction. If you'd rather take the bus, ride Tri-Met #9 to the corner of Powell and 162nd.

From the restroom building, start up the paved Mountain View Trail through a meadow of buttercups and clover. Birds sing from hawthorn shrubs. The view of Mt. Hood is quite good, with flat-topped Mt. St. Helens to the north and Mt. Adams' white tip emerging above the foothills as you climb.

Pavement ends after 0.6 mile at a junction on the butte's broad summit. Here there are picnic tables in an old walnut orchard with ripe blackberries in August. For a shortcut, simply go straight 200 feet to a big gravel junction and turn right on the Goldfinch Trail. For a longer tour, turn left onto the Orchard Loop Trail for 0.8 mile. To follow the loop around the summit, keep right at all junctions until you reach a big gravel junction. Then go straight on the Goldfinch Trail.

Whichever route you've chosen, follow the Goldfinch Trail a mere 80 feet and turn left on the Mt. Hood Trail. This path soon dives into a lush forest of Douglas fir, bigleaf maple, and droopy red cedar, with white wildflowers in spring, including candyflower, fringecup, and solomonseal. Beware of trailside nettles and expect a bit of mud in wet weather.

After half a mile turn right on the Cedar Grove Trail. Follow this path 0.2 mile to a 4-way junction at a creek culvert. Signs may be missing here, but cross the creek and turn right onto the Cougar Trail. After climbing another 0.2 mile the trail forks at a ridgecrest. Keep left for another 0.2 mile to a meadow, where you'll reach a road junction.

If the reservoir construction project in the meadow here is completed, you can continue straight 0.6 mile to your car. If the construction site is still fenced, turn right on the Goldfinch Trail 0.4 mile to the Mountain View Trail and follow this paved path left 0.6 mile down to your car.

Other Options

For a bike trip nearby, tie into the Springwater Trail Corridor. This paved path follows a former railroad line west from Powell Butte 6.1 miles to Tideman Johnson Park, and east 6.5 miles (a mile past Hogan Road). A good place to start is at Gresham's Main City Park. From there, bike 4.2 miles west to the signed Powell Butte junction, and keep right on the Pioneer Orchard Trail to the summit.

11   Oxbow Park

Easy
3.9-mile loop
200 feet elevation gain
Open all year
Use: hikers, horses, bicycles

Left: Mossy maples by the trail.

Just 7 miles east of Gresham the whitewater Sandy River winds through a gorge where patches of ancient forest still remain. The trails in popular Oxbow Park are never far from the swift, 200-foot-wide river with its eroding bank, brushy islands, and log jams. Hikers can picnic on pebble beaches, look for great blue herons, discover beaver sign, and watch drift boats negotiate the riffles. The park charges a $5-per-car fee, allows no pets, and closes at legal sunset except for the campground.

Drive 16 miles east of Portland on Interstate 84, take Wood Village exit 16, go south on 238th Drive (which becomes 242nd Drive and then Hogan Drive) for 2.7 miles to Division Street. Turn left on Division (which becomes the Oxbow Parkway) for 5.5 miles to a 4-way junction. Then turn left following a park sign, and descend 1.6 miles to an entrance toll booth. Continue 2.2 miles along the river past numerous pullouts, picnic areas, and hiking signs. After passing Group Area D, park at an unmarked boat ramp parking area on the left.

The Sandy River has undercut nearly a mile of riverbank here, rerouting some trails and closing some roads. To start your hike, walk straight ahead on a closed campground road along the fresh riverbank cliff. Stumps exposed in this sandy bank have been carbon dated to 1780, the year a Mt. Hood eruption sent a mudflow down the river, burying forests.

After 0.2 mile, opposite campsite #19, turn left at a rail fence to find the actual trail. This path switchbacks down through a mossy forest of red cedars, Douglas

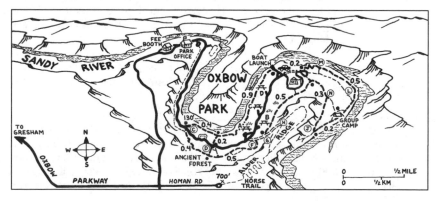

LUPINE AND PAINTBRUSH wildflowers pioneer the
blast zone at Mt. St. Helens' Johnston Ridge (Hike #21).

RANGERS give nature talks about volcanic activity on the Johnston Ridge Observatory's patio (Hike #21).

MOUNT SAINT HELENS

This uneasy volcano blew its summit into the sky in 1980 and extruded a steaming lava dome in 2004-2007, but trails and climbing routes are open.

COLDWATER LAKE (Hike #20) was created by a gigantic mudflow unleashed by the 1980 eruption.

FROM WINDY RIDGE, trails extend to Loowit Falls at the lip of the volcano's crater (Hike #28).

NORWAY PASS (Hike #29) overlooks Spirit Lake, where drift logs remain from the 1980 eruption.

THE BOUNDARY TRAIL to Badger Peak offers views of Mt. St. Helens from the east. (Hike #30).

CAPE HORN (Hike #39) has a lower loop along the Columbia (above) that's closed in spring, but the trail to the Nancy Russell Overlook (below) is open all year.

MOUNTAIN BIKERS and hikers share views of Mt. Hood from Hood River Mountain (Hike #157).

MIDDLE LEWIS RIVER FALLS is the smallest of three giant cataracts on an easy river trail (Hike #31).

WATER OUZELS

Naturalist John Muir called the water ouzel "the mountain streams' own darling, the hummingbird of blooming waters." Although it doesn't look aquatic, the robin-sized water ouzel (or American dipper, *Cinclus mexicanus*) spends much of its life on the bottoms of raging whitewater streams.

Watch beside any Columbia Gorge creek and you'll spot one of these slate-gray daredevils whirring along above the water, giving a distinctive *zeet-zeet* cry. Next, the bird is likely to land on a rock, bob a few times, and then plunge underwater for up to two minutes at a time, looking for insect larvae among the pebbles. The ouzel lives only where creeks run wild and white.

UPPER McCORD CREEK FALLS (Hike #49) is one of many Columbia Gorge falls visible only by trail.

AT COYOTE WALL (Hike #60) cliffs with ponderosa pines overlook the dry eastern end of the Columbia Gorge.

AT CASCADE LOCKS, travelers pay a $1 toll to cross the modern Bridge of the Gods, a 1926 steel span.

THE CHERRY ORCHARD TRAIL (Hike #62) traverses oak savannahs overlooking the Columbia Gorge.

WAHTUM LAKE (Hike #54) is a popular backpacking stop on the Pacific Crest Trail above Eagle Creek..

INDIAN POINT (Hike #53) overlooks the Columbia River from Nick Eaton Ridge at Herman Creek.

BRIDGE OF THE GODS

A native legend tells of a "Bridge of the Gods" across the Columbia River. In the legend, tribes on either side of the river met on the bridge to trade peacefully — until one day an evil spirit named Loowit changed herself into a beautiful maiden, camped on the bridge, and drove the chiefs of the two tribes to a jealous war.

This so angered the great spirit Tyee Sahalie that he changed all the principal characters into mountains. The two rival chiefs became Mount Hood and Mount Adams, while Loowit became Mount St. Helens. But they kept fighting, hurling lava bombs at each other. Finally their earthquakes destroyed the bridge.

Geologists say the legend may date to a gigantic landslide that dammed the Columbia River for several weeks at Cascade Locks 550 years ago.

THE KLICKITAT RAIL TRAIL (Hike #63) follows a railbed with trestles into a roadless Washington canyon.

41

THE TIMBERLINE TRAIL

Circling Mt. Hood from Timberline Lodge, the 39.3-mile Timberline Trail is a classic route for backpackers, and for day hikers who sample it in sections. A missing bridge interrupts the loop near Cloud Cap until at least 2015 (see pages 250-251).

PARADISE PARK (Hike #77) is a day's hike west of Timberline Lodge on the Timberline Trail.

WIND-GNARLED KRUMMHOLZ struggles on Barrett Spur above the Timberline Trail at Elk Cove (Hike #84).

TIMBERLINE LODGE (Hike #77), a spectacular 1937 hotel, is a starting point for several Mt. Hood hikes.

THE COOPER SPUR SHELTER (Hike #83) overlooks Mt. Hood's Eliot Glacier above the Timberline Trail.

CAIRN BASIN (Hike #73) has a historic stone shelter by a timberline meadow on the edge of a 2011 wildfire.

McNEIL POINT'S SHELTER (Hike #23), a mile above the Timberline Trail, is in a fragile alpine meadow.

WINTER AT MOUNT HOOD

With four downhill ski areas and 16 sno-parks for Nordic skiers and snowshoers, Mt. Hood is the most heavily used winter sports area in Oregon. Timberline Lodge's lifts top out at the 8500-foot level, but Mt. Hood Meadows has more powder snow.

THE SILCOX HUT (Hike #77), a mile above Timberline Lodge, offers snacks and lodging when it's open.

A SNOWBOARDER carves a half-pipe at Timberline Lodge in August. The ski area is open year round.

WHISTLING WILDLIFE

Two different denizens of the timberline area are likely to whistle at passing hikers. The pika or "rock rabbit" is about the size of a guinea pig. The marmot is

Pika.

about the size of a very obese cat. Both live in rockslides and whistle as a warning to their comrades that someone is in the area.

Marmot.

MOUNT HOOD dominates the wildflower slopes at timberline on Barrett Spur (Hike #84).

firs, sword ferns, and cottonwoods. At a junction with a post marked "M", go straight across a gully. For the next half mile the trail curves around the corner of a giant oxbow riverbend. When the trail forks at a rail fence barricade, keep left along the riverbank through a group campsite with a picnic shelter.

After another 0.2 mile you'll reach a trail junction in the forest at a post marked "J." The river trail peters out beyond this junction, so turn right for 0.2 mile to a wide graveled path at a post marked "N." Turn left on this wide trail 0.1 mile to a large Y-shaped junction.

If you're getting tired, you could fork to the right, taking a shortcut back through the campground to your car. If you're up for a longer loop hike, however, keep left at junctions for the next 0.5 mile, until you climb to a gravel road at a post marked "G."

Turn right on the gravel road 300 feet to a post marked "F". Then turn uphill to the left on a steepish trail overhung with maidenhair fern and bleeding hearts. This path ambles through an ancient forest with Douglas firs 5 feet in diameter. Keep left at all junctions for 0.9 mile. Just before the trail turns left across a small metal footbridge, go straight on the paved road 200 feet to a restroom building. Turn right through a parking lot to post "C", where a riverbank trail begins. Follow this path along the river 1.3 miles, passing several picnic lawns, to return to the boat launch by your car.

Other Options

For a longer hike, add a 1.6-mile loop atop Alder Ridge, a plateau with treetop osprey nests and a clifftop river overlook. Start by walking up the old road at the post marked "G". Look for the start of the loop trail at "H", 50 yards before road's end.

Horseback riders should start tours of Oxbow Park from the equestrian trailhead at the end of Homan Road. The $5 park fee is waived here, which would make this upper trailhead attractive for hikers too, except that then the day's hike ends with an uphill climb.

The eroding Sandy riverbank has exposed stumps from a 1780 Mt. Hood eruption.

12 Tualatin Hills Parks

Easy (Tualatin Hills)
4.5-mile loop
100 feet elevation gain
Open all year
Use: hikers, bicycles

Easy (Cooper Mountain)
2.2-mile loop
250 feet elevation gain

The two largest preserves of the Tualatin Hills park district are oases of wildness in Beaverton's suburbia. They're close enough you might visit both in a day.

Start with the 222-acre Tualatin Hills Nature Park—once a Catholic school's private preserve known as St. Mary's Woods. Here you can step off a MAX train and stroll for two hours past lilypad ponds, cedar groves, and marsh birds without once seeing a city street. Then drive 5 miles south to Cooper Mountain, where a new nature park with far-ranging views has restored a native oak savannah with spring wildflowers. Dogs are not allowed in either park and bicycles are limited to the few paved paths.

To find Tualatin Hills Nature Park by car, take freeway 217 to Canyon Road/ Beaverton exit 2A and head west on Canyon Road (which becomes the Tualatin Valley Highway) for 2.6 miles. At 160th Avenue turn right on Millikan Way for 0.4 mile to the park entrance on the left. Park here, walk through a covered breezeway between the restrooms and an Interpretive Center (with displays, programs, and a library), and then bear right on the paved Oak Trail.

The Oak Trail does indeed pass oaks, but the woods also include giant ponderosa pines, twisted little yews, wild hazel, and stately Douglas firs. Early April brings a gaudy rush of yellow wood violets, pale spring beauties, star-flowered solomonseal, and big three-petaled trilliums. Listen for the melodious warble of redwing blackbirds and the tirelessly cheery babble of Pacific wrens.

After 0.7 mile the Oak Trail crosses its third boardwalk, a scenic bridge over marshy Cedar Mill Creek. At the far end of this boardwalk the main trail veers right to the MAX station, but for the park loop you'll want to turn left on the barkdust Creek Trail. In rare winter floods, this route can be closed.

If you're coming here by MAX, take the blue Hillsboro line through Beaverton to the Merlo Road/SW 158th station, cross the tracks on a sidewalk to the left, and keep left on a paved path down into the woods. After 200 yards, just before the boardwalk over Cedar Mill Creek, turn right on the barkdust Creek Trail.

The Creek Trail skirts the Tri-Met bus barns through a forest of droopy-limbed red cedars and vine maples. After half a mile you'll reach a junction and face a choice. If you turn right on the Old Wagon and Vine Maple Trails you'll visit a lily pond. To shorten your hike by 0.7 mile, however, keep left on the Creek Trail.

On the far side of a zigzag bridge over Cedar Mill Creek, turn right and keep right at junctions for half a mile to tour more boardwalks and viewpoints on the Elliot, Big Fir, and Cougar Trails. Return on a loop via the Serviceberry Trail

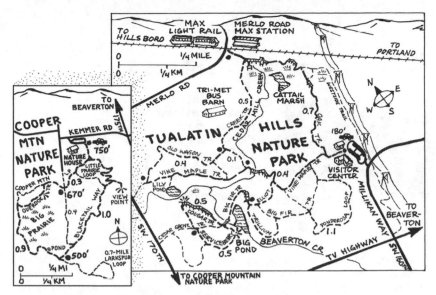

to the Big Fir Trail. Then keep right at junctions for 1.1 mile to return to your car at the visitor center. If you came by MAX, take the paved Oak Trail left 0.7 mile to find the station.

If you'd like to visit the area's other nature park (at Cooper Mountain) drive back to the Tualatin Valley Highway, head east a mile, and turn left (south) on 170th Avenue. After 2.1 miles you'll have to jog right on Rigert Road. Then continue south on 175th another mile to a flashing red light at the top of the hill, and turn right on Kemmer Road for 0.8 mile to the Cooper Mountain lot on the left.

The trail starts at the far right-hand end of the parking lot, beyond a playground and picnic area. For the recommended tour, keep right on the Cooper Mountain Loop for 0.4 mile. Then veer left onto the Overlook Trail, which has better views, and continue downhill around Big Prairie. Prescribed burns have restored native plants here, including a wildflower named farewell-to-spring (*Clarkia amoena*), which carpets the field with pink crosses in June.

At the 1.2-mile mark, fork left to stay on the Cooper Mountain Loop, but then keep right to climb Blacktail Way to a viewpoint on the way to your car.

Cooper Mountain from the Nature House.   *Opposite: The Merlo Road MAX station.*

13 Champoeg Heritage Area

Easy (around townsite)
3.2-mile loop
No elevation gain
Open all year
Use: hikers, bicycles

Moderate (to Butteville)
8.4-mile loop
No elevation gain

In 1843, when the Oregon Country didn't officially belong to any one nation, pioneers met at Champoeg, the earliest white settlement on the Willamette River, to discuss setting up a provisional government. At first it seemed the 100 white men at the meeting might reject the idea of government altogether. British traders and French-Canadian trappers feared the new American settlers would take control. When a line was drawn in the sand and sides were taken, the vote stood deadlocked, 50 to 50. Then a pair of French-Canadians threw in their lot with the Americans and Oregon has belonged to the US ever since.

Floods in 1861 and 1890 erased the old town of Champoeg. Today this scenic stretch of riverbank is a state heritage area with museums, monuments, picnic areas, and trails, A 3.2-mile hiking loop visits the most important sites, but it's tempting to extend the loop to 8.4 miles by hiking a paved path to the quaint old town of Butteville. For bicyclists, this paved path is the only option.

Drive Interstate 5 south of Portland 20 miles to Donald exit 278 and turn west, following signs 5.7 miles to Champoeg State Heritage Area's entrance. Expect to pay a $5 parking fee. Stop at the visitor's center to see the historical displays there. Additional exhibits are at the 1862 Donald Manson barn and farmstead beside the visitor center. You might also cross the entrance road to see the restored Robert Newell House Museum (open 1pm-5pm on weekends March through October, adults $4, children $2). Because it was on high ground, the 1852 Newell House was the only Champoeg home to survive the 1861 flood.

After inspecting the exhibits, get back in your car and drive into the park,

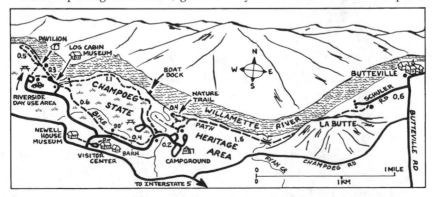

Barn and picnic area behind the visitor center.   Opposite: Monument at the pavilion.

keeping left to the Riverside Day Use Area. Park at the end of the Riverside loop.

Begin your hike by following the "Pavilion" trail sign to a monument and shelter built near the site of the famous 1843 meeting. Then walk through the pavilion to the Willamette—a broad, lazy river reflecting clouds, a few geese, and perhaps a great blue heron. Turn left here to explore a paved but scenic 0.4-mile loop path through a stand of 4-foot-thick cottonwoods. In spring look for wildflowers: fringecup, star-flowered solomonseal, and wild rose.

When this little loop returns to the pavilion, continue east along the riverbank. The trail ends at a paved road in front of a 1931 log cabin museum where an exhibit of pioneer artifacts is open 1pm-5pm on weekends March through October for $4.

Next continue 200 yards up the road to a curve where a paved bike path begins. Veer left here on the Champoeg Townsite Trail, a bark dust river path. After 0.6 mile the river path circles a group camping area with a boat dock. Then the path skirts the Oak Grove Day Use Area lawns and ends at a wide, paved bike path beside a road. To complete the 3.2-mile hiking loop, turn right on the bike path and follow it across the fields back to the log cabin museum and your car.

If, however, you'd like to walk the bike path toward Butteville, turn left when you reach the bike path, cross Champoeg Creek on the road bridge, and head left again. After 100 yards, be sure to detour left onto the lovely, 0.4-mile nature loop to the mouth of Champoeg Creek. A short spur trail of this graveled path passes an 1845 grave and deadends at the site of a pioneer gristmill. Then continue on the wide, paved bike path 1.5 miles along the river's edge to Schuler Road. Rustic Butteville is a half-mile roadside walk beyond. A lunch destination here is the 1863 Butteville Store, the oldest operating store in the state. Owned by Oregon State Parks and operated as a deli, gallery, and tiny museum, it also has a lawn with picnic tables for visitors, but is closed in winter.

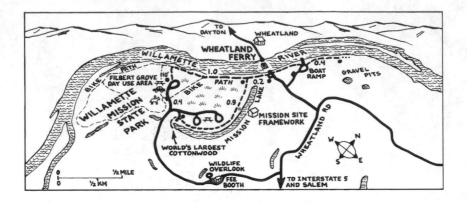

14   Willamette Mission Park

Easy
2.7 mile-loop
No elevation gain
Open all year
Use: hikers, horses, bicycles

This riverside loop through Willamette Mission State Park not only visits the nation's largest black cottonwood tree and the site of a historic 1834 settlement, it also includes a free ferry ride across the Willamette River and back.

To find the park, drive Interstate 5 north of Salem 9 miles to Brooks exit 263. Then head west on Brooklake Road for 1.8 miles, turn right onto Wheatland Road for 2.4 miles, and turn left at the Willamette Mission State Park sign. Follow the entrance road 1.8 miles, keeping left at all junctions, pay a $5-per-car fee at an entry booth, and park at the Filbert Grove Day Use Area—a picnic area set in an old hazelnut orchard. Some years the trees still produce a bumper crop of nuts that you can gather for free in autumn.

Equestrians and bicyclists have their own, separate loop trails through this park. A detailed map of the routes is at the equestrian trailhead, on the left just before the Filbert Grove parking area.

The hiking trail starts beside the restrooms at the far end of the Filbert Grove parking loop. Walk 0.2 mile to the riverbank and turn right on a paved bike path between the bank's cottonwood trees and a grassy field. Follow this promenade a mile to the Wheatland Ferry landing.

This is the oldest ferry landing in Oregon, dating to 1844 when mules winched a log barge across the river with ropes. The present steel vessel uses an overhead cable and electric engines. Pedestrians ride free, but car drivers pay about $2. The ferry runs from 5:30am to 9:45pm every day except Christmas and Thanksgiving—and about 30 or 40 days in winter when it closes for high water or repairs (call 503-588-7979 or check *www.co.marion.or.us/PW/ferries* for information).

The gravelly shore beside the landing is perfect for skipping rocks and watching the river. Children delight in finding tadpoles, frogs, and crawdads here. Look in the wet sand for the palm-sized tracks of great blue herons and the little hand-shaped tracks of raccoons. It's also fun to explore the riverbank beyond the landing; a path continues 0.4 mile before petering out.

To return to the loop, hike 300 yards back from the landing on the bike path and turn left onto a broad trail. This path leads through the woods to the shore of marshy Mission Lake. Before a flood changed the course of the Willamette River in 1861, this oxbow lake was the main channel. A framework across the lake depicts the mission built on the old riverbank by Methodist minister Jason Lee in 1834. In 1840, weary of the river's floods and the swampy environment, Lee moved operations to Chemeketa (now Salem), where he founded the Oregon Institute, which later became Willamette University. At the same time Lee gave up on teaching Indians and turned his attention to the children of white settlers.

After passing a monument near the mission site, the trail enters a developed picnic area in an old walnut orchard. Keep left at all junctions for half a mile to the trail's end at a road. A sign here points out the nation's largest black cottonwood—155 feet tall and over 26 feet in circumference. Walk along the road to return to your car, turning left at the first stop sign and right at the next.

The Wheatland ferry.   Opposite: Framework reconstruction of mission buildings.

Southwest Washington

Campgrounds

		Campsites	Water	Flush toilet	Open (mos.)	Rate range
1	**BATTLE GROUND LAKE STATE PARK.** Volcanic lake with campground close to Portland has trails, rowboats, showers, and 4 rental cabins ($59-69). Reservations: 888-226-7688 (*www.parks.wa.gov/reservations/*).	46	●	●	●	$12-37
2	**SUNSET FALLS.** On the East Fork Lewis River east of Battle Ground, this forest camp is a short walk downstream from Sunset Falls.	18	●		●	$12
3	**MERRILL LAKE.** Near Mt. St. Helens, but away from crowds, this camp is in old-growth Douglas fir woods on a fly-fishing lake. Tents only.	7			V-XI	free
4	**KALAMA HORSE CAMP.** With corrals and a loading ramp, this equestrian camp has lots of trails to Mt. St. Helens (see Hike #20).	17			V-XI	$8-12
5	**SEAQUEST.** A handy state park (showers! 5 yurts!) across from Mt. St. Helens' Silver Lk. Vis. Ctr. Res: 888-226-7688 *www.parks.wa.gov/reserve.asp.*	88	●	●	●	$12-37
6	**LOWER FALLS.** A lovely wooded camp at the gigantic waterfalls of the Lewis River (Hike #28).	44	●		V-IX	$15-35
7	**LEWIS RIVER HORSE CAMP.** Drab camp with 3 corrals and lots of trails in the beautiful Lewis River area.	9			V-XI	$5
8	**CULTUS CREEK.** This trailhead camp is a good base for huckleberry picking and treks into the Indian Heaven Wilderness.	50			VI-IX	$10-20
9	**PARADISE CREEK.** Camp under huge firs and cedars where a creek joins the Wind River. Res: 877-444-6777 (*www.recreation.gov*).	42	●		VI-IX	$18-34
10	**BEACON ROCK STATE PARK.** Woodsy camp near Hike #34 has 28 sites, best for tents. A new RV camp by the Columbia River is open all year.	39	●	●	●	$12-37

◁ *Beacon Rock.*

Cabins, Lookouts & Inns

		Rental units	Private bath	Breakfast	Open (mos.)	Rate range
1	**GOVERNMENT MINERAL SPRINGS.** 1937 guard station with kitchen and fireplace. Sleeps 9. Res: 877-444-6777 (*www.recreation.gov*).	1			●	$65
2	**CARSON MINERAL HOT SPRINGS.** This old-timey hot springs resort has clawfoot tub baths ($20), massages ($70), and a modern motel. Reservations at 509-427-8296 or *www.carsonhotspringresort.com.*	28	●		●	$75-219
3	**COLUMBIA GORGE RIVERSIDE LODGE.** Studios in 4 modern log cabins on Columbia River. Res: 509-427-5650 (*www.cgriversidelodge.com*).	8	●		●	$79-199
4	**SKAMANIA LODGE.** Modeled on Timberline Lodge, this massive, upscale lodge has Columbia Gorge views and a rustic Northwest ambiance. Reservations at 800-221-7117 (*www.skamania.com*).	254	●		●	$135-320
5	**BONNEVILLE HOT SPRINGS.** European-style spa resort with geo-thermally-heated rooms and natural hot springs mineral water. Most rooms have hot tubs. Res: 866-459-1678 (*www.bonnevilleresort.com*).	78	●	●	●	$159-499

Above right: Mt. St. Helens from the Johnston Ridge Observatory.

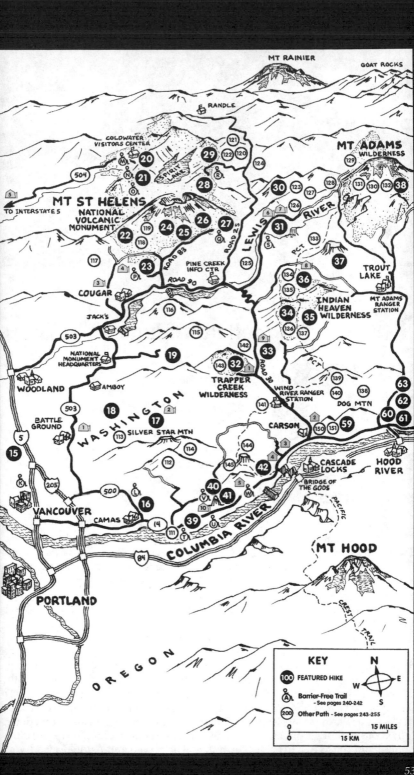

The Cathlapotle Plankhouse.   Below: Brush rabbit.

15   Ridgefield Refuge

Easy (to Boot and Carty Lakes)
2.7-mile loop
20 feet elevation gain
Open all year

Easy (Kiwa Trail)
1.5-mile loop
No elevation gain
Open May 1 to September 30

When Lewis and Clark camped at these Columbia River wetlands in 1805 and 1806 the flocks of birds were so loud that the explorers had trouble sleeping. They also found one of the largest Chinook villages on the river, 14 barn-sized plankhouses with 900 residents. Today the birdlife is still impressive, and there's a replica of one of the original cedar plankhouses. Two easy loop trails tour the wildlife refuge's highlights. Pets and bicycles are not allowed.

To start, drive Interstate 5 north from Vancouver 14 miles to Ridgefield exit 14 and take Pioneer Street west 3 miles into the city of Ridgefield. At a flashing light at the far end of downtown turn right on Main Avenue. After a mile turn left into the Ridgefield National Wildlife Refuge parking lot, where there's a $3 parking fee. Note that the entrance gate closes automatically each evening.

Walk a footbridge across the railroad tracks and keep right for 0.2 mile to the 37-by-78-foot plankhouse, a replica that took 3500 volunteer hours, 246 western red cedar logs, and $575,000 to build. A Portland State University excavation discovered hearth pits and post holes at the original riverside village that determined this building's dimensions. Visitors can tour the inside on weekend afternoons from late March to early November. The carved and painted woodwork inside was commissioned to reflect Chinookan style. Perhaps a dozen families of the Chinook's Cathlapotle band would have shared a house this size. The chief's family would have claimed the far end with the decorative artwork.

To continue from the plankhouse, follow "Oaks to Wetlands" pointers onward along the right-hand shore of Duck Lake. The path traverses grassy open woods with massive Oregon white oaks, snowberry bushes, wild Nootka roses, and brush rabbits that hop ahead of you on the trail. Goose honks and duck calls compete with the rumble of passing trains. Expect some mosquitoes in May.

If you keep right at all trail junctions you'll visit a viewpoint of muddy Boot Lake, tour a sunny basalt knoll, and return to the plankhouse after 1.5 miles. To see Lewis and Clark's campsite, veer to the right on a mowed path just before the longhouse, continue 300 yards, and turn right on a dike road 0.4 mile to a gate near Carty Lake. This route can be a little boggy and calls for boots, but it's where you'll see the best birdlife: great blue herons on stilt legs, redwing blackbirds clutching reeds, and swallows zooming overhead. The campsite is 100 yards beyond the gate, where a row of cottonwoods line the Lake River.

For the second easy loop in the refuge, drive back into Ridgefield, turn left on Pioneer Street for 0.4 mile, turn right on 9th Avenue for 0.6 mile, and turn right onto the refuge's 4.2-mile auto tour road. Expect a $3-per-car fee. Note that this road's gate closes automatically each evening. Also note that hiking is permitted only from May 1 to September 30. The rest of the year, people are allowed to leave their cars only to visit the bird blind.

After driving half a mile on the tour route you'll cross a one-lane bridge and turn right at the start of a loop road atop a dike. In another 1.3 miles you can park by a restroom on the left to see a bird blind. But for the Kiwa Trail, drive another 100 yards and park on the right. This broad gravel path crosses duckweed-filled Bower Slough to a junction at the start of a 1.5-mile loop. The Oregon ash woods here have tall grass, 6-foot stinging nettles, and creeping yellow bog buttercups.

If you turn left at the start of the loop the Kiwa Trail soon launches across a marshy lake on a boardwalk amid bird song and jungly squawks. At the far end of the second boardwalk, look for the foot-long arrowhead-shaped leaves of wapato along the lakeshore to the right. Lewis and Clark reported that native women would use their toes to dig up this plant's fleshy, edible roots, gradually filling a canoe as they waded along. When the loop trail returns you to your car, continue driving the auto tour counter-clockwise to complete your visit.

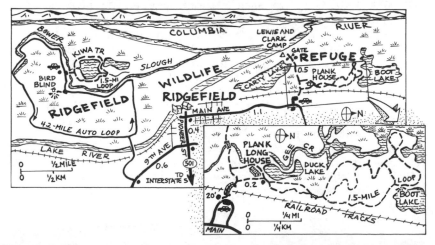

16 Lacamas Park

Easy (Round Lake to falls)
3.4-mile loop
200 feet elevation gain
Open all year
Use: hikers, bicycles

Moderate (Lacamas Lake path)
7 miles round trip
No elevation gain

When Ice Age floods roared down the Columbia River 12,000 years ago they took a shortcut across what is now Clark County. The channel they carved has since filled with forest-rimmed lakes and the waterfalls of Lacamas Creek. Although modern development has now encircled this scenery, with the mill town of Camas on one side and the housing tracts of Vancouver on the other, Lacamas Park remains a miniature wilderness — just the right kind of convenient, woodsy place for a winter stroll or an easy hike with the kids.

For a woodsy loop through Lacamas Park, turn off Interstate 205 just north of the Columbia River and take Highway 14 east for 7 miles to Camas exit 12. Follow the exit road 1.4 miles to town, continue straight on 6th Avenue for six blocks, turn left on Garfield Street, and follow "Hwy 500 West" signs for 1.2 zigzagging miles to the Lacamas Park parking lot on your right. On summer weekends the lot may be full, but you can drive 100 yards up the highway and turn right on Leonard Road to an overflow parking area. The C-Tran Camas bus also stops at Leonard Road. Pets must be on leash in the park.

The trail starts in a picnic area with barbecues, restrooms, and a playground. Take the lakeshore path to the right 0.3 mile through a Douglas fir forest, cross a footbridge beside a humming fish-screening device, and then cross a 50-foot-tall concrete dam built early in the early 20th century to provide power and water for the Camas papermill.

Beyond the dam is a confusion of paths. Stick to the lakeshore for 300 yards to a large signboard with a park map. At this point it's possible to opt for a very short, 1.6-mile loop by simply keeping left around the lake. For the longer loop, however, turn right for 100 yards to the turnaround of a gravel road. Here turn right again on an unmarked path 50 feet to a wire fence at an overlook of The Potholes. There you'll find a pair of circular green pools separated by a 20-foot waterfall and weirdly pockmarked bedrock. Floodwaters created these holes by swirling rocks in depressions in the soft rock.

At The Potholes, turn left along the fence and follow Lacamas Creek 0.6 mile downstream to a 150-foot metal footbridge above Lower Falls. The creek bank here, polished into chutes and pools, makes a nice lunch stop.

To continue the loop don't cross the footbridge, but instead walk left up an old gravel road for 100 yards and take an unmarked path uphill to the left. After 0.4 mile turn left on another old gravel road to return 0.8 mile to Round Lake. Along the way, optional, marked side paths lead to a patch of blue camas lilies

Lacamas Heritage Trail along Lacamas Lake.   Opposite: Trailhead sign.

(on the right) and 50-foot-tall Woodburn Falls (on the left). The camas blooms spectacularly from mid-April to mid-May, giving this entire area its name.

Back at the lake, follow the shore path 0.7 mile to the right and continue briefly on a paved road around to your car.

For a longer hike or bike ride, start at a different trailhead and tour Lacamas Lake instead. For this option, drive Highway 14 east of Interstate 205 for 5 miles to exit 10, turn left on 192nd Avenue for 3.5 miles, and turn right on 13th Avenue (which becomes Goodwin Road) for 0.9 mile to the Lacamas Heritage Trail parking lot on the right.

This wide graveled path skirts a golf course for a mile and follows the lakeshore for another mile to a private dock reserved for owners of the million-dollar homes above the trail. Continue along the lake 0.4 mile to a gazebo perched on the shore, a nice lunch stop. Then continue another 1.1 mile to a public dock and boat ramp at a parking area for Camas Heritage Park. This makes a good turnaround point, but you can also take a paved bike path along Lake Road 0.4 mile to the Lacamas Park trailhead at Round Lake, where you can launch the 3.4-mile loop described above.

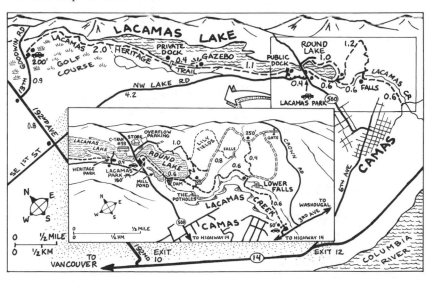

17   Silver Star Mountain

Difficult (to summit)
6.4-mile loop
1900 feet elevation gain
Open May to mid-November
Use: hikers, horses, bicycles

Difficult (to Indian Pits)
8.7-mile loop
2100 feet elevation gain

From Portland, Silver Star Mountain appears as a humble brown ridge. From the mountain's wildflower-spangled meadows, however, the view is proud indeed, encompassing four snowpeaks and a long, silver ribbon of Columbia River.

In 1902 the mountain was overswept by the Yacolt Burn, the largest forest fire in Washington history. Today, wildflower meadows thrive on the ridges where trees failed to reseed. A footpath on the mountain's north flank climbs to the summit by ducking through a natural rock arch. If you return on an abandoned road as a loop, the hike's only 6.4 miles. But it's worth adding a 2.3-mile side trip to visit a mysterious collection of Indian pits.

To find this northern trailhead, drive Interstate 205 north of the Columbia River for 4 miles to Orchards exit 30 and take Highway 500 (which becomes Highway 503), following signs 10 miles to Battleground. Continue north past Battleground on Highway 503 another 5.6 miles. At a pointer for Moulton Falls, turn right on NE Rock Creek Road for 8.6 miles. A quarter mile beyond Moulton Falls, turn right on NE Sunset Falls Road for 2 miles. Then turn right across a bridge onto NE Dole Valley Road for 2.4 paved miles, turn left on Road 1100 for 6.6 miles, and finally turn right on Road 4109 for 2.7 rough miles up to the trailhead turnaround at road's end *(GPS location N45°46.357' W122°14.674')*.

Start hiking on the level trail straight ahead. This path soon climbs to join an abandoned road. Among the vine maple and thimbleberry brush you'll find a conflagration of June wildflowers: yellow lupine, red paintbrush, blue iris, white

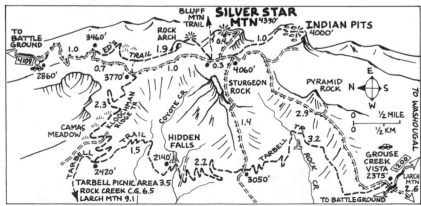

beargrass, and more. After a mile you'll reach an older trailhead turnaround. The old roadbed curves up to the right, and some hikers trudge up it to the summit. But if you're willing to tackle a scramblier, more scenic footpath, walk straight ahead, following a signpost for "Ed's Trail."

This path traverses a rock garden of windswept wildflowers, with views back to Mt. St. Helens' snowy rim. A few old road tracks and side paths confuse the route, but keep left at junctions to follow Ed's Trail along the ridge, through a doorway-sized rock arch, and up a pair of very steep switchbacks to a magnificent viewpoint atop a flat-topped rock pillar. Then Ed's Trail climbs to a 4-way junction with the old road *(GPS location N45°44.990' W122°14.535')*.

Walk up the old road 300 yards to a big 3-way road junction. Turn uphill to the left to scale Silver Star Mountain's twin summits, one of which still has foundations of a lookout tower. Soak in the view, and then hike back down to the 3-way road junction. If you're ready to head home, simply turn right on the old road back to your car. If you're intrigued by the Indian pits, however, turn left for 300 yards down to a big, possibly signless 4-way junction. A post on the left marks a footpath that leads up and down along a fabulous alpine ridgecrest for a mile to end at a rockslide with a sweeping view. The ancient stone walls and 6-foot pits here are thought to be vision quest sites where young Indian men fasted until they saw a guiding spirit. Do not remove anything. Return to the old road and follow it back to your car.

Other Options

For a longer loop hike, go straight across the 4-way junction when you return from the Indian pits trail, following an old rocky road steeply downhill past Sturgeon Rock. After 1.4 miles, turn right at a junction with the Tarbell Trail. This well-graded footpath descends 2.2 miles to Hidden Falls, a 92-foot cascade in a mossy grotto. Continue another 1.5 miles, turn right on the Kloochman Ridge Trail for a stiff, 2.3-mile climb through wildflower meadows, and then turn left on the abandoned road to return to your car.

Rock arch on Ed's Trail.   Opposite: Indian pit.

18   Moulton Falls

Easy (to Big Tree Falls)
1.7-mile loop
140 feet elevation gain
Open all year
Use: hikers

Moderate (to Bells Mountain)
4.9 miles round trip
1160 feet elevation gain
Use: hikers, horses, bicycles

Salmon leap up waterfalls in this woodsy Washington canyon. Start with a quick look at Lucia Falls. Then hike the easy loop from Moulton Falls to Big Tree Falls. For more exercise, add a climb up the Bells Mountain Trail.

From Portland, take Interstate 5 north across the Columbia River to Exit 2 and turn right on Highway 500 East. After 6 miles, continue straight on what now becomes Highway 503 for an additional 13 miles. Beyond Battle Ground 5.6 miles, turn right onto NE Rock Creek Road for 5 miles to the Lucia Falls parking lot on the right.

Although Lucia Falls' county park is too small for much of a hike, it's definitely worth getting out of your car. Walk to the left on a path across a lawn and then follow a wider trail 200 feet down to a viewpoint of the 15-foot cataract. Downstream to the right another 100 feet you can explore the lava bedrock beside the East Fork Lewis River. Fishing and swimming are not allowed.

After Lucia Falls, get back in your car and continue east on the paved road. Just 0.3 mile later, Hantwick Road veers off to the right. If you're bringing a bicycle or a horse, turn right here for half a mile to find a trailhead designed for cyclists and equestrians.

Hikers can drive the main road east from Lucia Falls 3.1 miles to a smaller Moulton Falls parking area on the right after a "Weight Limit 5 Ton" sign. If this lot is full, drive another quarter mile to a big overflow parking area up a hill to the right.

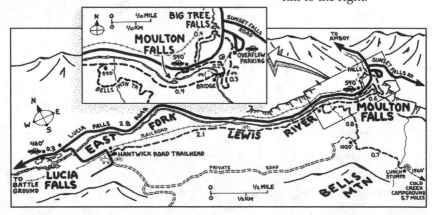

The East Fork Lewis River from the loop trail.   Opposite: Moulton Falls.

At the small Moulton Falls parking lot, first take a paved path 100 feet to the right to see the waterfall itself. Then return to the parking lot and take a sidewalk to the right alongside the paved road. Keep right at major junctions for 0.2 mile to a spectacular footbridge that's 120 feet long, and nearly as high.

Cross the bridge and continue straight on old road that has been converted into a hiker/biker/equestrian trail. Delicate maidenhair ferns line the cliffs along this broad, level path. Bigleaf maples, alders, cedars, and Douglas firs 3 feet in diameter have regrown here since the 1902 Yacolt Burn. Giant blackened snags on the hillside recall that colossal fire.

After 0.4 mile on this road/trail you'll reach a kiosk at the junction with the Bells Mountain Trail, a smaller path that climbs steeply up to the left. If you're hiking with children, turn back here. If you have extra energy, however, burn it off by gaining 1000 feet of elevation in 1.5 miles to the trail's high point, in a 2002 clearcut with stumps that serve as picnic tables. Young firs are starting to crowd the view of Mt. St. Helens, but this still makes a good turnaround point.

When you return to the high bridge and recross the river gorge, turn right on a small path—the start of a scenic loop back to your car. This trail heads upstream 300 feet to a gorge viewpoint and then turns uphill to the left, widening as it passes a picnic area. Ignore the overflow parking area and veer left down to a crossing of the paved road. On the far side of the road, the loop trail crosses a scenic metal bridge beside Big Tree Falls and then follows a creek back to the road near the Moulton Falls parking area, the end of the loop.

Other Options

If you'd like to continue beyond the viewpoint at the summit of the Bells Mountain Trail, the path descends 2.2 miles to a creek bridge and contours an additional 3.5 miles through the woods to Cold Creek Falls, a modest 6-foot cascade. Here the trail forks. To the left 0.2 mile is a trailhead at the Cold Creek Campground's day use area. Destinations to the right include Rock Creek Campground and Silver Star Mountain.

To shuttle a car to the Cold Creek trailhead, drive the paved road east from Moulton Falls 0.3 mile, turn right on NE Sunset Falls Road 2 miles, and turn right across a bridge onto NE Dole Valley Road. After 5.1 miles of pavement and an additional half mile of gravel, turn right through an unlocked yellow gate on a gravel road marked "L 1300". After 0.3 mile you'll pass a pullout for the Tarbell Trail. Continue 1.2 miles, keeping left at junctions, to the Cold Creek day use area. A Washington State Discover Pass is required to park here.

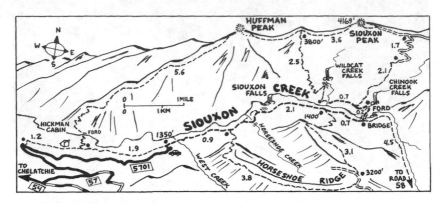

Siouxon Falls.   Opposite: Footbridge across Siouxon Creek at the 3.7-mile mark.

19   Siouxon Creek

Moderate
7.8 miles round trip
700 feet elevation gain
Open all year
Use: hikers, horses, bicycles

Ancient forest frames Siouxon Creek's green pools and waterfalls. The trail here follows the creek 3.9 miles to Chinook Creek Falls, where a cold ford turns back most hikers. And incidentally — the name *Siouxon* rhymes with *Tucson*.

The drive to Siouxon Creek is entirely paved. Take Interstate 205 north across the Columbia River to Orchards exit 30. Go right on Highway 500, which becomes Highway 503 through Battleground and makes three sharp corners in Amboy. When the highway ends, turn right on Cedar Creek Road. A total of 26.2 miles from the freeway — just past the Mt. St. Helens National Monument Headquarters — turn right on NE Healy Road for 9.2 miles to a fork. Watch your odometer, because road signs may be missing. At the fork, veer uphill to the left on Road 57 for 1.2 miles to a pass. Then turn left onto Road 5701 for 3.8 miles to a path on the left, 100 feet before road's end (*GPS location N45°56.760' W122°10.751'*).

Hike down the path and turn right on the Siouxon Creek Trail. This trail descends 0.2 mile to a footbridge over West Creek, passes three campsites, and then follows Siouxon Creek amid big Douglas firs and red cedars. After 1.4 miles the path bridges Horseshoe Creek between a pair of charming little waterfalls. Side trails to the left end at brushy viewpoints. Continue on the main trail 0.3 mile to Siouxon Falls, a 40-foot, S-shaped slide that sloshes into a huge green pool.

At the 3.7-mile mark the trail crosses a cascading little side creek on slippery, bare rock. Take care when you hop across, especially when the water is high in spring. Just beyond this crossing, turn left across a footbridge over a deep-pooled gorge. Mossy rock ledges beside the bridge serve as natural picnic tables if you're ready for a lunch stop. After resting here, continue a quarter mile to the ford below lacy, 50-foot Chinook Falls. The creek at this ford is calf-deep and 20 feet wide, so it's a good place to declare victory and return to your car the way you came.

Other Options

Backpackers or rugged day hikers can choose among three more difficult loops. For a sweeping view from Siouxon Peak's former lookout site, take the Chinook Trail just beyond Chinook Falls up to a jeep track, keep left to the peak, and return via the Wildcat Trail — altogether, a 18.4-mile loop gaining 3700 feet. For a 10.8-mile loop that gains 2600 feet, take the well-marked Horseshoe Ridge Trail up a steep, viewless crest, across a logging road, and back to Siouxon Creek. Finally, a 13-mile loop up Wildcat Creek passes within a cross-country scramble of Huffman Peak's scenic summit and follows a long, wooded ridge west to a difficult ford on a lower portion of the Siouxon Creek Trail, gaining 3900 feet in all.

20   Coldwater Lake

Easy (to lake access)
2.6 miles round trip
100 feet elevation gain
Open March through November

Moderate (to bridge)
9.4 miles round trip
200 feet elevation gain
Use: hikers, bicycles (Lakes Trail only)

Easy (Hummocks Trail)
2.4-mile loop
250 feet elevation gain

Most of Mt. St. Helens' summit slumped to the north and slid down the Toutle River valley during the mountain's 1980 eruption. The slide dammed 4-mile-long Coldwater Lake and left an eerie collection of 200-foot-tall hummocks strewn across the valley floor. You can view the results of this volcanic mayhem by hiking along the new lake's shore to a dramatic bridge over a gorge. Nearby, an easy loop trail tours the weirdly scenic Hummocks.

Drive Interstate 5 to Castle Rock exit 49 and take Highway 504 for 45 miles. Two miles beyond the turnoff for the Science & Learning Center at Coldwater, turn left to the Coldwater Lake picnic area. Remember that pets are not allowed on the trails.

Start by strolling the paved Birth of a Lake Trail 0.1 mile out to an impressive boardwalk pier with a view of Mt. St. Helens' truncated cone. Then turn around, keeping right at junctions for 0.2 mile left to a boat ramp parking lot. Continue clockwise around the lake on the shore path. Stumps on the hillside show that most of the area was clearcut before the 1980 eruption. The volcano's blast snapped the remaining trees. Today, wildflowers seem to dominate. Watch for white ox-eye daisies, purple foxglove, blue lupine, and yellow lotus.

A mile beyond the boat ramp you'll reach a lakeshore access point. If you're hiking with children, this is a good place to let them clamber on the driftwood logs of the beachless shore before heading back.

If you're going strong, continue on the trail to the far end of the lake. Along the way you'll pass a small waterfall in a rock gully, a panoramic peninsula, and the gravel fans of rockslides from the denuded slopes above. After 3.4 miles, turn right at a trail junction for the Coldwater Trail. In just 100 yards this path crosses a spectacular, 50-foot bridge over Coldwater Creek. Below, a cataract rages through a gorge of pink stone. This makes a good turnaround point.

To hike the loop trail through the Hummocks, drive onward on Highway 504 toward Johnston Ridge for a quarter mile and turn right to the well-marked parking area. The trail starts at the far end of the parking lot and heads straight toward Mt. St. Helens. The sand and rock piles left by the eruption's landslide here are being colonized first by a mat of moss and dwarf lupine, next by a meadow of grass and false dandelions, and then by a red alder forest with foxgloves. Ponds dot the uneven terrain. Elk like to browse the area.

After 0.7 mile turn right at a junction with the Boundary Trail. In another

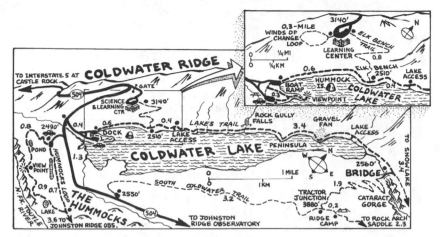

0.9 mile a short spur to the left accesses a viewpoint of the North Fork Toutle River's stripped-out floodplain. The final 0.8 mile of the loop passes a pond where beavers have gnawed saplings to build dams.

Other Options

If you're visiting on a weekend, you might start at the Science and Learning Center on Coldwater Ridge. If funding allows, this center will reopen in 2013 on weekends from mid-May through December. The center offers a great view, interpretive displays, and a short paved nature loop trail. For a longer hike, take the Elk Bench Trail downhill 0.8 mile to Coldwater Lake—but remember that you'll have to gain 630 feet of elevation on the return trip. Expect a fee to visit the learning center.

If you can arrange a car shuttle, consider hiking one-way from the Johnston Ridge Observatory (see Hike #21) down to Coldwater Lake. The Boundary Trail from the observatory to the Hummocks parking lot is only 4.3 miles. A more difficult route, to the Coldwater Lake boat ramp via the Lakes Trail, is 14.2 miles.

Mt. St. Helens from the Hummocks.   Opposite: Coldwater Lake.

Johnston Ridge

Easy (to great viewpoint)
3.8 miles round trip
400 feet elevation gain
Open early June through October

Moderate (to Harrys Ridge)
8 miles round trip
1000 feet elevation gain

Difficult (to Coldwater Peak)
12.8 miles round trip
2000 feet elevation gain
Open July through October

When Mt. St. Helens unexpectedly aimed its 1980 eruption toward this ridge, David Johnston, the Forest Service observer stationed here, had time to radio just five words: "Vancouver! Vancouver! This is it!" Today the most popular drive in the national monument leads to an observation building atop Johnston's ridge. The view of the volcano is both chilling and inspiring. But the panorama actually gets better the farther you hike from the visitor center: 1.9 miles to a bluff, 4 miles to Harrys Ridge, or 6.4 miles to Coldwater Peak.

Mt. St. Helens has steamed quietly since its latest dome-building phase ended in 2007. Future eruptions are expected, but are unlikely to be as violent as in 1980.

To drive here, take Interstate 5 to Castle Rock exit 49 and follow Highway 504 for 52 miles to its end at the Johnston Ridge Observatory. Start with a visit of the observatory itself, an interpretive center where you can buy the $8 wrist band that is required for adults when hiking in this area. If you have a NW Forest Pass, it's good for one free adult wristband. The observatory is open 10am-6pm daily from May through October. Remember that pets are banned on the trails. And be sure to bring plenty of water, because the route has none.

Mt. St. Helens from the Boundary Trail.   *Above: The Johnston Ridge Observatory.*

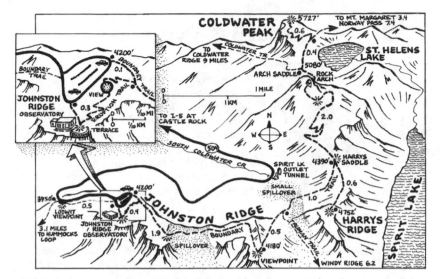

After touring the observatory, head uphill from the terrace on the paved Eruption Trail, which loops across a viewpoint knoll. After 0.3 mile, just before the paved path returns to the parking lot, turn right onto the unpaved Boundary Trail. (If you'd rather skip the visitor center's crowds and shorten the hike, start at a "Boundary Trail" signboard at the far end of the parking lot instead.)

The Boundary Trail ambles east along Johnston Ridge amid splintered logs. Blue lupine, red paintbrush, and purple penstemon brighten the stark slopes in summer. After half a mile the path dips to the Spillover, a barren saddle where a landslide from the volcano's 1980 eruption sloshed over the top of Johnston Ridge. The massive slide swept away soil and logs, but left behind wildflowers. At the 1.9-mile mark, the Boundary Trail switchbacks around the end of a ridge with the best view so far—including your first look at Spirit Lake and distant Mt. Adams. If you're hiking with children, make this your turnaround point.

For a longer tour, continue 1.5 miles on the Boundary Trail to Harrys Saddle. Here you face another choice. For the moderate hike, turn right on a path that climbs 0.6 mile up Harrys Ridge, with its close-up panorama of Mt. St. Helens and Spirit Lake. This ridge was named both for volcanologist Harry Glicken and for Harry Truman, the curmudgeon who died in his Spirit Lake Lodge during the 1980 eruption.

If you're up to a difficult hike, skip Harrys Ridge and continue straight across Harrys Saddle on the Boundary Trail, heading for the loftier viewpoint atop Coldwater Peak. After climbing 1.7 miles, the path ducks across a ridgecrest through a natural rock arch. Visible far below is blue St. Helens Lake, in a craggy mountain bowl lined with standing dead snags. Continue 0.3 mile down to a trail junction at Arch Saddle, keep right on the Boundary Trail for 0.4 mile, and turn uphill at a sign for the Coldwater Peak Trail.

Patches of snow linger until mid-summer on this steep, switchbacking path, but it's also a place to find vibrant alpine wildflowers: beargrass plumes and pasque flower anemones. Coldwater Peak's summit, once the site of a fire lookout, now has a small collection of antennas and solar panels. The dizzying view extends from Mt. Rainier to the Pacific.

22   Sheep Canyon

Moderate (to Toutle River)
7.6 miles round trip
1900 feet elevation gain
Open late June through October
Use: hikers, horses, bicycles

Difficult (to head of Sheep Canyon)
10.4-mile loop
1900 feet elevation gain

On the western edge of Mt. St. Helens' 1980 blast zone, this hike has a little of everything: intact old-growth forests, desolated canyons, wildflower-strewn timberline meadows, and a truly astonishing view of the mountain from the South Fork Toutle River's gorge, where the river has cut a sandy chasm into a half-mile-wide mudflow unleashed by the flash melting of the Toutle and Tallus Glaciers. Since then, smaller mudflows have periodically blocked car access to this hike's trailhead.

Drive Interstate 5 to Woodland exit 21 (north of Portland 25 miles) and turn right for 27.7 miles, following signs for Cougar. Half a mile before the town of Cougar, turn left onto Road 8100 at a sign for Merrill Lake. Follow this paved road 11.5 miles and then continue straight on gravel Road 8123 for 1.5 miles to the Blue Lake Trailhead at road's end.

The trail begins as a rock-lined path across a barren, sandy flood plain. After 850 feet, keep left at a junction to a crossing of Coldspring Creek. Next the route climbs along a ridge above mudslide-dammed Blue Lake through a forest of 5-foot-diameter hemlocks and noble firs. Look for the hand-sized triple leaves

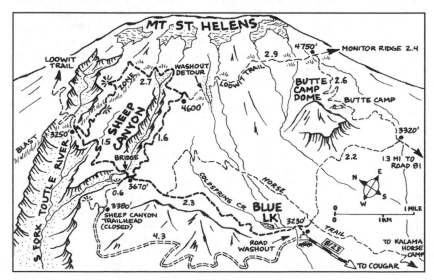

The South Fork Toutle River.   Opposite: Mt. St. Helens from a trailside meadow.

of vanilla leaf, a humble white wildflower that gives off a sweet smell as it wilts.

After 2.4 miles, turn left on the Sheep Canyon Trail for 200 yards, and then turn right to cross a spectacular footbridge above Sheep Canyon's gorge. Just before the bridge, you might detour briefly 200 yards left to a waterfall viewpoint.

Then return to the bridge and cross it. Beyond this point the trail becomes rougher and a little overgrown. Continue 1.5 miles, mostly downhill through big woods, to a Loowit Trail junction at the rim of the South Fork Toutle River's mudflow canyon. The loop route turns right here, but first detour a few hundred yards to the left for a view up the river's tiered canyon to Mt. St. Helens. The bouldery river is smaller and clearer now that the glaciers above are gone.

The river makes a good turnaround point for a moderate hike. If you'd like to return on a more challenging loop, however, walk back to the junction and climb the Loowit Trail up a long ridge into the 1980 blast zone, gaining better views all the way. Finally the trail levels out at timberline through meadows of bluebells, red paintbrush, blue lupine, and huckleberries. After traversing the head of Sheep Canyon you'll reach a trail junction. Turn right to complete the loop back to your car.

Other Options

For a longer, 13.5-mile loop, continue around the mountain counter-clockwise on the Loowit Trail another 2.3 miles, turn right on the Butte Camp Trail for 2.4 miles, and turn right for another 2 miles back to the Blue Lake Trailhead.

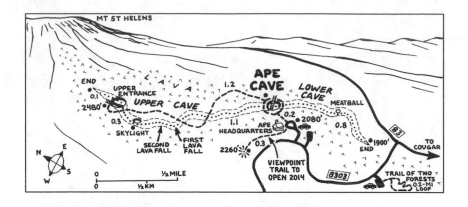

23   Ape Cave

Easy (Lower cave)
2 miles round trip
200 feet elevation gain
Open all year

Moderate (Upper cave)
3-mile loop
400 feet elevation gain

Easy (Trail of Two Forests)
0.2-mile loop
No elevation gain

The longest lava tube in the western hemisphere, Ape Cave features a 0.8-mile lower section that's easy to hike and a rugged, 1.4-mile upper section that's fun for adventurers. Want a shorter walk? Try the 0.2-mile Trail of Two Forests, where kids can crawl through a 50-foot rock tube left by tree trunks in a lava flow.

For Ape Cave, bring *at least* one lantern or flashlight for each person and be sure to dress warmly. Even on hot days the drafty cave remains a chilly 42° F. Pets, smoking, food, and beverages are banned in the cave. If you don't have a Northwest Forest parking pass you can buy one at the trailhead. There is no extra fee per person, but if you want to rent a lantern expect to pay $5. Although the cave is open all year, the entrance road is gated closed from December 1 to April 15, adding a mile to your hike each way and requiring a sno-park permit.

Ape Cave formed 1900 years ago when Mt. St. Helens erupted a runny kind of basalt lava known as pahoehoe. As the flow's crust hardened, the liquid lava underneath drained out along the course of a buried stream gully, leaving a 11,334-foot-long tube. In places the tube was so tall it pinched into two separate levels, one above the other. Watch along the walls for stripes, the "high-water marks" left by flowing lava. Also look for solidified puddles of the lava river on the cave floor, often with ripple patterns like cake batter poured in a pan.

As the lava ebbed, superheated gases blasted through the tube, remelting the walls' surface and leaving tiny, fragile stalactites known as "lava drips." Since then, earthquakes have shaken loose portions of the upper cave's ceiling. An eruption of Mt. St. Helens 450 years ago loosed a mudflow that spilled into the cave's main entrance and paved the lower cave with sand. Remarkably, the 1980 eruption had almost no effect here.

Discovered in 1946, Ape Cave was named for the Mt. St. Helens Apes, a group of Boy Scout cavers who took their tongue-in-cheek name from an alleged 1924 sighting of Sasquatch on the mountain's east flank at an otherwise unrelated valley, Ape Canyon (Hike #26).

To find the cave, drive Interstate 5 north of Portland 25 miles and turn right at Woodland exit 21, following signs for Cougar. After 35 miles (beyond the town of Cougar 6.7 miles), turn left onto paved Road 83. After another 1.7 miles, turn left on Road 8303 for 0.9 mile to a parking lot at "Ape's Headquarters," a staffed information cabin.

Take a short path to the cave's main entrance, go down the stone stairs, and a few hundred feet later descend a metal stairway to the cave's main floor. The route behind you (under the metal stairs) leads to the rugged upper cave while the route ahead of you goes to the easier lower cave. Explore the popular, 0.8-mile lower cave first. Then, if you'd like to get away from the crowds, return to the stairway and try the rougher upper cave.

The upper cave begins with a 40-foot-tall room, but the route then arduously clambers over the first of ten major rockfalls. At the 0.8-mile and 0.9-mile marks you'll have to climb up 8-foot lava falls using whatever handholds and footholds you can find. The skylight opening after 1.1 mile is too high to use as an exit, but continue 0.3 mile and you'll reach a metal ladder to the upper entrance, just before the cave ends. The above-ground trail back to the main entrance crosses a sparsely forested lava bed and mudflow.

After visiting Ape Cave, or if it's so crowded you can't find a parking spot there, drive back 0.7 mile on Road 8303 to park at the Trail of Two Forests. Here you can stroll a boardwalk across a lava flow. The 0.2-mile loop features tubular rock molds left when lava surrounded trees. Dogs are allowed here on leash.

Ape Cave's main entrance.   Opposite: Tree cast tunnel entrance on Trail of Two Forests.

24 Mount St. Helens Rim

Moderate (to Dryer Creek Meadows)
8 miles round trip
1100 feet elevation gain
Open late June through October

Very Difficult (to summit)
9.4 miles round trip
4500 feet elevation gain
Open mid-July to mid-October

From Mt. St. Helens' summit rim, the crater gapes like the broken edge of a shattered planet. Rock avalanches rumble in slow motion down 2000-foot cliffs to the steaming lava dome. On the horizon, the snowpeaks of Washington and Oregon float above the clouds. The volcano created this crater in a violent 1980 blast. After a dome-building eruption 2004-2007, climbing permits are again available. For current conditions, check *www.fs.fed.us/gpnf* or call 360-449-7800.

Between May 15 and October 31, only 100 people a day are allowed to hike to the rim, either by way of Butte Camp (Hike #119) or up the shorter, more popular Monitor Ridge route described here. The climb requires no technical climbing skills—only stamina and strong knees. Hikers start out on a well-graded forest path to timberline, then follow poles marking the way up a ridge of lava boulders, and finally trudge up a dune-like slope of ash. Goggles and face masks are advised because of blowing ash. Maximum party size is 12. Don't take pets.

If you're unsure about attempting the climb—or if you can't get a permit—an option is to take the round-the-mountain Loowit Trail to the wildflowers at Dryer Creek Meadows instead. This alternative skips the steep climbing, yet still visits Monitor Ridge's interesting lava fields and offers views to Mt. Hood.

Permits are always required for travel above the 4800-foot level. The permits cost $22 per person between April 1 and October 31, but are free the rest of the year. In winter the access road is gated closed 4.4 miles short of the trailhead. Permits must be reserved online at least one day in advance at *www.mshinstitute. org*. Summer weekends fill soon after the reservation system opens in February,

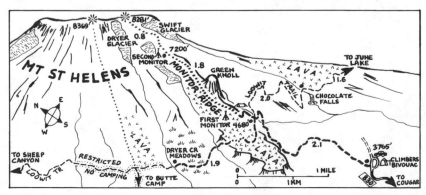

Dryer Creek Meadows.   Opposite: Mt. St. Helens' summit rim and distant Mt. Adams.

so consider a weekday trip. Permits have to be picked up at the Lone Fir Resort in Cougar (16806 Lewis River Road, 360-238-5210) by presenting your online payment confirmation.

To find the trailhead, drive Interstate 5 north of Portland 25 miles and turn right at Woodland exit 21, following signs for Cougar. After 35 miles (beyond the town of Cougar 6.7 miles), turn left on paved Road 83 for 3.1 miles. Then, following "Climbers Bivouac" pointers, turn left on Road 8100 for 1.7 miles and turn right on gravel Road 830 for 2.7 miles to a turnaround. Climbers determined to get an early morning start can either pitch their tents at a free, primitive campground here or backpack to a small, crowded, often waterless dale at timberline.

Start on the Ptarmigan Trail and climb steadily 2.1 miles to a junction with the Loowit Trail amid the pink heather and snow-bent firs of timberline *(GPS location N46°09.857' W122°11.434')*. If you're headed for Dryer Creek Meadows, turn left, follow the sometimes-faint Loowit Trail 0.9 mile across a rugged lava ridge, and continue another level mile through lovely August lupine fields to the mudflow gorge of the Dryer Glacier's outwash creek—a suitable turnaround point. If you're camping, note that most creeks on this mountain dry up from sunset to noon.

If you're climbing the mountain, walk straight across the Loowit Trail junction, following the steep climbers' route. The tread soon ends atop a rugged lava flow near one of the two tripod monitors that gave this ridge its name. The tripods' mirrors reflected laser beams to gauge the swelling of the mountain and thus predict eruptions.

Continue on a braided path marked by posts and then scramble up a ridge of boulders to the second monitor tripod. Shortly beyond this point the boulders end and the route ascends an ash slope between the Swift Glacier and a snow-field. Winds here often whip up gritty clouds of dust. When you reach the rim, don't venture too close to the unstable edge. Hiking is barred along the cliff to the right, but you can explore left as far as the Dryer Glacier headwall, which blocks safe access to what is technically the mountain's highest point.

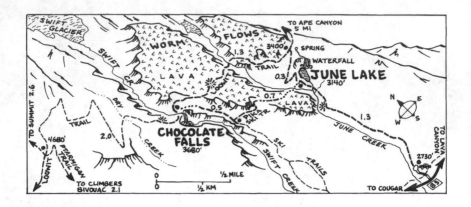

25   June Lake

Easy (to June Lake)
2.6 miles round trip
410 feet elevation gain
Open June to mid-November
Use: hikers, bicycles

Moderate (to Chocolate Falls)
5.8 miles round trip
1100 feet elevation gain
Open late June through October

The 1980 eruption had little effect here, but if you stroll through the woods to June Lake's 40-foot waterfall you'll see other proof that you're on a volcano. A mudflow dammed the lake about a century ago, and the waterfall drops off the edge of an ancient lava field. If you continue up to Chocolate Falls, you'll scramble across fresh-looking lava to a stripped-out gorge where an ash-choked waterfall sometimes runs as dark as chocolate milk.

Start by driving Interstate 5 north of Portland 25 miles to Woodland exit 21. Turn right, following signs for Cougar. After 35 miles (beyond the town of Cougar 6.7 miles), turn left onto paved Road 83 for 7.2 miles. At a "June Lake" sign, turn left for 200 yards to the trailhead turnaround. Bicycles are permitted, but are impractical on the lava beyond June Lake.

The first mile of the trail climbs gradually through a second-growth fir forest where huckleberry bushes hang heavy with blue fruit in late August. Expect to hear two common birds along the route. The tiny Pacific wren pours out a full ten seconds of cheerfully twittering musical madness from the vine maple underbrush. The robin-sized varied thrush pipes a single tone, like a slowly squeaking wagon wheel up in the firs.

At the 1.3-mile mark you'll cross the old mudflow—now a pleasant, sandy plain—to June Lake. A lacy waterfall splashes at the far side of the shallow pool amidst old-growth hemlocks.

The lake makes a lovely goal, but if you'd like a more challenging destination, walk to a "June Lake" sign 100 feet left of the shore and look for a path angling up into the woods ahead. This trail switchbacks up 0.3 mile to a junction just above the sudden spring that feeds June Lake's entire waterfall. Turn left on the Loowit Trail, a path that soon climbs across the Worm Flows—lava fields so rugged that hikers arc left to hop from boulder to boulder, following rock cairns and trail posts. Views extend across the lava to Mt. St. Helens' snowy rim.

After crossing three lava fields in 1.3 miles, the Loowit Trail dips to Chocolate Falls, a dramatic pair of 40-foot plumes in a canyon scoured by floods from the 1980 eruption (*GPS location N46°09.480' W122°10.448'*). Since the Swift Glacier's demise, the falls dry up at night, but run a silty brown from about 11:30 am to sunset.

Other Options

For a longer hike, continue as far as you like on the 29.5-mile Loowit Trail, which circles Mt. St. Helens at timberline. To the west of Chocolate Falls the route climbs 2 miles through woods to a climbers' campsite at the Ptarmigan Trail junction beside Monitor Ridge (see Hike #24). To the east of June Lake the Loowit Trail crosses lava fields and mudflow gullies for 5 miles to Ape Canyon (Hike #26).

June Lake's waterfall. Opposite: Chocolate Falls at 11:30 am, just after it starts flowing.

Ape Canyon

Difficult (to Plains of Abraham)
9 miles round trip
1300 feet elevation gain
Open July through October
Use: hikers, bicycles

Difficult (to Windy Ridge)
26.2-mile loop
2800 feet elevation gain

Mountain bikers and hikers all puff while climbing this trail, on a forested ridge beside a mile-wide mudflow with views up to Mt. St. Helens' decapitated rim. The top of the trail offers a view down Ape Canyon's eerie, 300-foot-tall rock slot at the edge of the 1980 blast zone. Before turning back, hikers generally continue another 0.8 mile to a clifftop spring at the Plains of Abraham, a once-desolate cinder plain that's now a field of blue lupine. Mountain bikers generally don't turn back at all—they continue on a challenging 26.2-mile loop via Windy Ridge and the Smith River Trail.

Ape Canyon won its name in 1924 when an ape-like creature threw rocks at two miners in a cabin here. In 1982 an old-timer confessed that he and another boy had staged the entire incident. But in the meantime the Sasquatch tale inspired a local Boy Scout group to name Ape Cave (see Hike #23), a lava tube 8 miles away on the mountain's south flank. Today, visitors are often confused that the canyon and cave are otherwise unrelated and are located so far apart.

To start, drive Interstate 5 to Woodland exit 21 (north of Portland 25 miles), and turn right, following signs for Cougar. After 35 miles (beyond the town of Cougar 6.7 miles), turn left on Road 83 for 11.2 paved miles to the Ape Canyon Trailhead on the left, just a few hundred yards before the road ends at Lava Canyon.

The Ape Canyon Trail starts out along a cliff overlooking the Muddy River's vast lahar—a flow of mud, rock, and ash unleashed when the volcano's 1980 eruption melted much of the Shoestring Glacier. The forest beside the moonscape

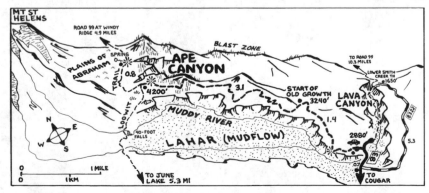

lahar was unscathed by the blast. However, the first 1.4 miles of the trail's route are still recovering from a 1968 clearcut. Deer and elk frequently browse the vine maples and alder here. Look for red paintbrush, dwarf blue lupine, and purple asters, too. Then the path dives into an impressive old-growth stand of 6-foot-thick hemlocks and Douglas firs hung with gray-green witch's hair lichen. White June wildflowers here include delicate inside-out flower and vanilla leaf.

At the 4-mile mark the trail enters the blast zone of trees killed by superheated air. Ahead, the lahar's mudflow plain snakes up toward the gray volcano, serrated by gullies. To the right, Ape Canyon's still-green valley gradually narrows to a slot-like chasm framing a view of snowy Mt. Adams.

The path joins the round-the-mountain Loowit Trail in a pumice plain with two signposts *(GPS location N46°11.731' W122°08.102')*. Unless you're bushed, it's worth turning right here to follow the Loowit Trail 0.8 mile through the Plains of Abraham's lupine to a spring atop a rock cliff.

If you're biking, plan to continue on the loop, because if you race back down the Ape Canyon Trail you'll bowl over the people puffing uphill. For the loop, keep right at junctions for another 4.9 miles to the Windy Ridge Viewpoint, follow paved Road 99 for 1.8 miles to the Upper Smith Creek Trailhead, turn right on the Smith Creek Trail for 10.3 miles down to the Lower Smith Creek Trailhead, and take gravel Road 8322 for 5.3 miles back up to find your car.

Lupine on the Plains of Abraham.   Opposite: Ape Canyon and distant Mt. Adams.

27

Lava Canyon

Easy (to suspension bridge)
1.3-mile loop
300 feet elevation gain
Open mid-April to mid-November

Moderate (to The Ship)
3.3 miles round trip
1100 feet elevation gain

This spectacular trail descends a mudflow-scoured chasm past waterfalls and ancient lava cliffs. An easy loop circles the upper gorge, crossing the canyon twice on scenic footbridges. More adventurous hikers can continue downstream on a narrower tread that descends a dizzying 40-foot ladder en route to a lava outcrop called The Ship. Pets are not allowed.

The rock formations in Lava Canyon are remnants of a Mt. St. Helens lava flow that coursed down the Muddy River's valley 3500 years ago. The basalt lava fractured into a honeycomb of pillar-like columns as it cooled. When the river then cut down through the flow it carved waterfall chutes and left free-standing lava towers such as The Ship. Later stream debris buried the formations until the 1980 eruption, when the melting Shoestring Glacier loosed a gigantic *lahar* (mudflow) that washed Lava Canyon clean.

Drive Interstate 5 north of Portland 25 miles to Woodland exit 21 and turn right, following signs for Cougar. After 35 miles (beyond the town of Cougar 6.7 miles), turn left onto paved Road 83 for 11.3 miles to a turnaround at road's end.

The path is wide and paved for its first 0.4 mile, with viewpoint decks and interpretive signs. Then turn right to cross a metal footbridge. Below the span are a series of frothing waterfalls and churning river cauldrons. Hang tight to small children from here on. The path downstream follows a basalt cliff for 0.3 mile and then recrosses the gorge on a high, scary-looking

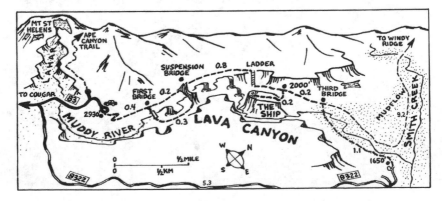

The suspension footbridge.   *Opposite: Waterfalls in Lava Canyon.*

suspension bridge.

For the short loop, turn left after crossing the suspension bridge and return to the car. For a more rugged hike (not suitable for children), turn right and continue downstream past a string of colossal waterfalls. The steep trail crosses cliffy slopes with no railings, and the tread can be slippery in wet weather, so be sure to wear boots with good soles. Climb down a 40-foot metal ladder and a few hundred yards later turn right on a side trail that scrambles 0.2 mile to a viewpoint atop The Ship, a 100-foot-tall lava block in mid-canyon. Then return to the main trail.

Before returning to your car you might want to continue briefly downstream to the trail's third bridge, in a 1980 mudflow plain that's regrowing with dwarf lupine wildflowers and scattered fir trees. An elk herd commonly ranges here.

Other Options

If you can arrange a short car shuttle, you can hike the Lava Canyon Trail one way, all downhill. To leave a car at the lower trailhead, turn off Road 83 just 0.8 mile before the Lava Canyon Trailhead and follow gravel Road 8322 downhill for 5.3 miles to its end at the Lower Smith Creek Trailhead.

28   Windy Ridge

Easy (to Windy Ridge Viewpoint)
0.2 mile round trip
200 feet elevation gain
Open late June through October

Moderate (to Loowit Falls)
9.2-mile loop
900 feet elevation gain

Difficult (to Plains of Abraham)
11.4-mile loop
1400 feet elevation gain

For a close look into the mouth of Mt. St. Helens' steaming crater, start at the Windy Ridge parking area. A staircase climbs 200 feet to a popular viewpoint, but longer trails lead right up to the crater's outlet—a badlands chasm below 200-foot Loowit Falls. A trail planned for 2015 will climb to an even closer viewpoint above Loowit Falls. Hikers are not allowed to explore off trail.

To find the trailhead, drive Interstate 5 to Woodland exit 21 (north of Portland 25 miles), turn right toward Cougar, and continue a total of 88 paved miles, following signs for Windy Ridge. Along the way, you'll drive Highway 503 through the town of Cougar, continue straight on what becomes Road 90 to the Pine Creek Information Station, go straight on Road 25 for 25 miles, and turn left on Road 99. Follow this paved road for 16 miles to its end. Pets and camping are banned.

When you park at the Windy Ridge Viewpoint the most obvious and popular trail is a long flight of steps scaling a 200-foot butte to the right. If you join the crowds puffing up these stairs you really will gain a sweeping view of Spirit Lake and the volcano. But to leave the hordes behind—and see the mountain closer up—start your hike by walking up a gated gravel road on the opposite side of the parking area. This old road, now a wide trail, traverses a ridge where

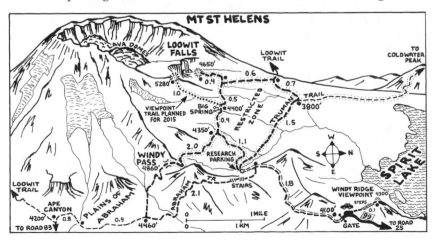

scattered trees have taken root since the 1980 blast. Wildflowers have flourished; look for blue lupine, pearly everlasting, purple daisy-shaped asters, and clumps of big purple penstemons.

After 1.8 miles the Abraham Trail joins on the left—the return route of an optional loop. Continue to road's end at a parking area for research vehicles. Head left across the pumice plain on the Windy Trail, which climbs a mile to the round-the-mountain Loowit Trail. Because this route crosses a restricted zone under scientific study, hikers must stay within 10 feet of the trail.

Turn right on the Loowit Trail across a creek gully. A quarter mile later, splash across the outlet of Big Spring in a willow thicket. Just beyond, a side trail to the left may open in 2015, climbing a mile to the best crater viewpoint of all. If it's not built, simply go straight 0.9 mile up to the Loowit Falls viewpoint. The lava dome, out of sight in the crater above, heats this steamy waterfall.

You can return from Loowit Falls on either of two loops. For the easier loop, hike down from the Loowit Falls viewpoint 0.4 mile, turn left on the Loowit Trail, and then keep right at junctions to the Truman Trail. This route takes you down toward Spirit Lake, with interesting views of the volcano's crater over your shoulder.

A longer loop visits the dramatic Plains of Abraham. For this option, hike down from the Loowit Falls viewpoint 0.4 mile and keep right at junctions for 2.9 miles, climbing over Windy Pass to the Plains of Abraham, a rock-strewn desert colonized by blue lupine and other flowers.

Camping is permitted, but the only water is a weird creek of what looks like chocolate milk oozing from the ash. Turn left at a well-marked junction, recross the creek, and traverse a glorious ridge packed with July wildflowers and views of Mt. Adams before dscending two sets of steps to join the trail back to the car.

Spirit Lake from the trail near Loowit Falls.   Opposite: Loowit Falls.

29 Spirit Lake & Norway Pass

Easy (to Harmony Falls)
2.4 miles round trip
700 feet elevation **loss**
Open late June through October

Moderate (to Norway Pass)
4.4 miles round trip
860 feet elevation gain
Use: hikers, bicycles

Difficult (to Mt. Margaret)
11 miles round trip
2240 feet elevation gain
Open late July through October

When Mt. St. Helens' summit slid into Spirit Lake in 1980 it launched a gigantic wave that sloshed 800 feet up the lake's far shore, obliterating three youth camps and denuding the slopes. Today wildflowers and small trees have returned to this landscape, but hikers can still see the pale high-water mark left by the wave and the vast jumble of driftwood it washed into the lake.

Today the only access to Spirit Lake's shore is on the popular 1.2-mile Harmony Falls Trail. For a better view of the lake, you can hike the Boundary Trail 2.2 miles up to Norway Pass—or you can continue to the top of Mt. Margaret for the best view of all. Pets are not allowed on these trails.

Start by driving Interstate 5 to Woodland exit 21 (north of Portland 25 miles). Turn right toward Cougar and follow signs for Windy Ridge a total of 85 paved miles. Along the way, you'll follow Highway 503 through the town of Cougar, continue straight on what becomes Road 90 to the Pine Creek Information Station, go straight on Road 25 for 25 miles, and turn left on Road 99 for 13.1 miles to the Harmony Viewpoint (2.8 miles before road's end at Windy Ridge).

The 1.1-mile Harmony Trail descends from the viewpoint amid thickets of sweet-smelling white alder with blue huckleberries, salmonberries, candyflower,

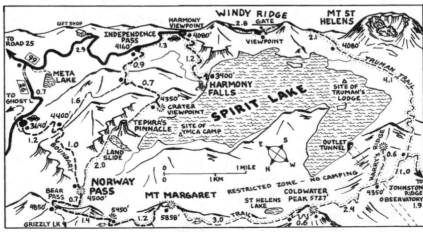

and devils club. The path dips past a drippy cliff and then traverses a sandy plain with flotsam logs left from the gigantic wave. Finally descend along Harmony Creek's stairstep falls to the shore, 200 feet above Spirit Lake's old level. Off-trail hiking, camping, and venturing out on the driftwood logs are banned.

If you'd like to hike to the bigger view at Norway Pass, drive 4.2 miles back on Road 99. Just after Meta Lake turn left on Road 26, a paved road that's been made very rough by a slump. After 0.7 mile, pull into Boundary Trailhead to the left.

The trail to Norway Pass sets out through blast-zone blowdown that is regrowing with huckleberries, strawberries, willow brush, and some spire-shaped firs. After 1.2 miles you'll switchback up to the right at a trail junction. Avalanche lilies bloom here just after the snowmelt, and in August the huckleberry bushes are loaded with fruit.

The spectacular view across Spirit Lake to the volcano suddenly opens up at Norway Pass, a great spot for lunch. Hillsides of blowdown trees have regrown with hummingbird-friendly brush: thimbleberry, tiger lilies, and paintbrush. The tiny birds zoom and chip angrily at each other, defending this valuable territory.

The side trail from Norway Pass to Independence Pass is often closed by slides, so for a longer hike, stay on the Boundary Trail toward Mt. Margaret. After 0.7 mile you'll climb to Bear Pass, where views extend north to Grizzly Lake and Mt. Rainier. Another 1.4 miles brings you to a backpacker campground in a high swale. Maximum camping group size is four, camping is allowed in designated sites only, and campfires are not allowed. The required backpacking permits are free, available at the Johnston Ridge Observatory, the National Monument headquarters in Amboy, and the Cowlitz Valley Ranger District office.

Beyond the campground 1.1 mile, a short spur to the right climbs to the panoramic view atop Mt. Margaret.

Mt. St. Helens from Norway Pass.   *Opposite: Spirit Lake from Harmony Falls.*

30   Badger Peak

Moderate (to Badger Lake)
8.6 miles round trip
1300 feet elevation gain
Open mid-July through October
Use: hikers, horses, bikes

Difficult (to Badger Peak)
10.2 miles round trip
2000 feet elevation gain

This convenient but overlooked section of the 56-mile Boundary Trail between Mt. St. Helens and Mt. Adams is currently open to motorcycles. The policy is damaging and annoying, but the hike is great and the trail is worth saving. Visit here to witness some of the unbelievably beautiful wilderness scenery in Washington that should not be abandoned to motor vehicles.

The Boundary Trail follows the crest of the Dark Divide, with views of Mt. Rainier, Mt. St. Helens, and Mt. Admas, to a little subalpine lake that makes a great lunch stop. A side trail climbs to the rocky site of a former fire lookout, where views spin around the compass.

Start by driving Interstate 5 to Woodland exit 21 (north of Portland 25 miles). Turn right toward Cougar and follow signs for Windy Ridge for 46 paved miles, following Highway 503 through the town of Cougar and continuing straight on what becomes Road 90. At the Pine Creek Information Station, reset your odometer and continue straight on Road 25 another 21 miles toward Windy Ridge. At a large "Boundary Trail Trailhead" sign in Elk Pass, park in a lot on the left.

From the trailhead messageboard, follow a rutted path 300 feet into the woods to a T-shaped junction with the Boundary Trail. All of the trails in this area have been eroded into grooves by motorcycle tires, but the odds are low that you will actually meet motorized traffic.

Turn left on the Bounday Trail, cross the paved road, and enter an old-growth forest of hemlock and fir, some as large as 6 feet in diameter. White avalanche

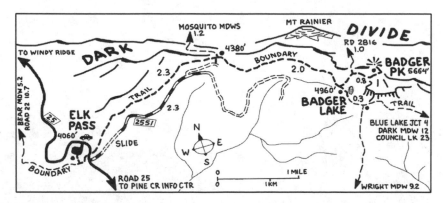

lilies carpet the forest floor in July as the last of the snowpack melts. Also expect vanilla leaf, devils club, bracken, and coolwort.

After a mile the trail traces a forested ridgecrest with glimpses left to the white tip of Mt. Rainier. At the 2.3-mile mark, go straight at trail junctions in a broad saddle. The Boundary Trail climbs gradually for the next 2 miles to a small sign for the Badger Ridge Trail, on a large tree immediately before Badger Lake's meadow.

First cross the grassy meadow to take a look at Badger Lake, a shallow, 300-foot-long pond flanked by shaggy-barked Alaska cedars *(GPS location N46°17.131' W121°53.928')*. This is a good place to eat lunch and gather your energy for the climb up Badger Peak.

When you're ready, recross the meadow to the big tree with the Badger Ridge Trail sign. The 0.8-mile side path climbs steadily up to a rock crag with 360° views from Mt. St. Helens in the west, Mt. Rainier to the north, Mt. Adams to the east, and Mt. Hood to the south. Butterflies often rendezvous up here. Iron anchor bolts and three survey markers remain from the lookout building that once stood on Badger Peak's small, flattened summit.

Other Options

It's slightly quicker, but a bit tedious, to return from Badger Lake on a loop. Hike back 2 miles from the lake to a junction in a broad saddle *(GPS location N46°17.840' W121°55.751')*, take a trail left 100 feet to an old logging road, and keep right on roads 2.3 miles to your car.

Alaska cedar at Badger Lake.   Opposite: Mt. Adams from Badger Peak.

Upper Lewis River Falls.   Opposite: Middle Lewis River Falls.

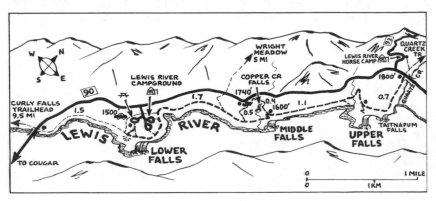

31 Lewis River Falls

Easy
7 miles round trip
500 feet elevation gain
Open all year
Use: hikers, horses, bicycles

The Lewis River thunders over three colossal falls along this riverbank path. Because a paved road parallels the route, it's easy to plan a car (or bicycle) shuttle and hike the 3.5-mile trail one way — but the path's pretty enough you probably won't mind hiking it twice.

Drive Interstate 5 north of Portland 25 miles, turn right at Woodland exit 21, and follow signs for Mt. St. Helens for 46.7 miles. Along the way, you'll follow Highway 503, go through the town of Cougar, and continue straight on what becomes Road 90. Just beyond the Pine Creek Information Station, turn right toward Carson on what is still Road 90 and follow this paved road for 14 miles to the Lower Falls Recreation Area on your right. Keep right to the picnic area loop and park by the restrooms.

A graveled trail sets off through Douglas fir woods with lots of pointy-leaved Oregon grape, dark-berried salal, and vine maple. After 100 yards take a right-hand fork of the trail that leads to an overlook of Lower Falls, where the Lewis River takes a magnificent Niagara-like plunge into a huge green pool.

Several trails from the nearby campground confuse things a bit here, but if you simply follow the riverbank upstream and ignore all left-hand forks you can't go wrong. After half a mile the graveled path turns to duff. In another mile you'll cross a footbridge above Copper Creek's 20-foot, double-humped waterslide into the Lewis River. You can visit another of Copper Creek's waterfalls by taking a 0.6-mile-longer loop to the left on well-marked side trails — but save this detour for the return trip.

Continue along the Lewis River past Middle Falls, a 100-foot-long, milky-looking slide. The river trail soon ducks below a huge, overhanging cliff and enters a grove of massive old-growth Douglas firs and red cedars up to 10 feet thick. About 0.8 mile past Middle Falls you'll pass a trailside campsite with a bouldery beach and a glimpse ahead to Upper Falls. This is the only beach on the hike where kids can safely play by the river.

Next the trail bridges Alec Creek and climbs above Upper Falls, where a side trail leads to the 80-foot cascade's lip. The final 0.7 mile of the Lewis River Trail passes humble Taitnapum Falls and follows Quartz Creek to a bridge on Road 90, just 2.7 miles by road from your car.

32   Observation Peak

Moderate (from Road 5800)
5.6 miles round trip
1390 feet elevation gain
Open June to mid-November

Difficult (from Trapper Cr Trailhead)
15-mile loop
3200 feet elevation gain

Halfway between the Columbia River and Mt. St. Helens, the Trapper Creek Wilderness is a warren of hiking paths along woodsy creeks and ridges. Several trails climb 6 miles or more to reach the old lookout site at Observation Peak, with views from Mt. Jefferson to Mt. Rainier, but a little-known trailhead gets you there in less than 3 miles—and allows explorers to take a side trip to a higher, better viewpoint atop Sisters Rocks.

To find this back-door trailhead, drive Interstate 84 to Cascade Locks exit 44, pay a $1 toll to cross the Bridge of the Gods, turn right on Highway 14 for 5.9 miles, and turn left through Carson on Highway 30 for 14.5 miles to a junction. The lower Trapper Creek trailheads are straight ahead, but turn right for the shortcut trail, following a Mt. St. Helens pointer onto what is still Highway 30. After 2 miles fork left onto one-lane Dry Creek Road 64 for 4.1 miles of pavement and another 2 miles of gravel. Then fork left onto gravel Road 5800 and keep left at forks for the next 2 miles to a small parking area on the left with a sign for the Observation Trail *(GPS location N45°56.994′ W122°02.390′)*.

The path climbs a windy ridge of ancient Douglas fir and western hemlock. In June expect white beargrass and bunchberry blooms. In August expect ripe blue huckleberries and inedible red bunchberries. After 1.1 mile, where the trail crests a summit, take a spur trail 50 feet left to a boulder pile with a nice view east to Mt. Adams. Listen for the *meep!* of pikas (rock rabbits) in the rockslide below.

Then continue on the main trail, descending 0.7 mile to a saddle with two

Observation Peak from Sisters Rocks.   Above: Forest along the Observation Trail.

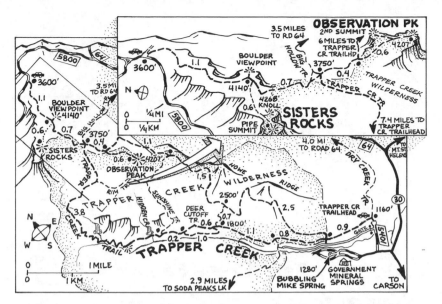

junctions. Go straight, ignoring both the Big Hollow Trail to the left and the Trapper Creek Trail to the right. After 0.4 mile you'll reach another saddle with a junction. Veer uphill to the right for 0.6 mile to trail's end at Observation Peak *(GPS location N45°55.239' W122°01.486')*.

The peak overlooks the entire Trapper Creek Wilderness. Clusters of blue gentians and bluebells bloom on the knoll. Observation Peak also has a second summit that you can visit on the return trip. After hiking back 0.3 mile, take a spur to the right that climbs 200 yards along a cliff edge to a spectacular summit atop rock fins. Then return to the main trail and follow it back to your car.

If you'd rather start your hike at a lower, more convenient trailhead, drive Highway 30 north through Carson for 14.5 miles to a junction, go straight on Mineral Springs Road for 0.4 mile, and turn right on gravel Road 5401 to its end at the Trapper Creek Trailhead.

Set out on Trapper Creek Trail 192. For a moderate 7.2-mile hike, loop back when you reach the second junction with the Deer Cutoff Trail. For a more challenging 15-mile loop, follow the Trapper Creek Trail a total of 7.4 miles, turn right for a mile up to Observation Peak, return 0.6 mile to a junction, and turn right on a well-graded return trail down Howe Ridge.

Health-conscious tourists were first attracted to the Trapper Creek area by Bubbling Mike, a metallic-tasting soda spring. A 3-story spa hotel from the early 1900s burned in 1934, but the spring remains. Volunteers from the Portland Mazamas outdoor club built many of the trails in the area.

Other Options

The area's best viewpoint, at Sisters Rocks, requires some scrambling, so it's for adventurers only. Hike the Observation Trail from the upper trailhead 1.1 mile. Beyond the boulder viewpoint crest 20 feet ignore a spur to the left and instead take a faint, unofficial path to the right (westward) through the open woods of a broad ridge for 0.4 mile. When the path emerges at a bare knoll, turn right and follow a rocky ridge another 0.2 mile to the viewpoint atop Sisters Rocks, a crag marked by an iron pipe *(GPS location N45°56.048' W122°02.774')*.

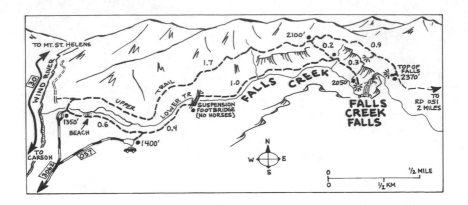

33   Falls Creek Falls

Easy (lower trail)
3.4 miles round trip
650 feet elevation gain
Open April 1 to November 30
Use: hikers, bicycles

Moderate (to top of falls)
6.3-mile loop
1150 feet elevation gain
Use: hikers, horses, bicycles

The Lower Falls Creek Trail crosses a suspension footbridge over a mossy gorge on its way to a colossal, 200-foot waterfall. For a loop, return via a longer, upper path along the forested canyon's rim.

Start by driving Interstate 84 to Cascade Locks exit 44. Pay a $1 toll to cross the Bridge of the Gods, turn right on Highway 14 for 5.9 miles, and then turn left through Carson on Highway 30 for 14.5 miles. Next, following a sign for Mt. St. Helens, turn right on paved Wind River Road 30 for 0.8 mile. Then turn right onto gravel Road 3062 for 2 miles and fork to the right onto Road 057 for half a mile to road's end, where there's a turnaround for the Lower Falls Creek Trail.

The path begins in a second-growth forest where ancient stumps still show the springboard notches left by timber fallers with crosscut saws. Soon the path enters old-growth woods with Douglas firs five feet in diameter. Also look for larch (or *tamarack*), a tree that usually grows east of the Cascades. This conifer packs 17 to 21 needles in each cluster, but loses them in fall, so it looks dead all winter.

After 0.4 mile the path crosses Falls Creek on a 30-foot suspension footbridge. Frilly stalks of maidenhair fern waft from the gorge cliffs below. Continue 1.3 miles upstream, climbing to trail's end at a viewpoint beside Falls Creek Falls. The 3-tiered cascade starts with a hidden 50-foot falls, spreads across a 70-foot fan, and finally thunders 80 feet into a rock punchbowl.

If you'd like to return on a loop, walk back from the falls 0.3 mile and turn uphill to the right on a signed connector trail that climbs steeply up a ridge 0.2 mile to the Upper Falls Creek Trail. To visit a viewpoint near the top of the falls, turn right on this upper trail 0.9 mile and take a spur 100 yards to the right. Although you can't see much of the falls from this clifftop perch, the view of the valley below is nice. A very rough scramble trail does continue down to the actual falls, but it's too steep to risk. Instead declare victory here and head back down the Upper Falls Creek Trail.

After descending 2.6 miles through the woods, turn left at an unmarked trail junction just before an abandoned road, cross the creek on a wide footbridge, and turn left again along a creekside trail. Soon you'll pass a small gravel beach, a good place for kids to play in the water on a hot day. When the path rejoins the Lower Falls Creek Trail, turn right 150 yards to your car.

Other Options

Because the suspension footbridge on the lower trail is closed to horses, equestrians start at the end of Road 3062 and take the Upper Falls Creek Trail instead. After passing the top of the falls, this path levels off for 2 viewless miles to its end at gravel Road 051.

Falls Creek Falls.   Opposite: The suspension footbridge.

34   Thomas Lake

Easy (to Thomas Lake)
1.4 miles round trip
300 feet elevation gain
Open mid-June to mid-October
Use: hikers, horses

Moderate (to Blue Lake)
6.8 miles round trip
900 feet elevation gain

Children and lake-lovers of all ages enjoy exploring the five lakes clustered in the forest within the first mile of the Thomas Lake Trail. For a longer hike, cross Indian Heaven's glorious heather-and-huckleberry meadows to sapphire Blue Lake, backed by the cliffs of Gifford Peak. Maximum group size is 12 (including horses) and camping near the lakes is limited to 15 sites designated by posts.

To find the trailhead, drive Interstate 84 to Cascade Locks exit 44, pay $1 to cross the Bridge of the Gods, turn right on Highway 14 for 5.9 miles, and turn left through Carson on Highway 30 for 5.8 miles. Following signs for Panther Creek Campground, turn briefly right and then jog left on what becomes Road 65. Follow this curvy, one-lane paved road for 11 miles to an X-shaped junction called Four Corners. Go straight on paved Road 65 for 2 miles and then fork to the right on a gravel continuation of Road 65 for 6.7 miles to the signed Thomas Lake Trail parking area on the right.

The trail begins in a partially logged area with a view of Mt. St. Helens, but soon climbs into uncut woods of lichen-draped mountain hemlock and Pacific silver fir. Blue huckleberries ripen here in August. Mosquitoes can be thick in July.

After 0.7 mile the path squeezes between three lakes. Just beyond a little footbridge, explorers might want to try a side trail to the right that leads past several heavily used campsites and continues faintly 0.5 mile around Thomas Lake. Otherwise continue on the main trail 100 yards to a major, unmarked fork.

The left-hand fork deadends in 0.2 mile at Eunice Lake. If you've set a more distant goal, keep right and climb up a steep, rough switchback to a wooded plateau. After another half mile you'll pass a pond on the left. Immediately opposite this pond, on the right-hand side of the trail, a faint side path leads 100 yards over a small ridge to hidden, rarely-visited Brader Lake.

Beyond this point the main trail has a few more steep, rocky pitches before leveling off amid heavenly alpine meadows. Turn right at a 4-way junction, ramble 0.8 mile to a T-shaped junction at a pond, and turn right for a final half mile through the woods to the Pacific Crest Trail at the end of Blue Lake.

Other Options

The lake-dotted high meadows invite exploration. For a loop along an abandoned trail, turn left at the T-shaped junction 0.5 mile before Blue Lake, pass a "Trail Not Maintained" sign, and take the easily followed path 1.7 miles through

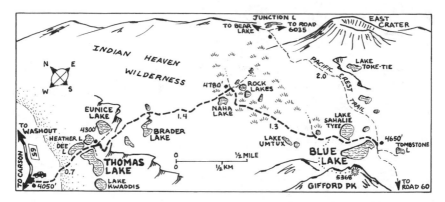

the meadows to Junction Lake (also accessible via Hike #35). Then turn right on the PCT for 2 woodsy miles to Blue Lake.

Adventurers with compass in hand can also bushwhack to a rare viewpoint atop Gifford Peak. From Blue Lake, hike back past Sahalie Tyee Lake to the Thomas Lake Trail's highest point in the forest and strike off to the left up a wooded ridge, gaining 700 feet in 0.8 mile.

Thomas Lake.   Opposite: Cascades frog.

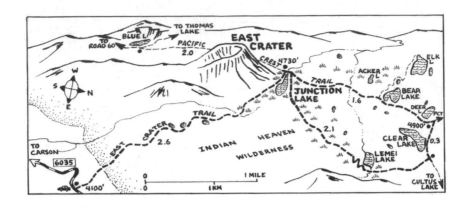

Junction Lake.   Opposite: Clear Lake.

35 Junction Lake

Easy (to Junction Lake)
5.2 miles round trip
700 feet elevation gain
Open mid-June to mid-October
Use: hikers, horses

Moderate (to Lemei Lake)
9.2-mile loop
900 feet elevation gain

The East Crater Trail provides the easiest route to the famous alpine meadows of the Indian Heaven Wilderness. And once you reach huckleberry-rimmed Junction Lake, it's tempting to make an additional 4-mile loop on the Pacific Crest Trail past four other large lakes and vast fields of heather.

Drive Interstate 84 to Cascade Locks exit 44, pay $1 to cross the Bridge of the Gods, turn right on Highway 14 for 5.9 miles, and turn left through Carson on Highway 30 for 5.8 miles. Following signs for Panther Creek Campground, turn briefly right and then jog left on what becomes Road 65. Follow this curvy, one-lane paved road for 11 miles to an X-shaped junction called Four Corners. Turn right on gravel Road 60 for 8.6 miles, and then follow an "East Crater Trail" pointer left onto Road 6030 (which becomes Road 6035) for 4.2 miles to the well-marked trailhead on the left, 100 feet before a "Road Closed Ahead" sign *(GPS location N45°58.880' W121°45.484')*.

The path's first 1.4 miles climb gradually through unremarkable mountain hemlock woods—a long stretch for hikers with small children. But then you pass three tadpole-filled ponds and the meadowed openings become larger and larger, leading over a low pass to Junction Lake. The heather blooms here in July—a month when mosquitoes are a real problem. In August the huckleberries ripen, while the crisp nights of September turn the huckleberry leaves gold and red. If you're backpacking, be sure to camp in the woods and not in the fragile meadows.

To continue on the loop, go to the Pacific Crest Trail junction at the far end of the lake, turn right across the outlet creek, and promptly turn right on the Lemei Lake Trail. This path ambles through heather and past grassy-banked Lemei Lake. After 2.1 miles turn left on the Indian Heaven Trail, which leads between a huge rockslide and Clear Lake. Then turn left on the PCT to complete the loop. Short side trails to the right of the PCT lead down to forest-rimmed Deer and Bear Lakes, as well as to unseen Elk Lake.

Other Options

To explore more of this high country, either take a side trip from Clear Lake north 0.4 mile to Cultus Lake (see Hike #36), or take the PCT south from Junction Lake 2 miles to Blue Lake (see Hike #34). Adventurers who are careful to use compass can also bushwhack due south a mile from Junction Lake up the steep, forested flank of East Crater to a viewpoint on the volcano's east rim. In the middle of the crater is an eerie, hidden meadow with a rarely visited pond.

36   Cultus Lake

Moderate (to Cultus Lake)
4.4 miles round trip
1100 feet elevation gain
Open July to mid-October
Use: hikers, horses

Moderate (to Lake Wapiki overlook)
6.8 miles round trip
1600 feet elevation gain

The Indian Heaven country features alpine meadows, sparkling lakes, and world-famous huckleberry fields—but because this Wilderness lacks a major Cascade mountain it seldom draws crowds. The trail to Cultus Lake makes up for this by sneaking views of not-so-distant Mt. Adams. And if you hike an extra 1.2 miles through the heather you'll get even better views from craggy Lemei Rock, an ancient volcano that cups Lake Wapiki within its crater.

Until the 1920s Indians came to this high country each August to pick berries, hunt, and race horses. Natural and set wildfires maintained the berry fields and meadows. Even today the non-Wilderness huckleberry fields northeast of Highway 24 are reserved for Indians. Then as now, mosquitoes are a problem in July.

Drive Interstate 84 to Cascade Locks exit 44, pay a $1 toll to cross the Bridge of the Gods, turn right on Highway 14 for 5.9 miles, and turn left through Carson on Highway 30 for 14.5 miles. Next, following a pointer for Mt. St. Helens, turn right on paved Wind River Road 30 for 15.8 miles. When pavement ends at a junction near the Lone Butte Sno-Park, follow a "Sawtooth Berry Field" sign to stay on Road 30 for another 7.9 miles to a T-shaped junction with Road 24, and then turn right for 4.2 rough gravel miles to the Cultus Creek Campground *(GPS location N46°02.799' W121°45.407')*. Park at the far end of the campground loop by a sign for the Indian Heaven Trail.

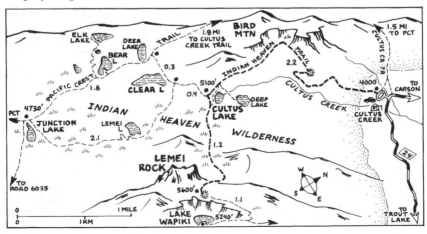

Lemei Rock from its base.   Opposite: Lemei Rock from Cultus Lake.

The trail climbs steeply through Douglas fir woods for a mile to a view of several peaks—from left to right, Sawtooth Mountain, Mt. Rainier, the Goat Rocks, and Mt. Adams. Then the path continues uphill to a small meadow below Bird Mountain's cliffs before leveling off for a mile. You'll reach a trail junction at your first glimpse of Cultus Lake. Explore to the left if you wish— the path deadends in 0.3 mile at Deep Lake. Otherwise keep right around beautiful, alpine Cultus Lake to a junction with the Lemei Trail. In Chinook jargon, the old trade language of Northwest tribes, *lemei* means "old woman" and *cultus,* oddly enough, means "worthless."

For a longer hike, take the Lemei Trail up through a mile of gorgeous heather meadows, switchback up to the base of Lemei Rock's summit crags, and continue a few hundred yards to the red cinder rim of the old crater overlooking lovely Lake Wapiki, Mt. Adams, and Mt. Hood. If you're eager for a swim, it's 1.1 miles further down to the meadows and sandy beach at Lake Wapiki, but remember to save energy for the return climb.

Other Options

Two moderate loop trips also begin with the hike to Cultus Lake. For a 9.2-mile meadow tour of six lakes, continue straight on the Indian Heaven Trail to the Pacific Crest Trail, turn left to Junction Lake (also accessible via Hike #35), and turn left on the Lemei Lake Trail. For a woodsy 6.2-mile loop around Bird Mountain, take the Indian Heaven Trail to the PCT, turn right for 1.8 level miles, and turn right on the Cultus Creek Trail over a low pass for the steep descent to your car.

37 Sleeping Beauty

Moderate (from Road 5800)
3.2 miles round trip
1410 feet elevation gain
Open July to early November

Stonework ramps enable the trail to scale the final switchbacks to the former fire lookout site on Sleeping Beauty, a crag with an astonishing close-up view of snowy Mt. Adams. The trail is steep but steady, so it usually demands just one hour of good exercise to reach the top.

From Interstate 84 in Hood River, take White Salmon exit #64, pay a $1 toll to cross the Columbia River bridge, and turn left on Washington Highway 14. After 1.4 miles, turn right on "Alt 141" toward Trout Lake. In another 2.3 miles you'll merge left onto Highway 141. Continue 20.5 miles.

Beyond the Trout Lake general store 1.6 miles, turn right on Trout Lake Creek Road 88. After another 4.6 miles, turn right on Road 8810. This wide gravel road turns left at a T-shaped junction after 1.1 mile. Continue another 5 miles and turn right on smaller, rougher gravel Road 040 for 0.4 mile to a pair of parking pullouts on the right, opposite a small messageboard for the Sleeping Beauty Trail *(GPS location N46°05.107' W121°39.500')*.

The trail slaloms up through a second-growth forest of Douglas fir and vine maple. After 0.2 mile the path shifts to switchbacks in old-growth woods with trees 6 feet in diameter. Here you'll find a ground cover of vanilla leaf, pathfinder plant, thimbleberry, bracken, and wild strawberry.

At the 1.2-mile mark you'll reach a T-shaped junction in a broad, forested saddle. Lots of blue huckleberries ripen here in August. Turn right for the final 0.4-mile climb to the summit. This part of the hike is the payoff: a spectacular

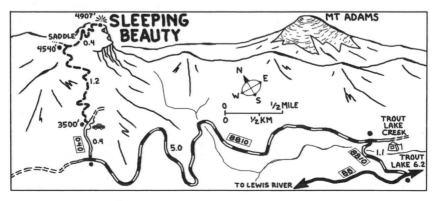

series of switchbacks between sheer rock cliffs.

The trail ends at a great viewpoint, but confident hikers will want to continue beyond the end of the official trail 100 feet, scrambling up a bare rock slope to Sleeping Beauty's actual summit. Three concrete foundations and an awkward cable railing remain from the old lookout. To the west stands the truncated cone of Mt. St. Helens. Mt. Rainier is not visible, and Mt. Hood is hiding behind the broad massif of the Indian Heaven Wilderness. But the view of Mt. Adams is so close it's scary, with the Goat Rocks on the craggy horizon to the left.

Mt. Adams from Sleeping Beauty.   *Opposite: Sleeping Beauty from the south.*

38 Mount Adams Meadows

Easy (from Bird Creek Meadows Trailhead)
3.1-mile loop
900 feet elevation gain
Open mid-July to mid-October

Difficult (from South Climb Trailhead)
11.4 miles round trip
1500 feet elevation gain
Use: hikers, horses

When the Yakama Nation won back jurisdiction over the southeast flank of Mt. Adams in 1972, they agreed to allow public access to the Bird Creek Meadows area. Today two different routes cross these spectacular, stream-laced wildflower meadows to Hellroaring Viewpoint, a cliff looking up the barrel of a gigantic canyon to Mt. Adams' glaciers.

The easy route to this alpine paradise, from a trailhead on the Indian Reservation, involves a terrible access road. Still, it's the most popular way. To find it, drive Interstate 84 to Hood River Bridge exit 64, pay $1 to cross the Columbia, turn left on Highway 14 for 2.4 miles, and then turn right on Highway 141 for 21 miles to the town of Trout Lake. At a major fork here you'll have to choose between pointers for Carson or Randle. Veer right toward Randle. Now follow "Bird Creek Meadows" signs, keeping right at forks at the 0.7- and 2-mile marks. Then continue 2.6 paved miles and another 6.3 gravel miles to a fork where the road suddenly worsens. Veer left for 4 miles on a rough, narrow track to Mirror Lake. Then continue straight a mile to the Bird Creek Meadows parking area *(GPS location N46°09.224' W121°25.498')*. Expect to pay $5 per car at a fee box here.

Take the "Round the Mountain Trail," a wide path that starts at a picnic table and heads up into the woods. Ignore side trails for 0.9 mile. Then turn uphill to the right through the meadows for a mile up to Hellroaring Viewpoint. To return on a loop, turn right on a path along the canyon rim. Horses are allowed only on the Round the Mountain Trail.

The longer route to Bird Creek Meadows uses a less awful access road and requires only the usual Northwest Forest parking pass. To find this trailhead follow "South Climb" signs. From Trout Lake, drive toward Randle on Road 23 for 1.3 miles, fork to the right for 0.7 mile, fork left on paved Road 80 for 3.8 miles, and fork to the right on gravel Road 8040 for 5.4 miles to the Shorthorn Trailhead — the place to stop if you're pulling a horse trailer. Otherwise drive onward, turning up to the right on Road 500 for 2.6 steep, rough miles to the trailhead on the left, just before road's end *(GPS location N46°08.139' W121°29.872')*.

Some of the trees here burned in 2008, and the rest burned in 2012. The trailhead area also serves as the primitive Cold Springs Campground, where climbers bivouac in the woods before launching predawn ascents of Mt. Adams.

As you hike up the dusty South Climb Trail, you'll mostly meet mountain climbers. Leave them behind after 1.3 miles by turning right on the Round the Mountain Trail. This relatively level timberline path traverses a lava flow, leaves the burn zone, crosses the Indian Reservation boundary, and suddenly enters

Mt. Adams from Hellroaring Viewpoint.   Opposite: Iceberg Lake near Sunrise Camp.

a world of wildflower meadows. Consider detouring briefly to the right on the Bird Lake Trail to see Crooked Creek Falls. Then continue another 0.8 mile to the start of Bird Creek Meadows' picnicking zone and turn left for a mile up to Hellroaring Viewpoint.

Backpacking on the Reservation is allowed only at Sunrise Camp, a climber bivouac on a scenic cinder flat beside the Mazama Glacier. This also makes a good day-hike goal. From Hellroaring Viewpoint follow an increasingly faint trail up the ridge 1.7 miles to an iceberg-filled lake. A cross-country route continues to the right past a waterfall for 1.2 miles to Sunrise Camp. Along the way you're almost certain to see ptarmigans and mountain goats. Tenters need to bring a $10 permit from a fee box at one of the Reservation trailheads.

Other Options

Scaling Mt. Adams is not a hike. Special gear and training are required for safety. Anyone venturing above 7000 feet on the Forest Service side of the mountain must first pick up a climbing permit at the ranger station in Trout Lake. To sample the high country, adventurous hikers can follow the South Climb Trail until it peters out at the 8400-foot level beside the Crescent Glacier.

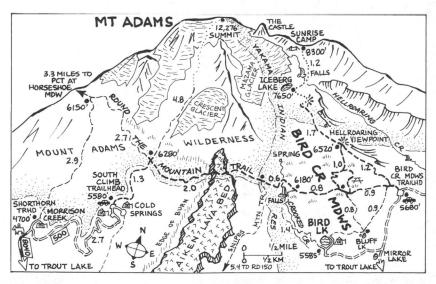

Columbia Gorge

Cabins, Lookouts & Inns	Rental units	Private bath	Breakfast	Open (mos.)	Rate range
① BRIDAL VEIL LODGE. Bed & breakfast inn on 30 acres in waterfall country. Reservations: 503-695-2333 *(www.bridalveillodge.com).*	2	●	●	●	$129
② INN AT THE GORGE. Walk to downtown Hood River from this bed & breakfast in a 1908 Queen Anne home at 1113 Eugene Street. Some kitchenettes. Reservations: 877-852-2385 *(www.innatthegorge.com)*	5	●	●	●	$119-159
③ HOOD RIVER HOTEL. In a historic downtown district, this restored 1913 hotel (102 Oak St.), furnished with antiques, has a hot tub, 9 kitchen suites, and Italian restaurant. Res: 541-386-1900 *(www.hoodriverhotel.com).*	41	●	●	●	$99-234
④ HOOD RIVER BnB. Three blocks from downtown at 918 Oak Street, this bed & breakfast inn has a deck, gazebo, and river views. Reservations: 541-387-2997 *(www.hoodriverbnb.com).*	4	2	●	●	$85-135
⑤ OAK STREET HOTEL. Built 1909, this renovated bed & breakfast in downtown Hood River has a view. Res: 866-386-3845 *(www.oakstreethotel.com).*	9	●	●	●	$109-149
⑥ VILLA COLUMBIA. Bed & breakfast in a downtown Hood River 1911 Craftsman home at 902 Oak St. Res: 800-708-6217*(www.villacolumbia.com).*	5	●	●	●	$179-199
⑦ PANORAMA LODGE. This log home on Hood River Mtn (see Hike #157) has a Mt. Hood view. Res: 888-403-2687 *(www.panoramalodge.com).*	5	●	●	●	$80-235

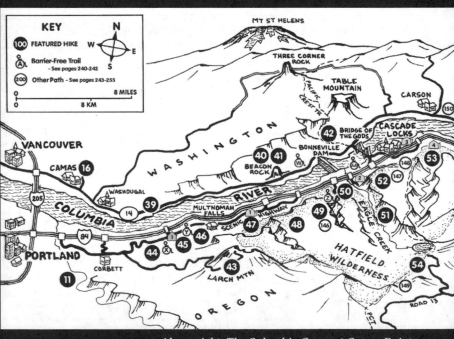

KEY

⬤ FEATURED HIKE

Ⓐ Barrier-Free Trail
— See pages 240-242

Ⓞⓞⓞ Other Path — See pages 243-255

0 ——— 8 MILES
0 ——— 8 KM

Above right: The Columbia Gorge at Crown Point.

Campgrounds

		Campsites	Water	Flush toilet	Open (mos.)	Rate range
1	**AINSWORTH STATE PARK.** Wooded park near Multnomah Falls includes some nice walk-in campsites. Showers. See Hike #43 map for trails.	49	●	●	III-X	$13-20
2	**EAGLE CREEK.** At trailhead for Hikes #47 and #48, this was the first Forest Service camp built in the US, in 1915. Now has some freeway noise.	17		●	V-IX	$15
3	**CASCADE LOCKS MARINE PARK.** The camping lawn of this riverfront city park in Cascade Locks is a popular stop for long-distance Pacific Crest Trail hikers. Showers. Winter rates are just $15, but then there are no showers or water, and the lawn can be soggy.	15	●	●	●	$15-25
4	**HERMAN CREEK HORSE CAMP.** A rustic campground with spacious sites, loading dock, and hitching rails, half a mile from the Herman Creek Trailhead (Hike #50).	7			V-IX	$10
5	**WYETH.** Secluded among maples along Gordon Creek, this camp was an early settlement site and was later used as a CCC camp in the 1930s.	14		●	V-IX	$10
6	**VIENTO STATE PARK.** Popular with windsurfers, this Columbia riverfront camp has showers, but also has noise from trains at night.	74	●	●	IV-X	$13-20
7	**TUCKER.** County park on a grassy riverside flat 5 miles south of Hood River. Showers.	90	●	●	IV-X	$18-25
8	**MEMALOOSE STATE PARK.** Near a Columbia River island where Indians interred their dead, this camp has showers and some freeway noise. Reservations: 800-452-5687.	110	●	●	III-X	$15-24

◁ *The 1913 Hood River Hotel.*

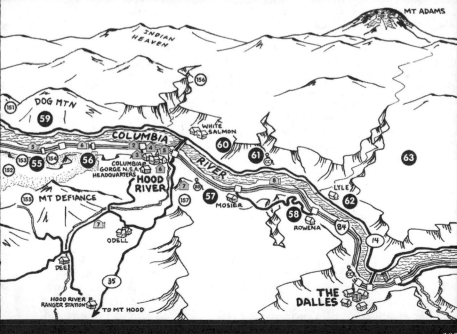

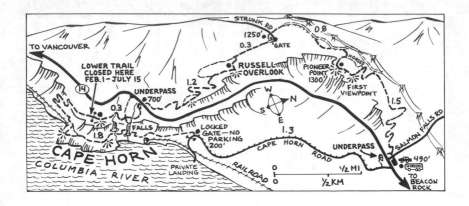

39 Cape Horn

Easy (to Pioneer Point)
3 miles round trip
870 feet elevation gain
Open all year

Moderate (to waterfalls)
7.2-mile loop
1300 feet elevation gain
Open July 16 to January 31

This spectacular trail explores Cape Horn, a landmark bluff towering above the Columbia River on the Washington side of the Columbia Gorge. For an easy hike, climb to a clifftop viewpoint with wildflowers. A grander loop that passes waterfalls and a train tunnel is closed from February 1 to July 15 to protect the peregrine falcons that nest on riverside cliffs.

When a housing subdivision threatened to mar Cape Horn with 16 mansions in the early 1980s, local activist Nancy Russell led the Friends of the Columbia Gorge to stop the development by buying the lots. One 5500-square-foot home was built nonetheless, but 20 years later the Friends bought it and tore it down. The site now has a stone-walled viewpoint honoring Russell.

The Columbia Land Trust, another local non-profit group, secured rights-of-way to make Cape Horn's loop trail possible. Volunteers hacked out the original tread. The Columbia Gorge National Scenic Area has since improved the trail and built pedestrian tunnels for highway crossings.

To drive here from Vancouver take Highway 14 east 26 miles through Camas and Washougal. Between mileposts 26 and 27, turn left on paved Salmon Falls Road and immediately pull into a Park & Ride lot on the right *(GPS location N45°35.337' W122°10.698')*. For a small fare you can ride the Skamania County bus here, but not on weekends or holidays. On weekdays it leaves the Fisher's Landing transit center in Vancouver at 7:00am (and 12:35pm on Friday), and returns at 5:32pm.

Walk across Salmon Falls Road from the parking lot to the trail. Keep uphill to the right. The path dives into a lush bigleaf maple forest with sword ferns and vine maple. April and May bring a profusion of flowers: 4-foot stalks of blue larkspur, red bleeding hearts, and pink-striped (edible) candyflower.

After crossing a small creek the trail switchbacks up a mile to the first of three cliff-edge viewpoints overlooking the Columbia Gorge. Look for Wahkeena Falls (Hike #46) on the far shore, a mile upriver, with the broad, wooded arc of Larch Mountain (Hike #43) on the horizon behind. The little crag in the river below you is Phoca Rock. The third and highest viewpoint, Pioneer Point, blooms with camas in spring. This final viewpoint makes a good turnaround point.

Beyond these viewpoints the trail crosses a broad, wooded summit and joins an old road. Follow this abandoned forest lane left. After 0.6 mile you'll reach paved Strunk Road *(GPS location N45°35.134' W122°11.922')*. Cross the road, take a trail left 200 feet, and turn right on a wide gravel path. After 0.2 mile, turn left on a trail to the Russell Overlook patio. This is another possible turnaround point.

If you're continuing, turn right along the clifftop path. This trail descends through the woods 1.2 miles to a pedestrian underpass beneath Highway 14. On the far side of the road, the path crosses two creeks to a viewpoint in 0.3 mile, where the trail closure from February to mid-July takes effect.

If the route is open, you'll switchback down a rockslide. A horse bypass trail veers left, but hikers can keep right to the top of a railroad tunnel. The next mile of the trail is a hiker's amusement ride, roller-coasting up and down along the riverside cliffs, ducking past a waterfall, and popping out at unexpected viewpoints. The fun ends at Cape Horn Road. Because there's no room to park a shuttle car here, walk 1.3 miles up the paved road to complete the loop.

Cigar Rock and the Gorge from Cape Horn.   Opposite: The Nancy Russell Overlook.

40 Hardy Ridge

Difficult
8.5-mile loop
2200 feet elevation gain
Open all year
Use: hikers, horses, and bicycles (hikers
    only atop the ridge).

If you've visited Beacon Rock State Park, on the Washington side of the Columbia Gorge, you may have seen the crowds hiking to viewpoints atop Beacon Rock or Hamilton Mountain (Hike #41). Hardy hikers can climb to an uncrowded alternative—a rocky ridgetop wildflower garden that actually looks down on the park's other viewpoints. Although the loop starts at an equestrian trailhead and mostly follows old forest roads, trails on the ridge itself are open only to hikers.

To find the equestrian trailhead from Portland, take Interstate 205 north across the Columbia River and turn right on Highway 14 for 28.5 miles. Opposite Beacon Rock, and immediately before the park headquarters building, turn left on paved Kueffler Road. After one mile fork to the right on to a gravel road for 0.4 mile to a huge parking turnaround. (If you're driving to the park from the east, take Interstate 84 to Cascade Locks exit 44, pay $1 to cross the Bridge of the Gods, and turn left on Highway 14 for 7 miles.)

You'll need a Discover Pass for your car in this Washington State Park. The permit costs $10 a day if you buy it at the trailhead fee box. Yearly passes for $35 are available at outdoor stores, at 866-320-9933, or at *discoverpass.wa.gov*.

At the far end of the parking loop, you can start your hike either on the trail or on the gated road, because they soon join. Covered with fir needles, the old road climbs gradually through a forest of Douglas firs and bigleaf maples with

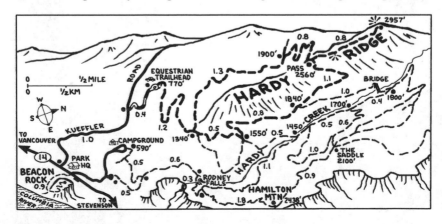

Hikers on Hardy Ridge.   Opposite: Mt. Hood from the viewpoint summit in April.

an understory of wild hazel, bracken, and Oregon grape.

At an X-shaped junction after 1.2 miles, hikers part ways with other trail users. Bicyclists and equestrians should go straight for about two miles to a large, horse-friendly bridge across Hardy Creek. Signs and mapboards describe the area's large network of usable trails.

If you're on foot, however, you'll want to turn left at this first X-shaped junction, heading for Hardy Ridge. After hiking on a road another 1.3 miles, you'll reach a "Hardy Ridge Trail" sign. Turn right on a steeper, narrower footpath that switchbacks 0.8 mile up to a junction in a windy saddle atop Hardy Ridge. Keep left, climbing along the ridge's spine.

The rocky slopes here bloom with yellow glacier lilies in April, pink wild onions in May, fuzzy cat's ears in June, orange tiger lilies in July, red paintbrush in August, and white yarrow until fall.

If it's blustery, you might follow the ridgecrest just 0.2 mile, turning back at a viewpoint knoll with some shelter from the wind. Otherwise continue a full 0.8 mile to a summit capped with pink phlox blooms *(GPS location N45°40.182' W122°01.803')*. Here views sweep south across the Columbia Gorge to Mt. Hood, east across Table Mountain to the top half of Mt. Adams, and south to the tip of Mt. Rainier.

To return on a loop, hike back along the ridge 0.8 mile to the saddle, but then turn left. This path descends 0.6 mile to an old road. Heeding pointers for the equestrian trailhead, follow the road 1.3 miles, turn right at a T-shaped junction, and go straight for 1.7 miles to your car.

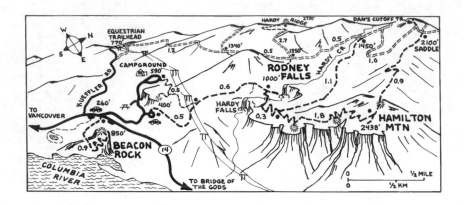

41   Beacon Rock Park

Easy (to Beacon Rock)
1.8 miles round trip
600 feet elevation gain
Open all year

Easy (to Rodney Falls)
2.2 miles round trip
600 feet elevation gain

Difficult (to Hamilton Mountain)
7.6-mile loop
2000 feet elevation gain

Beacon Rock State Park boasts two of the Columbia Gorge's most famous and popular trails: a switchbacking path up Beacon Rock's 848-foot-tall block of basalt, and a longer trail that passes beautiful Rodney Falls before climbing steeply to cliff-edge viewpoints on Hamilton Mountain.

Lewis and Clark named Beacon Rock in 1805 while paddling past its cliffs. In 1915 a man named Henry Biddle bought the rock and arduously constructed a well-graded trail to the top, incorporating 47 switchbacks and dozens of railed catwalk bridges. When the Army Corps of Engineers suggested the monolith be blown up for use as a jetty at the mouth of the Columbia, Biddle's family tried to make the area a state park. At first Washington refused the gift. But that decision quickly changed when *Oregon* offered to accept.

To find the park, take Interstate 205 north across the Columbia River and turn right on Highway 14 for 28.6 miles. If you're driving here from the east, take Interstate 84 to Cascade Locks exit 44, pay $1 to cross the Bridge of the Gods, and turn left on Highway 14 for 6.9 miles.

You'll need a Discover Pass for your car in this Washington state park. The permit costs $10 a day if you buy it at the trailhead fee box. Yearly passes for $35 are available at outdoor stores, at 866-320-9933, or at *discoverpass.wa.gov*.

To climb Beacon Rock, park in one of the roadside pullouts on either side of Beacon Rock (near milepost 35) and walk 50 yards along the highway to the signed trailhead, halfway between the parking areas. Although nearly all of the 0.9-mile route has railings, parents may want to hold small children's hands to make sure they stay on the path. From the top, the view stretches from Crown Point to Bonneville Dam. Far below, Burlington Northern's toy trains chug by. Tiny powerboats cut white V's in the Columbia's green shallows.

If you'd rather take the Hamilton Mountain Trail, turn off Highway 14 opposite Beacon Rock, drive 0.3 mile up a paved road toward the campground, and then veer to the right into a trailhead parking lot. This road is gated closed on winter weekdays, adding 0.4 mile to the hike.

The path climbs through a second-growth Douglas fir forest with red thimbleberries, blue Oregon grape, and bracken fern. Soon you pass under a powerline, where a trail from the campground joins on the left. At the 1-mile mark a side trail to the right descends to a poor viewpoint of Hardy Falls. Continue on the main trail a few hundred yards and go left on a side trail that ends at a railed cliff beside Rodney Falls, a fascinating, 50-foot cascade trapped in an enormous rock-walled bowl. Return to the main trail and switchback down to a footbridge below the falls—a good turnaround point for hikers with children.

If you're continuing, switchback uphill, keep left at an unmarked fork (the right-hand path descends to the creek above Hardy Falls), and climb 0.2 mile to a fork marking the start of the loop. Keep right on a steep, switchbacking trail up a cliff-edged ridge with dizzying views across the Columbia Gorge. After 1.8 miles you'll finally reach a T-shaped junction at the summit ridgecrest. The path to the right promptly deadends at Hamilton Mountain's summit, where the view is partly obscured by brush.

To continue the loop, turn around and follow the ridgecrest trail past better viewpoints of Mt. Hood, Mt. Adams, and Table Rock. After 0.9 mile, turn left down an abandoned road. Keep left on the road for a mile to a meadow at a creek crossing. Here veer left onto a level path through a cool alder forest. After 1.1 mile, this path joins the main trail. Turn right to return to your car.

Cliffs on the trail up Hamilton Mountain.   *Opposite: Beacon Rock from Highway 14.*

Moderate (to Aldrich Butte)
3.6 miles round trip
1100 feet elevation gain
Open all year

Difficult (to Table Mountain)
8.6-mile loop
3380 feet elevation gain

Table Mountain launched a gigantic landslide 550 years ago that shoved the Columbia south, left a ragged cliff, and sparked the legend of a "Bridge of the Gods" that made it briefly possible to cross the Columbia River with dry feet. Today the Pacific Crest Trail crosses a steel Bridge of the Gods on its way to Table Mountain's cataclysmic cliff.

Although the PCT is the best developed path in the area, a rougher shortcut opened in 2008, shaving miles off the hike to Table Mountain. And if your knees shiver at the propsect of the steep final pitch up "Heartbreak Ridge" to the top of the cliff, choose the moderate hike to Aldrich Butte's viewpoint instead.

From Vancouver, drive Highway 14 east through Camas for 38 miles, almost a mile past the North Bonneville exit. If you're coming from Interstate 84, take Cascade Locks exit 44, pay $1 to cross the Bridge of the Gods, and turn left on Highway 14 for 3.5 miles. In either case, turn off between mileposts 38 and 39 at a sign for Bonneville Hot Springs, duck to the north under the railroad tracks, turn right on paved E. Cascade Drive for 0.8 mile, and turn right into the entrance for the hot springs resort. After 100 yards, turn left on a gravel road and park in a gravel lot *behind* the hotel (*GPS location N45°39.304' W121°57.582'*).

Start by walking uphill on a gravel road that angles away from the resort hotel. After 150 yards you'll climb to a T-shaped road junction. Turn left for just 17 steps to find a faint path up to the right through a blackberry bramble, passing a tree with an overgrown sign, "PCT 2.2, Table Mt. 4." After a few hundred feet of blackberry bushes, the trail enters shady Douglas fir woods with sword fern

The Columbia Gorge from Aldrich Butte.   Above: Table Mountain's summit cliffs.

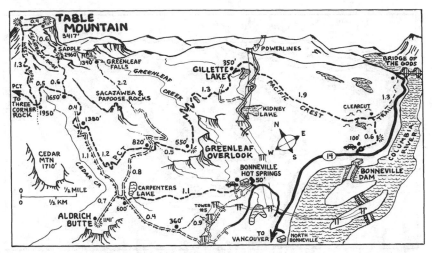

and Oregon grape. This shortcut path was built by volunteers, so expect a few steep spots and fallen logs. Boots are recommended, especially in wet weather.

After 1.1 mile the path crosses the outlet creek of the meadow at Carpenters Lake and ends at an old dirt road *(GPS location N45°39.499′ W121°58.449′)*. Turn right along the road 200 feet to a fork. Then turn uphill to the left for 250 feet to a second fork in the road. Here you face a decision.

For a moderate hike, turn left on an old road that climbs 0.7 mile to a viewpoint on Aldrich Butte *(GPS location N45°39.229′ W121°58.767′)*. Foundations here recall an antiaircraft gun battery that defended Bonneville Dam in World War II. The bare edge of the knoll still offers sweeping views of the Bonneville Dam area, with Beacon Rock to the west and Dog Mountain to the east.

If you'd rather tackle the difficult scramble up Table Mountain, however, turn *right* at the second fork in the road. This route ambles up 1.1 mile to the Pacific Crest Trail, where you turn left and continue uphill an easy 0.4 mile.

Look for a small sign marking a steep path that crosses the PCT. This is the Heartbreak Ridge Trail, named for its unforgiving grade. Turn right on this brutal chute for 0.6 mile to a stunning viewpoint in a cliff-edged saddle. This is an acceptable place to declare victory and turn back. If you're still going strong, the trail traverses left a quarter mile and peters out in a rockslide. Scramble up 500 feet to the resumption of the trail at the upper left corner of the boulder field. From there keep right at junctions 0.3 mile to a summit viewpoint atop the cliff where the landslide cut loose 550 years ago.

To return on a loop, follow trails back to the west across Table Mountain's summit plateau 0.4 mile. Bear left to find the West Ridge Trail, a slightly less precipitous chute back down to the PCT. Then turn left to complete the loop.

Back at your car, consider splurging $20 (on weekends, $30) for a half-hour soak in one of Bonneville Hot Springs' decadent clawfoot tubs.

Other Options

If you don't like rough trails (or if you have a horse), access this area at the Bonneville Trailhead, 2 miles west of the Bridge of the Gods on Highway 14. The path climbs 0.6 mile to the PCT. Then turn left 1.9 miles to green Gillette Lake, a pleasant picnic spot.

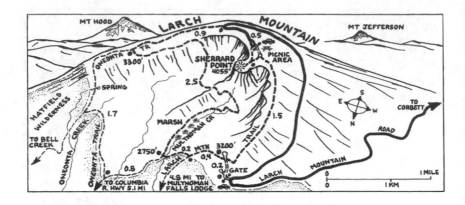

43 Larch Mountain Crater

Moderate
6.4-mile loop
1300 feet elevation gain
Open May through November
Use: hikers, horses, bicycles

The panoramic viewpoint atop this 4055-foot volcano deserves its fame. Mount Hood looms across the Bull Run Valley while four other snowpeaks mark the horizon. But the charms of Larch Mountain's crater are less well known. A moderate 6-mile loop explores a huge old-growth forest, a meadow of marsh marigolds, and a mossy creek hidden in the throat of the old volcano.

Larch Mountain had a much smaller crater when it stopped erupting some 4 million years ago. During the Ice Age, however, a glacier scoured the peak into an enormous bowl, breached the mountain's north flank, and exposed Sherrard Point — the volcano's central lava plug. When the ice melted, a lake was left that gradually silted in to become a marshy meadow. Trees around the meadow grew to giant size, protected from fire and windstorms by the crater's wall.

Rather than start this loop from the crowded parking area at the summit — which would mean ending the hike with an uphill trudge — it's more fun to start at a secret trailhead near the crater's base.

To find this lower trailhead, take Interstate 84 east of Portland to Corbett exit 22, drive steeply up a mile to Corbett, turn left on the old Columbia River Highway for 2 miles, and then fork to the right on the paved Larch Mountain Road for 11.6 miles. Watch for a sharp curve to the right with a "20 MPH" warning sign and a guardrail. Park along the road's shoulder after the end of the guardrail (*GPS location N45°32.964' W122°05.515'*).

Mt. Hood from Sherrard Point.   Opposite: Sherrard Point from the crater.

If this area is full, don't block the gate. There's more parking 100 yards ahead on the right. Then walk past the gate on a small, rough side road. Keep uphill to the right for a quarter mile. A hundred yards before the road ends you'll see a trail crossing the road. This is the start of the loop.

Turn left on the downhill trail for 0.4 mile. Then turn right onto the Multnomah Creek Way trail and continue down to a 40-foot bridge over Multnomah Creek. The water that later rages over Oregon's tallest falls flows peacefully here amid red cedar, skunk cabbage, and salmonberries. Turn right and follow the creek upstream past a marshy meadow with a view ahead to Sherrard Point's crag. The trail climbs through an ancient grove of hemlock trees.

When you reach a ridgecrest junction, turn right on the Oneonta Trail and climb the ridge. In May this trail is lined with a stunning display of white lilies — both large-leaved trilliums and droopy-headed avalanche lilies. After 0.9 mile the trail ends at the Larch Mountain Road. Walk up the road 0.3 mile to its end and keep right on a paved path to Sherrard Point's railed viewing platform *(GPS location N45°31.962' W122°05.257')*.

To continue the loop, walk back from Sherrard Point but keep right at all junctions. You'll cross a road turnaround, skirt a picnic area, and descend a forested ridge to your car.

Other Options

To experience the Columbia Gorge from top to bottom, hike from Larch Mountain's 4055-foot summit to the old Columbia River Highway, virtually at sea level. If you can arrange a car shuttle it's a 6.7-mile one-way romp down to the Multnomah Falls Lodge (see Hike #46). Without a shuttle it's wisest to start at the bottom for the long, difficult climb.

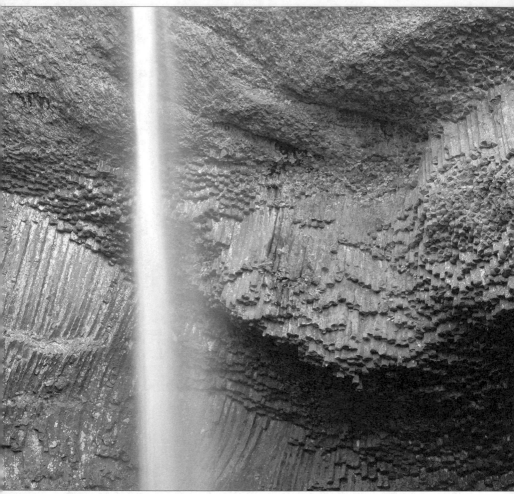

Lower Latourell Falls.   Opposite: Footbridge at Lower Latourell Falls.

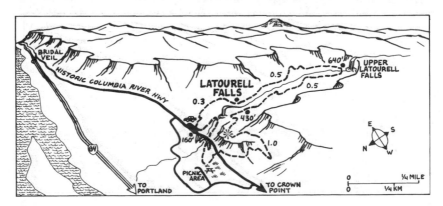

44 Latourell Falls

Easy
2.3-mile loop
600 feet elevation gain
Open all year

Closest to Portland of the Columbia Gorge's great waterfalls, Lower Latourell Falls plunges 249 feet over the lip of an eroded lava flow. An easy 2.3-mile loop trail climbs to the top of the falls, continues to a secluded, 100-foot upper falls, and returns by way of a picnic area.

From Portland take Interstate 84 to Bridal Veil exit 28, turn right on the historic Columbia River Highway, and drive 2.8 miles to the Latourell Falls parking area on the left. If you're coming from Hood River, take exit 35 and follow the old highway 10 miles.

Start on the broad paved path leading *uphill to the left* from the lot. Pavement ends just beyond a first viewpoint. The trail climbs through bigleaf maple woods lush with greenery: delicate black-stalked maidenhair fern, little white-starred candyflowers, stinging nettles, and waterleaf, a low-growing but handsome plant with sharply lobed, foot-wide leaves. In early summer, the trail itself is overhung with edible salmonberries. Shaped like raspberries, these mild-flavored fruits are the pinkish-orange color of fresh salmon.

Pass a viewpoint at the top of the falls and continue upstream. In late spring look here for two closely related pink wildflowers: bleeding hearts (with arching fronds) and corydalis (with tall stalks of pink hoods).

At the 0.8-mile mark the trail crosses a bridge at the splash pool of Upper Latourell Falls, a spiraling cascade that arches over a shallow cavern. Continue on the loop trail. The route heads back downstream half a mile and switchbacks up to a nice viewpoint of the Columbia River. To the west you'll see Rooster Rock, a long splinter of lava that broke off from Crown Point's cliffs only a few thousand years ago and landed upright in the river mud.

Next the loop trail descends to the highway. Cross the road and take the stone steps down to the grassy picnic area. In the middle of the lawn turn right on a paved path that ducks under the 100-foot arch of the highway bridge and emerges at spectacular Lower Latourell Falls. Notice the strangely splayed hexagonal pillars in the falls' cliffy face. This rock began as basalt lava pouring through the Columbia Gorge from Eastern Oregon. Here the lava puddled up. As it slowly cooled, it shrank and fractured into a characteristic honeycomb pattern known as columnar basalt. The resulting pillars are splayed because the surface they cooled against was uneven.

Beyond Lower Latourell Falls, continue on the loop trail up to your car.

45 Angels Rest

Moderate
4.6 miles round trip
1500 feet elevation gain
Open all year

Angels Rest juts like a balcony above the western Columbia Gorge. While the viewpoint makes an excellent goal by itself, it's also tempting to extend the hike by exploring the adjacent plateau. One option is to add an easy 2.4-mile loop to a creekside picnic site. Better yet, arrange a short car shuttle and continue to Wahkeena Falls for a 6.4-mile, moderate one-way hike. Dogs must be on leash.

From Portland, drive Interstate 84 east, take Bridal Veil exit 28, and park a few hundred yards later at the junction with the old Columbia River Highway. If you're driving here from the east, take exit 35 and follow the old highway 7.3 miles. If the parking lot is full, drive 300 feet west on the old Columbia River Highway and turn left on Palmer Mill Road to an overflow parking area.

The Angels Rest Trail starts at stone steps by a huge trail sign across the road from the west end of the main parking area. The path sets off uphill through a fern-filled forest where large white trilliums bloom in early spring. After half a

Angels Rest.   Above: Fairy bells.   Opposite: Picnickers at the viewpoint.

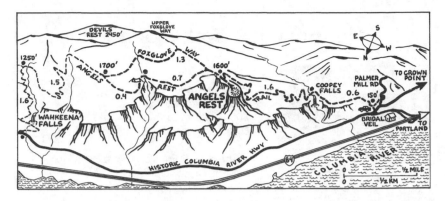

mile you'll get a glimpse of 100-foot Coopey Falls. Then the trail climbs past an upper, 30-foot cascade and crosses Coopey Creek on a scenic footbridge. By late spring larkspur crowds the woods here with chest-high stalks of blue flowers.

Beyond Coopey Creek the path climbs in earnest, switchbacking up a ridge and traversing a rockslide. Beware of poison oak growing from beneath the trailside rocks. Finally the trail reaches a windy crest with an unmarked junction. Turn left to Angel Rest's miniature mesa, with views of the Columbia River on three sides. Look for Crown Point's observatory to the west. Then return as you came.

Other Options

If you'd like to continue beyond the viewpoint, walk back along the ridgecrest past the first junction until you reach a fork in the trail. Keep left toward Wahkeena Falls for 0.7 mile and hop across a creek to a lovely campsite with a picnic table. A side trail to the left leads to a 20-foot cascade. This makes a good turnaround point.

If you can arrange a short car shuttle, you can hike 6.4 miles to Wahkeena Falls without backtracking. From Angels Rest simply keep left at every junction and you'll pass the creekside picnic site, Wahkeena Spring, and Fairy Falls en route to the Wahkeena Falls trailhead described in Hike #46.

46 Multnomah & Wahkeena Falls

Easy (to top of falls)
2.2 miles round trip
700 feet elevation gain
Open all year

Moderate (from Wahkeena Falls)
5.4-mile loop
1600 feet elevation gain

Oregon's tallest waterfall, Multnomah Falls was the state's most popular tourist attraction until it lost that title to a casino. Still, thousands of visitors pull off the freeway each day to snap photos of the 620-foot, two-tiered cascade. Hundreds of them continue up the paved 1.1-mile trail to the top of the falls—a classic little hike. To beat the crowds here, consider the longer, even prettier loop that begins at the quiet Wahkeena Falls trailhead nearby.

For the short hike to the top of Multnomah Falls, drive Interstate 84 east of Portland to Multnomah Falls exit 31, park, and walk under the overpass. The historic stone lodge on your right was built in 1925 for the grand opening of the scenic Columbia Gorge-Mount Hood highway loop. Walk straight toward the falls to find the paved trail switchbacking up to a stone bridge between the two segments of Multnomah Falls' long cascade.

The trail here has seen more than its share of natural drama. In 1991 a forest fire swept across the path, stopping just short of the lodge. In 1996 a bus-sized chunk of the waterfall's cliff broke loose, landed in the splash pool, and sprayed rock splinters past the bridge. In 1998, torrential rainstorms launched a gigantic landslide of rocks, mud, and trees that wiped out the trail and kept it closed for

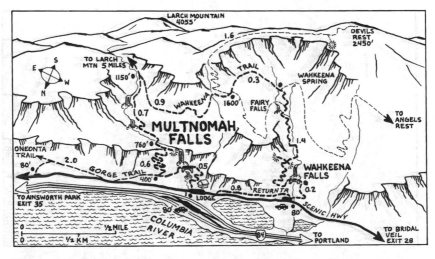

Wahkeena Falls.   Opposite: Fairy Falls along the Wahkeena Trail.

a year. If your courage holds, continue on the reopened path past the stone bridge. Keep right at junctions to climb to a fenced overlook on Multnomah Falls' lip. The dizzying view aims down the cataract to the toy-sized lodge and its ant-like crowds.

If you have the time to try a quieter, prettier route to the top of Multnomah Falls, start at the Wahkeena Falls trailhead instead. To find it, drive the freeway to Bridal Veil exit 28 and turn left along the old Columbia River Highway 2.6 miles to the Wahkeena Falls Picnic Ground pullout on the right.

The Wahkeena Trail starts at a footbridge and climbs to the right 0.2 mile to an elegant stone bridge below Wahkeena Falls, a 242-foot triple cascade in a sculpted chute. Continue on the unpaved, steep path 2.6 miles up to the Larch Mountain Trail. Then turn left along Multnomah Creek for 0.7 mile, passing many smaller falls on the way down to the Multnomah Falls viewpoint. After marveling at the view, continue down the 1.1-mile path to the lodge and turn left along the old highway, where you'll find a return trail back to your car.

Other Options

Devils Rest is a more challenging goal from Wahkeena Falls, requiring a 7-mile round trip and 2400 feet of elevation gain. Although the summit of this forested knoll has no views, a side trail 0.2 mile before the top leads to a Gorge overlook. Ascend the Wahkeena Trail 1.9 miles until it levels off, and then take the marked Devils Rest Trail to the right.

An even tougher climb is the 13.6-mile round trip from Multnomah Falls to the panoramic view atop 4055-foot Larch Mountain (see Hike #43).

47 Oneonta and Horsetail Falls

Easy
2.7-mile loop
400 feet elevation gain
Open all year

Next door to busy Multnomah Falls but usually overlooked by tourists, this delightful trail explores a cavern *behind* Ponytail Falls and then loops around Oneonta Gorge, a mossy chasm so narrow that Oneonta Creek fills it wall to wall. What's more, an optional 1.8-mile side trip leads to breathtaking Triple Falls, where three plumes of water plunge 120 feet at once.

Drive Interstate 84 east of Portland to Ainsworth Park exit 35 and follow the old scenic highway 1.5 miles back to the large Horsetail Falls Trailhead parking area. The trail starts beside 176-foot Horsetail Falls and climbs along a mossy slope of little licorice ferns. In late spring tiny white candyflowers and pink geraniums crowd the path.

After 0.2 mile turn right on the Gorge Trail, which soon ducks behind 80-foot Ponytail Falls (alias Upper Horsetail Falls). The lava flow that created this falls' stony lip also buried a layer of soft soil. The falls have washed out the underlying soil, creating the cavern.

Beyond the falls 0.4 mile take a right-hand fork for a quick viewpoint loop out to a cliff edge high above the highway. The view extends up the Columbia to Beacon Rock, but keep children away from the unfenced edge. Then continue on the main trail another 0.4 mile, switchback down to a dramatic metal footbridge above 60-foot Oneonta Falls, and climb to a junction with the Oneonta Trail.

Turn left here if you'd like to take the optional side trip up to Triple Falls and the perfect spot for lunch: a footbridge in a scenic creekside glen at the top of

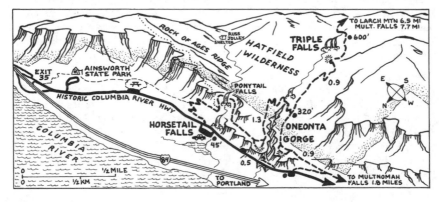

Tunnel at the mouth of Oneonta Gorge.   Opposite: Ponytail Falls.

the falls. If you're hiking with children, however, you'd best skip Triple Falls and simply turn right to continue the loop, following the Oneonta Trail 0.9 mile down to the highway.

To complete the loop, walk to the right along the road to the mouth of slot-like Oneonta Gorge. Here you'll follow the original route of the historic Columbia River Highway, crossing the creek on an old concrete bridge to a short tunnel through the gorge's rock cliffs. Filled with rubble for fifty years, the tunnel reopened to pedestrians in 2012. Continue 0.3 mile along the highway to your car.

Other Options

The best way to see the inside of Oneonta Gorge is to put on sneakers and wade hip-deep up the creek from the highway bridge. In late summer when the water's not too icy or swift, adventurers can explore half a mile through the 20-foot-wide chasm to an otherwise hidden, 100-foot falls.

A delightful, longer loop hike from Horsetail Falls extends all the way to Multnomah Falls, gaining 2800 feet in 12.2 miles. Start by hiking to Triple Falls, but continue another 2.9 miles upstream on the Oneonta Trail, turn right for 2.2 miles on the Franklin Ridge Trail, and turn right again for 2.6 miles on the Larch Mountain Trail. Beyond the viewpoint at the top of Multnomah Falls 0.6 mile, turn right on the Gorge Trail for 2.3 miles to return to your car.

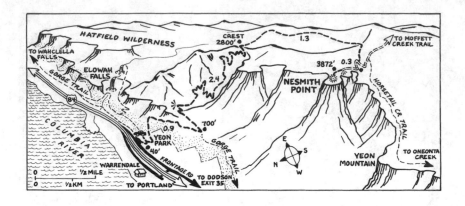

48   Nesmith Point

Difficult
9.8 miles round trip
3800 feet elevation gain
Open April through November

Mountain climbers often use the challenging trail to Nesmith Point as a spring conditioning trip because the goal—the highest point in the cliffs lining the Columbia Gorge—is snow-free by April. But this hike offers other rewards than mere exercise. Expect a variety of wildflowers, the solitude of a high valley's natural amphitheater, and of course a bird's eye view across the Columbia to the snowpeaks of Washington. Dogs must be on leash.

Nesmith Point's promontory was unnamed until 1915, when the Portland Mazamas club suggested it memorialize James Nesmith, a burly Oregon Trail pioneer whose wagon raft was driven ashore near here by high winds in 1843. Nesmith was forced to wait out the storm reading *The Merry Wives of Windsor*.

If you're coming from Portland on Interstate 84, take exit 35 for Ainsworth Park, turn left toward Dodson for just 200 feet, and turn sharply right onto Frontage Road. (If you miss the Frontage Road turnoff you'll end up back on the freeway.) Then follow Frontage Road 2 miles to a big paved pullout on the right—the Yeon Park trailhead for Nesmith Point. If you're driving here from Hood River, take Warrendale exit 37, duck left under the freeway, and turn left for 0.4 mile to the trailhead *(GPS location N45°36.738' W122°00.273')*.

Start on the uphill trail and keep right at junctions, climbing through a lowland forest brightened in summer by chest-high, orange tiger lilies. In 0.9 mile meet the Gorge Trail and turn left. The path climbs relentlessly for the next 2.4 miles, switchbacking up a steep, narrow valley with occasional views out to Beacon Rock and Mt. Adams. Finally climb past huge old-growth cedars in a natural amphitheater at the canyon's head. Then, at a sunny ridgecrest, the forest abruptly shifts to high-elevation fare: small Douglas fir, beargrass, and huckleberries.

After reaching the ridgecrest, climb more gradually along a tilted plateau for 1.3 miles to an abandoned dirt road that leads up to the summit, once the site of a fire lookout tower. Unfortunately trees have grown up, leaving only a view west down the Columbia River to Portland's haze and Silver Star Mountain (Hike #17), the tall brown hump on the horizon. But don't despair; a better viewpoint is nearby. Continue past the old lookout's foundation pier and down into the woods 200 yards. You'll pass the lookout's abandoned outhouse, descend through a forest carpeted with May-blooming trilliums, and emerge at a cliff edge with an aerial view of Beacon Rock's riverside monolith, snowy Mt. Adams, and flat-topped Mt. St. Helens.

Other Options

By arranging a short car shuttle you can descend on a less steep but longer path that leads to the Oneonta Trailhead described in Hike #47. From Nesmith Point walk down the dirt road 0.4 mile, turn right on the Horsetail Creek Trail for 5.6 miles, and then turn right on the Oneonta Trail for 2.9 miles to the highway. The hike's total length is 13.8 miles. Don't attempt this route in spring when high water makes a bridgeless crossing of Oneonta Creek hazardous.

Fog on the trail to Nesmith Point.   Opposite: View across the Columbia River.

49 Elowah and Wahclella Falls

Easy (to Elowah Falls)
3 miles round trip
600 feet elevation gain
Open all year

Easy (to Wahclella Falls)
2 miles round trip
380 feet elevation gain

Moderate (both falls, with car shuttle)
7.3 miles
1100 feet elevation gain

Two of the Columbia Gorge's best waterfalls are hidden in canyons with short trails. A 3-mile hike to airy, 289-foot Elowah Falls includes a detour past a Gorge viewpoint to an additional 100-foot falls. Just down the road, the 1-mile path to thundering Wahclella Falls loops through a charming, canyon-end grotto.

For a quick afternoon stroll, choose just one of these hikes. If you're doing both you can connect them with a short drive or with a level, 3.1-mile trail. The trail route includes a new paved section of the Historic Columbia River Highway State Trail that opens in August 2013.

If you're hiking with children, Wahclella Falls is safest. Otherwise, start with the hike to Elowah Falls. To find the Elowah Falls trailhead from Portland, take Interstate 84 to exit 35 for Ainsworth Park, turn left toward Dodson for just 200 feet, and then turn sharply right onto Frontage Road for 2.1 miles to Yeon Park's big paved parking pullout on the right.

If you're driving here from the east, take Interstate 84 to Warrendale exit 37, duck left under the freeway, and turn left for 0.3 mile to Yeon Park.

At the Yeon Park trailhead the wide, paved Historic Columbia River Highway State Trail sets out to the left. But start your hike by taking the unpaved Elowah Falls trail uphill to the right. After a few feet, ignore a right-hand fork to Nesmith Point. Hike the main, level trail another 0.4 mile, and then switchback up to the right on a side trail that climbs along a dramatic, railed ledge blasted out of sheer cliffs. The aerial view here extends from Elowah Falls across the Columbia to

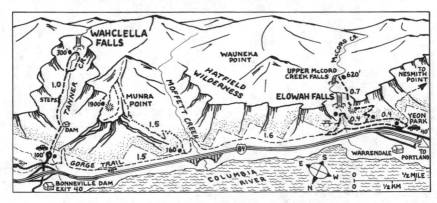

Upper McCord Creek Falls.   Opposite: Wahclella Falls.

Beacon Rock and Hamilton Mountain (Hike #41). Continue to trail's end at a creekside glen above Upper McCord Creek Falls' 60-foot fan.

Then hike back 0.7 mile to the main Elowah Falls trail and turn right for 0.4 mile to an enormous cliff-rimmed amphitheater at the base of the falls, a gauzy ribbon so tall that breezes waft it about. The seven layers of basalt visible in the cliffs are evidence of the many lava flows that surged down the Columbia Gorge in the past 15 million years only to be cut back by the river.

If you're walking onward to the Wahclella Falls Trailhead, simply hike straight past Elowah Falls on the Gorge Trail, which connects with the paved historic highway trail.

If you'd rather drive to Wahclella Falls, walk back to the Yeon Park trailhead. Then back to Interstate 84, head east 3 miles to Bonneville Dam exit 40, turn to the south (away from the dam), and keep right for 100 yards to a turnaround and parking area.

The Wahclella Falls trail begins on an old gated road alongside bouldery, maple-shaded Tanner Creek. The old road ends at a small water intake dam for the Bonneville fish hatchery. Continue on a trail into the ever-narrowing canyon. Along the way you'll pass a side creek's 60-foot fan-shaped falls.

When the trail forks after 0.8 mile, keep left for 0.2 mile to the wave-tossed pool at the base of Wahclella Falls. The falls itself has two tiers, with a plunge in an upper slot followed by a 60-foot horsetail. Listen here for the *zeet-zeet* of water ouzels, remarkable robin-sized birds that dive into the creek, flapping their wings underwater so they can run along the streambed eating insect larvae.

Beyond Wahclella Falls, the trail continues on a short downstream loop, ducking under a 20-foot cavern and winding past house-sized boulders left from a 1973 landslide.

The Tooth Rock Viaduct.   Below: Marker at the trailhead.

50 Tooth Rock and Wauna Point

Easy (to Tooth Rock viaduct)
2-mile loop
130 feet elevation gain
Open all year
Use: hikers, bicycles

Moderate (to Wauna Viewpoint)
4.8 miles round trip
900 feet elevation gain

Difficult (to Wauna Point)
10 miles round trip
3250 feet elevation gain

When engineer Samuel Lancaster laid out the original Columbia River Highway in 1913, he decided not to tunnel through Tooth Rock, a basalt shoulder of Wauna Point that juts out over the river. Instead he perched the narrow roadway on a perilous-looking viaduct, a half-bridge clinging to the cliff's face. The resulting viewpoint was so impressive that Model T drivers often stopped to gawk—and were sometimes rear-ended by the next car.

Today, Interstate 84 roars through a modern tunnel in Tooth Rock's base. But high above, the fragile old viaduct has been restored for hikers and bicyclists as part of the Historic Columbia River Highway State Trail. For an easy 2-mile loop, take this paved path across the viaduct and return on an unpaved upper path. For a longer hike, continue up to 1050-foot Wauna Viewpoint. For the best view of all, tackle the tough hike to 2160-foot Wauna Point itself.

Start by driving Interstate 84 east of Portland to Bonneville Dam exit 40. Then follow signs half a mile to the Historic Columbia River Highway trailhead's large parking lot. Set off on foot (or by bicycle) on the wide, paved trail to the right, paralleling the noisy freeway 0.8 mile to the viaduct, where views extend across the river from Beacon Rock to the Bridge of the Gods.

Beyond Tooth Rock 0.2 mile the paved path ends at a concrete staircase. To return on a loop, walk back 40 feet from the staircase and take a small trail uphill. This path soon becomes an even older roadbed that crosses the top of Tooth Rock. Beware of 3-leaved poison oak on this route. After climbing 0.4 mile you'll reach a junction, and face a decision. To return to your car, go straight. To continue on the longer hike to Wauna Viewpoint, turn uphill to the left.

This upper path climbs 200 yards to the switchback of a gravel road. Keep left to find the continuation of the trail. After another 0.4 mile turn right at a sign for Wauna Viewpoint and switchback up through the woods on a somewhat over-grown path. The knoll at trail's end, beside a powerline, features red paintbrush flowers and a view extending from the pools of the Eagle Creek Hatchery to Mt. Adams. There is no direct route from Wauna Viewpoint up to Wauna Point.

The rugged hike to Wauna Point has been made longer since the old access road 777 was closed by a gate. So start at the same trailhead as for Tooth Rock, but after hiking 0.2 mile on the paved path, turn uphill to the right for 0.5 mile until you reach a switchback of old Road 777. Follow this narrow gravel lane uphill 1.2 miles to the old Tanner Butte Trailhead.

From this old trailhead, a path climbs past four lacy, 20-foot waterfalls in a mossy glen of alder, bleeding hearts, and columbine. The trail twice crosses under huge, crackling powerlines and then climbs steadily through Douglas fir woods carpeted in spring with delicate star-flowered solomonseal. After 2.3 steep miles the path forks, with the Tanner Butte Trail continuing to the right.

If you're headed down the rugged bushwhacking route to Wauna Point, however, keep left past a "Trail Not Maintained" sign for 0.3 mile to another junction. Turn left again on a steep, narrow downhill path that switchbacks under a cliff and scrambles half a mile down a precarious, rocky ridgecrest to Wauna Point, a knife-edge promontory overhanging the Gorge. The dizzying view extends across the river to Table Mountain and Mt. Adams.

Other Options

For a backpacking trip, try the 14.3-mile loop to Dublin Lake. The rough, chal-lenging route gains 4250 feet. Start as for Wauna Point, but keep right on the Tanner Butte Trail an extra 2 miles. Continue straight past the Tanner Cutoff Trail junction 150 yards and turn left 0.3 mile down to the woodsy lake. To con-tinue, return to the faint Tanner Cutoff Trail junction, take this steep trail 2.3 miles downhill, turn right on the Tanner Creek Trail to Road 777, follow it 2.9 miles back to the old Tanner Butte Trailhead, and continue down the road to your car.

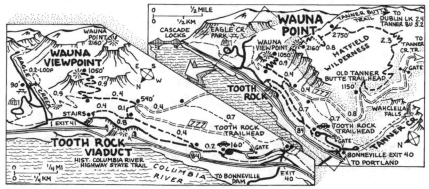

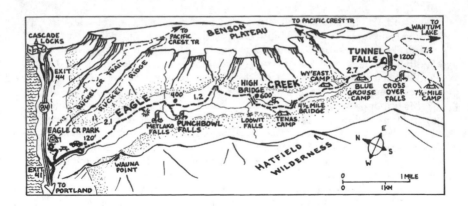

51

Eagle Creek

Easy (to Punchbowl Falls)
4.2 miles round trip
400 feet elevation gain
Open all year

Moderate (to High Bridge)
6.6 miles round trip
600 feet elevation gain

Difficult (to Tunnel Falls)
12 miles round trip
1200 feet elevation gain

Built in the 1910s to accompany the opening of the Columbia River Highway, the Eagle Creek Trail is one of Oregon's most spectacular paths, passing half a dozen major waterfalls. The trail is also something of an engineering marvel. To maintain an easy grade through this rugged canyon, the builders blasted ledges out of sheer cliffs, bridged a colossal gorge, and even chipped a tunnel through solid rock behind 120-foot Tunnel Falls.

Today the trail is so popular the parking lot fills by 10am on sunny weekends, leaving latecomers to park half a mile away. Although this is a great place to backpack, tenting along the first 7.5 miles is only allowed within four designated camp areas, where competition for weekend space is keen. Campfires are strongly discouraged. An additional caution to parents: trailside cliffs make this no place for unsupervised or hard-to-manage children. Dogs must be on leash.

If you're coming from the Portland area, take Interstate 84 to Eagle Creek exit 41, turn right, and keep right along the creek for half a mile to road's end. Because the Eagle Creek exit is only accessible from the west, travelers from Hood River will have to take Bonneville Dam exit 40 and double back on the freeway for a mile. Leave nothing of value in your car because break-ins are a problem here.

The trail starts along the creek but soon climbs well above it along a slope of cedars and mossy maples. Look for yellow monkeyflowers and curving fronds of maidenhair fern overhanging the path. After 0.8 mile the trail traverses a cliff with cables as handrails. At the 1.5-mile mark several short side trails to the right lead down to a viewpoint of 100-foot Metlako Falls in the distance.

Continue on the main trail 0.3 mile to a ridge-end junction with the Lower Punchbowl Trail, a 0.2-mile side trail down to a broad, 15-foot falls with a bedrock bank suitable for sunbathing. Hike upstream to a gravel beach to peer ahead to picturesque, 30-foot Punchbowl Falls in a huge, mossy rock bowl.

If you're game for a longer hike, return to the Eagle Creek Trail and continue 1.2 miles to High Bridge, a metal footbridge across a dizzying, slot-like chasm. Here the creek has exposed a long crack in the earth—the fault along which this valley formed. For a nice lunch spot, continue 0.4 mile to Tenas Campground (on the right) and Skooknichuck Falls (on the left). For a still longer hike continue a couple miles further, duck behind Tunnel Falls, and 200 yards later gain a view ahead to the valley's last great cascade, Crossover Falls.

Other Options

A classic 2- to 3-day backpacking trip continues to Wahtum Lake. Snow closes this 26.8-mile loop from mid-November until June. Start by hiking up the Eagle Creek Trail 13.3 miles to Wahtum Lake (see Hike #54). Then veer left on the PCT for 6.3 miles to the Benson Plateau, and turn left to descend the Ruckel Creek Trail (see Hike #52) back to your car.

Punchbowl Falls.   Opposite: Cable handrail along the Eagle Creek Trail.

52   Ruckel Creek

Difficult
9.6 miles round trip
3700 feet elevation gain
Open April through November

The challenging Ruckel Creek Trail climbs nearly 4000 feet to the forested Benson Plateau. The path approaches Ruckel Creek only twice, instead visiting Indian-dug pits, a clifftop viewpoint, and meadowed slopes dotted with late spring wildflowers

From Portland, take Interstate 84 to Eagle Creek exit 41, turn right, and park by the restroom at the Eagle Creek Park entrance. Because the Eagle Creek exit is accessible only from the west, drivers coming from Hood River will have to take Bonneville Dam exit 40, duck left through an underpass, and get back on the freeway eastbound for a mile.

From the parking area at the park's entrance, walk up the paved road toward the campground 150 yards to a sign marking the Gorge Trail on the left. Follow this path 0.2 mile up beside the campground to a fork signed for Buck Point. Keep straight on the Gorge Trail for 0.3 mile and then turn right on the Columbia River Highway Trail.

After 200 yards this paved bike path crosses Ruckel Creek on a picturesque concrete bridge—a remnant of the old scenic highway. Turn right here on a creekside path that switchbacks steeply uphill, heads under a powerline, and 0.3 mile later crosses a strange, hummocky, moss-covered rockslide. The pits here were dug at least 1000 years ago, evidently as vision quest sites for young Indian men.

Next the path switchbacks up for a grueling mile to a viewpoint atop a sheer 500-foot cliff overlooking the Bridge of the Gods, Table Mountain, and Mt.

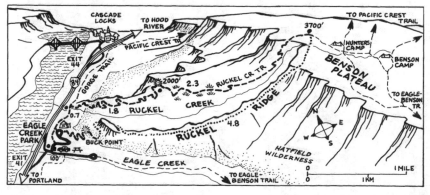

Bonneville Dam from Ruckel Ridge near Buck Point.   Opposite: Snowberry.

Adams. The trail's next 1.5 miles are relatively level, through grassy slopes of purple cluster lilies and red paintbrush. Finally climb very steeply again to the Benson Plateau. After just 150 yards through this level forest the trail forks. Turn right past a "Trail Not Maintained" sign for another 150 yards to splashing Ruckel Creek — a perfect lunch spot and turnaround point.

Other Options

The hardiest of adventurers can turn this hike into a loop by starting out on the Ruckel Ridge Trail, a very rough, unmaintained path along a rocky crest with numerous viewpoints. Park at the same trailhead, but turn right when you reach the Buck Point Trail junction beside the Eagle Creek Campground. Cut through the campground to site #5 and hike up to the right past a big sign for the Buck Point Trail. This path climbs 0.6 mile to Buck Point, a viewpoint beneath a powerline. Continue down to the right past a "Trail Not Maintained" sign to a rockslide. Take a faint trail up this slide, following cairns and watching for loose rocks. Traverse left around the base of a cliff and then climb steeply to a viewpoint on the ridgecrest. From here on the unofficial Ruckel Ridge Trail is a bit clearer, but you'll have to step over logs and use your hands as you clamber up and down along the narrow crest for another 3 miles. When you finally gain the level Benson Plateau, the trail vanishes in the woods. Follow cairns and blazes 0.3 mile left to the Ruckel Creek crossing described above. Shortly afterwards, turn left on the Ruckel Creek Trail to complete the loop.

Herman Creek

Moderate (to Three Spires)
4.8 miles round trip
1020 feet elevation gain
Open all year
Use: hikers, horses

Difficult (to Indian Point)
8-mile loop
2600 feet elevation gain

Herman Creek's huge canyon and nearby Nick Eaton Ridge offer hiking options for nearly everyone. For a relatively easy hike, cross a bridge to a waterfall and three rock spires. For a more difficult loop, climb to the viewpoint atop Indian Point's rock pinnacle, returning through the steep wildflower meadows of Nick Eaton Ridge. Mountain goats from Eastern Oregon were reintroduced into this area in 2005.

From Portland, take Interstate 84 to Cascade Locks exit 44 and drive straight through town 2 miles. Just when you reach the on-ramp for the freeway east, go straight onto a paved road marked "To Oxbow Fish Hatchery." Follow this road 1.8 miles, turn right at Herman Creek Campground, and drive up through the campground, keeping right to the trailhead parking loop at the far end. If you're driving from Hood River it's quicker to take Herman Creek exit 47 and head toward the Oxbow Hatchery for 0.7 mile to the trailhead turnoff. On winter weekdays, when the campground road is gated closed, you'll have to walk a few hundred extra yards.

The trail begins in a cool forest of Douglas fir and bigleaf maple. Look for white inside-out flowers and bold orange tiger lilies in summer. The path switchbacks up across a powerline access road fringed with poison oak, and then climbs

Herman Creek's footbridge.   Above: The Columbia Gorge from Indian Point.

another 0.4 mile to a well-signed fork.

If you're interested in the easier option, veer right onto the Herman Creek Bridge Trail and descend slightly for 0.4 mile to the 75-foot metal span, where you can relax beside the rushing stream's bouldery banks. Then continue up through the woods on the far side 0.8 mile and turn right on the Pacific Crest Trail for 0.4 mile to a small creek where you can look up a narrow side canyon to Pacific Crest Falls, a pair of little cascades. Continue 0.2 mile to Three Spires, a rock formation that makes a good turnaround point.

If you're aiming for a longer hike, however, hike 0.6 mile up from the trailhead and *fork to the left,* continuing up the Herman Creek Trail. This path soon joins an old dirt road and follows it uphill to the right for 0.6 mile to Herman Camp, a primitive tentsite. Turn left off the road onto the signed Gorton Creek Trail, which climbs steadily for 2.6 miles before switchbacking up to a junction on a ridge end. To continue the loop you'll turn uphill to the right here on the Ridge Cutoff Trail, but first continue straight 50 yards on the Gorton Creek Trail to find a small, unmarked side path to the left that leads 0.1 mile down to Indian Point, where views extend from Hood River to Mt. St. Helens. The frightening, final 30-foot scramble up an exposed rock pinnacle requires the use of your hands. Turn back here if you're uncertain.

To complete the loop return to the Ridge Cutoff Trail, follow it 0.6 mile, and take the Nick Eaton Trail down a steep ridgecrest through rock gardens of summer blooms: purple penstemon, blue lupine, red paintbrush, and lavender plectritis. Views include the tip of Mt. Hood and Bonneville Dam.

Other Options

To explore more of Herman Creek, continue straight past Herman Camp on the old road. This route soon becomes a trail again and contours through old-growth woods with Herman Creek audible far below. Casey Creek makes a good goal. If you're backpacking, continue on a 26.4-mile loop to Wahtum Lake. Hike 11.2 miles up the Herman Creek Trail and turn left on the Pacific Crest Trail 1.6 miles to the lake (see Hike #54). Then turn around and take the PCT 12.1 miles north across the Benson Plateau to the Herman Creek Bridge Trail.

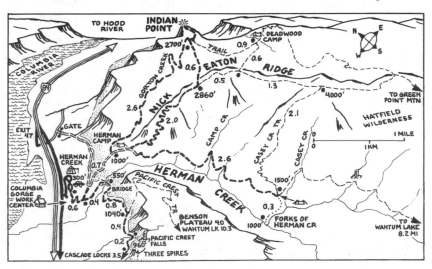

54   Wahtum Lake

Moderate (to Chinidere Mountain)
4.1-mile loop
1100 feet elevation gain
Open June to mid-November
Use: hikers, horses

The loop around this scenic lake climbs on the Pacific Crest Trail past patches of huckleberries and wildflowers to Chinidere Mountain, arguably the best viewpoint in the Hatfield Wilderness.

Drive Interstate 84 to West Hood River exit 62, head into Hood River 1.1 mile, turn right on 13th Street, and follow signs for Odell for 3.4 zigzagging miles. After crossing the Hood River Bridge take a right-hand fork past Tucker Park for 6.3 miles. Then fork to the right again toward Dee, cross the river, and turn left on the road to Lost Lake. After 5 miles veer right at a "Wahtum Lake" pointer, follow 1-lane paved Road 13 for 4.3 miles, and finally veer right again onto Road 1310 for 6 miles to a pass with primitive Wahtum Lake Campground. If you don't have a Northwest Forest Pass, you'll have to pay a $5 parking fee at this trailhead. A tent site is an extra $10.

Park by the message board and take the "Wahtum Express Trail" down 252 steps to the lake. Turn right on the Pacific Crest Trail and climb gradually away from the shore through a hemlock forest dotted with blue huckleberries in August. Earlier in summer expect wildflowers: 4-petaled white bunchberry, big trilliums, bleeding hearts, mint, and columbine. The rarest bloom of all is cutleaf bugbane, which grows here and at Lost Lake (Hike #74), but nowhere else on earth. Look for its salmonberry-like leaves and 5-foot plumes of tiny white starbursts.

After 1.6 miles the PCT forks. Head uphill to the right past a "Chinidere Mountain" sign on a steepish 0.4-mile switchbacking path to the former lookout

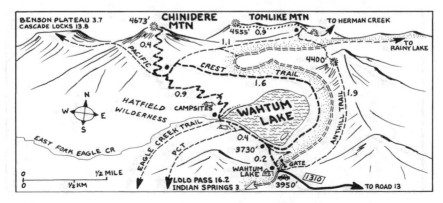

Wahtum Lake.   Opposite: Cutleaf bugbane.

site's bare summit amid alpine wildflowers: blue gentian, red paintbrush, and purple aster. The 360-degree view includes the entire route of your hike, as well as snowpeaks from Jefferson to Rainier. Mt. St. Helens rises above the broad Benson Plateau, while Mt. Adams looms above Tomlike Mountain's barren ridge. *Chinidere* was the last reigning chief of the Wasco Indians, and his son was named *Tomlike.* Appropriately, *wahtum* is an Indian word for lake.

To finish the loop, return to the PCT, head left for 100 feet, and turn right on a continuation of the Chinidere Mountain Trail. This path switchbacks 0.9 mile down past several campsites. Cross Wahtum Lake's log-jammed outlet creek as best you can and turn left on the Eagle Creek Trail. Turn left past some more campsites, join the PCT, pass a nice bathing beach, and then turn right to climb back to your car.

Other Options

For a slightly wilder 6.6-mile loop, visit Tomlike Mountain instead. Descend to Wahtum Lake, turn right on the PCT for 1.5 miles and turn right on the Herman Creek Trail for 1.1 mile to a junction with the Anthill Trail. Continue straight 100 feet to a switchback at a ridge end. Leave the trail at this corner and bushwhack left, straight out the ridgecrest. The first few hundred yards are a tangle of small trees, but then it's mostly easy walking along the open rock crest, following cairns 0.9 mile to the summit. To complete the loop, return via the Anthill Trail, which has a nice viewpoint of Wahtum Lake.

Backpackers often stop at Wahtum Lake on 2- or 3-day loop trips via Eagle Creek (see Hike #51) or Herman Creek (see Hike #53). Camping is banned on the fragile lakeshore, but nice sites have been designated nearby.

Moderate (to Hole-in-the-Wall Falls)
2.5-mile loop
600 feet elevation gain
Open all year

Very Difficult (to summit)
12.1-mile loop
4800 feet elevation gain
Open mid-June through October

One of the most physically demanding paths in Oregon, the Mount Defiance Trail gains nearly 5000 feet of elevation on its way to the highest point in the Columbia Gorge. But the trail begins with an easier option—a short, steep loop that visits waterfalls, viewpoints, and creek valleys at the mountain's base.

Take Interstate 84 east of Cascade Locks 10 miles to Starvation Creek Trailhead exit 55. If you're coming from Hood River, you'll have to take Wyeth exit 51, turn around, and drive back on the freeway 3 miles to access Starvation Creek Trailhead exit 55. While you're here, be sure to take the 100-yard paved path past the restrooms to the base of 186-foot Starvation Creek Falls. The falls earned their name when two trains were trapped near here in an 1884 blizzard. Stranded passengers were offered $3 a day to dig out the track while waiting for skiers to arrive with food from Hood River.

To find the Mount Defiance Trail, walk back toward the freeway and follow its noisy shoulder west. The trail veers into the woods, passes mostly-hidden Cabin Creek Falls, and after 0.8 mile crosses a footbridge below Hole-in-the-Wall Falls, which plummets 100 feet from a tunnel. This oddity was created in 1938 when the Oregon Highway Department, upset that Warren Creek Falls wetted

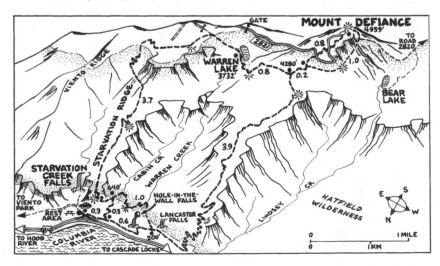

Mt. Hood from Mt. Defiance.   Opposite: The Columbia River from Starvation Ridge.

the old Columbia River Highway, diverted the creek through a cliff.

In another 0.1 mile reach a junction with the Starvation Ridge Trail. Turn left if you'd like to take the easy loop. This path climbs to a crossing of Warren Creek and then switchbacks up over a grassy ridge to a cliff overlooking the parking area, the river, and Dog Mountain (Hike #59). Continue across Cabin Creek and soon veer left on the Starvation Cutoff Trail to return to your car. Take care if you attempt this dangerous part of the path, because it's steep and strewn with slippery pebbles!

If you'd prefer the difficult loop, follow the Mount Defiance Trail from Hole-in-the-Wall Falls straight 0.2 mile to 20-foot, fan-shaped Lancaster Falls. After another level half mile the trail suddenly launches upward, climbing 3 miles along a densely wooded ridgecrest. Finally reach a junction with the Mitchell Point Trail (route of the return loop). Continue uphill to the right for 0.2 mile, watching carefully for an unmarked side trail to the right. Take this new scenic route across massive rockslides overlooking Bear Lake, and curve left up to the microwave relay towers at the summit.

To return on a slightly shorter loop, walk past the fenced microwave building and a smaller tower to an old wooden trail sign. Take a path downhill that crosses a dirt road twice. When you return to the Mitchell Point Trail junction turn right toward Warren Lake. This route descends 0.8 mile to the pretty lake, rimmed with rockslides and pines. Though mud-bottomed, Warren Lake is a fine spot to swim or camp.

Beyond the lake the trail continues straight and level for half a mile to an important but unmarked junction where you'll want to turn left onto the Starvation Ridge Trail. If you miss the turnoff, the Mitchell Point Trail ends 50 yards later at a dirt road. The Starvation Ridge Trail, on the other hand, barrels down a wooded ridgecrest for over 3 miles, passing two excellent viewpoints. At the bottom turn right on the Starvation Cutoff Trail to return to your car.

Other Options

A shorter, 1.6-mile trail climbs to Mt. Defiance from the south, gaining just 1200 feet of elevation. From Hood River, take 13th Street south, following signs for Odell 3.4 miles. After crossing a bridge, fork right past Tucker Park for 6.3 miles and continue on gravel Road 2820 for 10 miles to a sign for the Mt. Defiance Trail. Keep right at trail junctions, unless you'd like a side trip to Bear Lake.

56   Mitchell Point

Moderate (to Mitchell Point)
2.2 miles round trip
1040 feet elevation gain
Open all year

The old Columbia River Highway once tunneled 390 feet through Mitchell Point in an elegant, arched gallery hewn from solid rock. Views from the cliff "windows" spanned the Columbia Gorge to Dog Mountain. Although a much-regretted 1966 demolition order destroyed the tunnel, a freeway overlook recaptures the old view, and a rugged little trail climbs to an even better viewpoint atop Mitchell Point's stony crest.

From Cascade Locks take Interstate 84 east 14 miles to the Mitchell Point Overlook at exit 58. Since this rest area is only accessible from the west, travelers from Hood River will have to take Viento Park exit 56 and double back on the freeway 2 miles.

The Columbia River from Mitchell Point.   *Above: Mitchell Point from the overlook.*

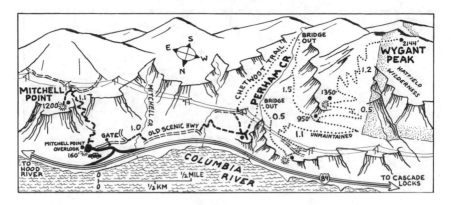

Park at the far left end of the overlook's parking area, where interpretive signs describe the old tunnel and an abandoned log flume still visible across the river. Then walk across the big parking lot and take an obvious paved trail uphill. The paved path soon turns to gravel and briefly follows the old Columbia River Highway's route. Then the trail switchbacks to the left, climbing steeply through a Douglas fir forest. At times poison oak crowds the narrow tread with its triple leaflets, so it's best to wear long pants.

After 0.9 mile the trail forks beneath the first wire of a powerline. Go left, paralleling a service road uphill 200 feet. At a crest, turn left on a trail along a bare ridgecrest up 0.2 mile to Mitchell Point's summit, where views cover the entire sweep of the Columbia Gorge from White Salmon to Table Mountain. Do not venture beyond the trail's high point! The narrow, rocky hogback beyond is dangerous and does not have better views.

Return to your car as you came.

Other Options

The Mitchell Point trailhead is also the starting point for the Wygant Peak trail system, but lack of maintenance has made most of the trails in that area dangerously rough, confusing, and overgrown with poison oak. The only rec-ommended portion is the first mile along the old route of the historic Columbia River Highway. Beyond that, powerline work has obscured the tread and both bridges over Perham Creek are missing.

To hike this first mile of the scenic old highway from the Mitchell Point trail-head, walk down toward the freeway and take an old gated road that parallels the freeway. The overgrown foundations below this road are the remains of Sonny, an oddly named railroad stop. The place's inhabitants tried to call it Mitchell, but Oregon already had a town by that name. Next they chose Little Boy after a local ranch, but this was rejected as awkward to telegraph. Sonny seemed the next best thing.

At a corner in the road, trail signs direct you onto a path that crosses Mitchell Creek and joins an abandoned section of the old Columbia River Highway for 0.3 mile. At the 1-mile mark, turn back at a junction with the abandoned Chetwoot Trail—unless you're wearing long pants and are prepared for route finding. Even at the summit of Wygant Peak, brush blocks views.

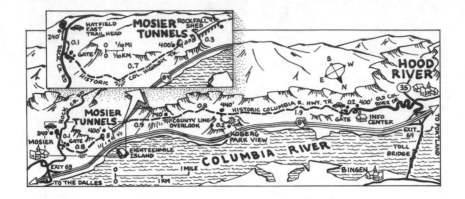

57   Mosier Twin Tunnels

Easy (from east trailhead)
1.8 miles round trip
160 feet elevation gain
Open all year
Use: hikers, bicycles

Moderate (entire trail)
9.4 miles round trip
960 feet elevation gain

Tunnels with gracefully arched rock windows pierce the basalt cliffs high above the Columbia River at Mosier. The twin tunnels were built in 1919-21 for the historic Columbia River Highway, one of America's earliest and most beautiful pleasure drives. When falling rocks from the cliffs above damaged several cars in 1953, engineers backfilled the tunnels and rerouted traffic onto a new, river-level route—now Interstate 84.

Still, many people remained nostalgic for the old highway, with its daring tunnels, grand panoramas, graceful curves, delicate bridges, and stonework railings. And so in 1995, workers began reopening portions of the original route as the Historic Columbia River Highway State Trail. Much of this paved path is best toured by bicycle, but the twin tunnels near Mosier are interesting enough to attract hikers as well.

To start, drive Interstate 84 east of Hood River 5 miles to Mosier exit 69. Head south 0.2 mile to the village of Mosier and turn left on Rock Creek Road for 0.7 mile to the large Hatfield Trailhead on the left. Expect a $5-per-car fee. Follow a paved path back along the shoulder 200 yards and cross the road to a gate where the actual trail begins.

The "trail," of course, is a paved highway that's closed to traffic. The engineers who designed this pioneer road specified that it be 14 feet wide, with a minimum 100-foot radius on curves, and a maximum grade of 5 percent. Though unusually generous for 1921, such specifications now make the highway seem narrow and twisty.

This portion of the old road sets off across a strange, hummocky landscape of basalt rock piles. Shade is scarce so remember to bring a hat. The rockfield was formed by the crumbling rimrock above, and has been colonized only by a few Douglas firs, ponderosa pines, and oaks. If you look carefully, you might notice that some of the rock piles are not natural. Thousands of years ago, native tribes arranged the rocks in walls and pits. These are believed to be vision quest sites, where young men fasted to obtain guidance from the spirit world.

After 0.8 mile you'll enter the tunnels. The first is 288 feet long, with two windows carved out of the cliff wall. The windows overlook a rocky island in the river below, with the town of Bingen and the Hood River toll bridge in the distance. Sailboarders ride the windy river's whitecaps far below.

The shorter, second tunnel was connected to the first by a concrete roof in 1999. Engineers built this roof — and the concrete shed covering the road for 700 feet beyond the tunnels — to protect trail users from rockfall. Because the structures also had to keep rocks from bouncing down onto the railroad tracks and freeway below, they were designed with massive, flat roofs capable of catching a 5000 pound rock that has fallen 200 feet.

If you're not ready to turn back yet, consider continuing up to County Line Overlook, where the old highway skirts a tall riverside cliff near the border of Wasco and Hood River counties. Still not tired? Then sally onward another 0.8 mile and turn right on a 0.2-mile side path to a viewpoint knoll overlooking Koberg Beach State Wayside.

If you plan to hike (or bike) the entire 4.7-mile trail, you might want to start from the Hood River side, where two former gravel pits have been converted to trailhead parking lots with visitor facilities. To find this trailhead, drive Interstate 84 to the east end of Hood River, take exit 64 and follow "Government Camp" signs 0.3 mile to a stop sign. Then turn left onto Old Columbia River Drive for 1.3 miles to road's end.

The view from one of the tunnels' rock windows.   Opposite: Inside the tunnels.

58 Tom McCall Preserve

Easy (to plateau ponds)
2.2 miles round trip
300 feet elevation **loss**
Open all year

Moderate (to McCall Point)
3.4 miles round trip
1100 feet elevation gain
Open May 1 to October 30

This cliff-edged plateau of oak grasslands and wildflowers is one of the Nature Conservancy's most dramatic preserves. The conservancy is a non-profit private organization that quietly purchases ecologically sensitive land. Their preserve here has two trails. A path easy enough for children explores several ponds on a lower plateau overlooking the Columbia River, while a steeper trail climbs to the breathtaking mountain viewpoint atop McCall Point.

The best time to visit this dry eastern end of the Columbia Gorge is spring, when flowers dot the slopes. Grass widows are at their showiest in mid March, while yellow balsamroot and blue lupine peak in early May. Avoid the heat of July and August. And remember to wear long pants if you're taking the upper trail, as it passes poison oak.

Take Interstate 84 east from Hood River to Mosier exit 69 and go straight through Mosier for 6.6 miles to the Rowena Crest Viewpoint parking area. If you're coming from The Dalles, take Rowena exit 76 and follow a winding section of the historic Columbia River Highway up to the viewpoint. Because this is a nature preserve, dogs, horses, and bicycles are not allowed. Camping and flower picking are also banned. Hikers must stay on designated trails.

The easy path to the lower plateau starts at a signboard on the opposite side of the highway from the viewpoint's entrance road. During the spring wildflower season, look here for sunflower-like balsamroot, purple vetch, blue bachelor buttons, and white yarrow. Ten-inch-long ground squirrels zip about

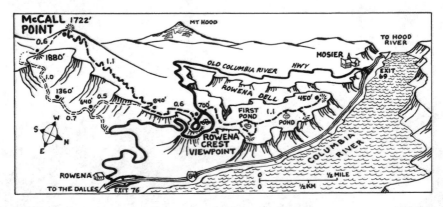

The plateau from Tom McCall Point.   Opposite: Tom McCall Point from the trailhead.

the fields from February to June but hibernate the other seven months. Where the path crosses a narrow neck leading to the plateau notice the old stone wall that once fenced sheep.

After 0.3 mile take a right-hand fork of the trail around a pond full of lilypads and cattails. Listen for the melodious warble of redwing blackbirds. The trail loops past a cliff-edge viewpoint and returns to the main trail. Continue out the plateau past a smaller, poison-oak-fringed pond, and reach trail's end at a cliff with a view across the Columbia to the town of Lyle at the mouth of the Klickitat River. Note the eight layers of basalt in the opposite cliffs, evidence of the repeated lava floods that deluged the Columbia Basin and created this plateau 10-17 million years ago.

To try the steeper path up McCall Point (open May through October), return to the parking area and look for a trail sign on the right at the start of the parking loop. This path climbs along the rim edge through meadows of balsamroot and groves of gnarled scrub oak with some poison oak. After climbing gently 0.6 mile to a signboard, the path switchbacks more steeply up to the right. Here the lower-elevation wildflowers are joined by red paintbrush and blue lupine. The trail switchbacks up to a summit meadow with glorious views of Mt. Hood, Mt. Adams, and the entire eastern Columbia Gorge. Return as you came.

Other Options

Adventurers who don't want to turn back at McCall Point can continue on a very rough loop. Continue 50 feet past the white post marking McCall Point's summit, fork downhill to the left to a saddle, and then follow faint trails, keeping left along the rim, for 0.6 mile to a viewpoint by a collapsed picnic table *(GPS location N45°39.883' W121°17.834')*. Continue along the rim, go through a fence opening, and keep left to find an old roadbed that descends a mile to a confusing junction. Veer downhill to the right on a steep roadbed for 0.7 mile to another confusing junction *(GPS location N45°40.381' W121°17.873')*. Then turn left on a relatively level, less used roadbed with some poison oak. This track crosses a rockslide, scrambles across some boulders, and skirts a cliff for half a mile to the signboard junction with the McCall Point Trail *(GPS location N45°40.580' W121°18.015')*. Turn right here for 0.6 mile to return to your car.

59 Dog Mountain

Moderate (to lower viewpoint)
3 miles round trip
1500 feet elevation gain
Open all year

Difficult (to summit)
6.9-mile loop
2820 feet elevation gain

The most spectacular wildflower meadows of the Columbia Gorge drape the alp-like slopes of Dog Mountain. In May and June these hills are alive with yellow balsamroot, red paintbrush, and blue lupine. Even flowerless seasons provide breathtaking views of the Columbia Gorge. Such beauty has made the steep climb popular, but with three trails to the top, you can choose your route.

From Portland, drive Interstate 84 to Cascade Locks exit 44, take the Bridge of the Gods across the river (paying a $1 toll on the way), and turn right on Washington Highway 14 for 12 miles. Between mileposts 53 and 54, at a large sign for the Dog Mountain Trailhead, park in a huge pullout on the left.

Which of the trails up Dog Mountain should you take? For the best views, head uphill on the steep, scenic route. Then you can return on a gentler, longer loop that's easy on the knees. So start out from the far, right-hand end of the parking lot on the Dog Mountain Trail. This path begins along an ancient road but after 100 yards turns sharply left and begins a relentless, switchbacking

Wind Mountain and the Columbia River from Dog Mountain.   Above: Balsamroot.

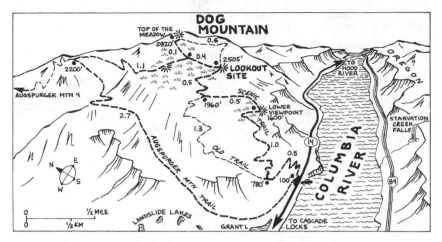

climb. Beware of lush, three-leaved poison oak along these lower slopes. Also notice early summer wildflowers: baby blue eyes, lupine, yellow desert parsley, and purple cluster lilies on onion-like stalks.

After half a mile the trail forks. Ignore the left-hand path—the precipitous, viewless Old Trail. Instead turn right, through a Douglas fir forest brightened in spring by big 3-petaled trilliums and tiny 6- or 7-petaled starflowers. This path climbs almost a mile before suddenly emerging at a viewpoint on a windswept, grassy knoll. In early summer, sunflower-like balsamroot and red paintbrush spangle this pleasant picnic spot—a satisfactory turnaround point for a moderate hike. The view extends across the chasm of the Columbia Gorge to Starvation Creek Falls and sometimes-snowy Mt. Defiance.

The grander meadows on Dog Mountain's summit are nearly twice as high as this lower viewpoint. If your legs are up to the challenge, continue half a mile to another junction with the Old Trail. Head uphill here at a gruelingly steep grade for half a mile to an old fire lookout site in a steep wildflower meadow. Take a sharp left turn here and keep heading uphill for another half mile to your destination: the top of the meadow, afloat in panoramic vistas from Hood River to Mt. Hood and Cascade Locks. Notice the flavorful assortment of wildflowers at this viewpoint: wild strawberry, chocolate lily, and wild onion.

Turn back after soaking in the view from the top of the meadow. (If you keep going, the trail ahead merely dives into viewless woods.) So turn around, hike back down through the meadow 200 yards, and turn right at a sign for Augspurger Mountain. This path descends a ridge with views of its own for 1.1 mile. Then turn left at a junction. For the final 2.7 miles back to your car, the Augspurger Mountain Trail gently spirals halfway around Dog Mountain, like the flight path of an airplane slowly coming in for a landing.

Other Options

If you're a frequent climber of Dog Mountain, consider tackling the faint, very rough route 6.7 miles to Augspurger Mountain, a 3667-foot peak with lesser views and less crowded meadows. Start at the same trailhead, but after 2.7 miles keep left. Confusing dirt roads and powerlines make a topographic map essential. A proposed extension to the trail would reach Grassy Knoll (see I like #140), providing a link to the Pacific Crest Trail.

The trail begins as an abandoned road below Coyote Wall.   Below: Mountain biker.

60   Coyote Wall

Easy (to fence)
3.7-mile loop
680 feet elevation gain
Open all year
Use: hikers, bicycles

Moderate (to top of meadow)
6.1 miles round trip
1520 feet elevation gain

When Ice Age floodwaters from Montana roared into the Columbia Gorge 12,000 years ago they backed up here, at a tilted stack of lava flows opposite Hood River. The floods stripped this landscape to bedrock, but now Coyote Wall's scenic, bare cliff blazes with wildflowers each spring.

The open slopes have become so popular that the Forest Service is decommissioning some unofficial trails and will be requiring that dogs be leashed December 1 through June 30. A trail along the western base of Coyote Wall was closed in 2012 to protect private property, but a new trail land is planned on public land farther west that will make possible an 8-mile loop.

Start by driving Interstate 84 to Hood River Bridge exit 64. Pay the $1 toll to cross the river. Then turn right onto Washington Highway 14 through Bingen for a total of 4.6 miles. Turn left on paved Courtney Road for 100 feet and pull into a gravel parking area along an abandoned road to the left *(GPS location N45°41.986' W121°24.228')*. Watch for poison oak, the triple-leafletted brush that's often disguised among this area's many genuine oak seedlings.

Walk back across paved Courtney Road, pass a locked green gate, and follow an abandoned road around the base of Coyote Wall's cliff for 0.7 mile. Turn uphill to the left at an old "Forest Visitors" sign on a gateless fence box on the left *(GPS location N45°41.939' W121°23.627')*.

Follow this trail for 150 yards, keeping uphill to the left. Then turn left on an old dirt road used by mountain bikes. In another 0.2 mile, veer left onto a slightly smaller path that curves along a rimrock cleft past a few ponderosa

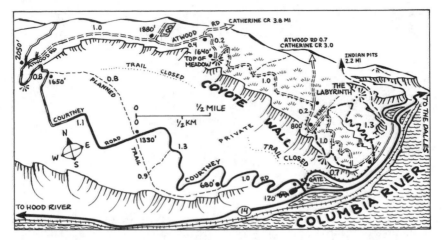

pines. Sunflower-like balsamroot and blue lupine bloom here in April. Wild onions bloom pink among the grass in summer.

Views across the Columbia River to Oregon improve as you climb. Keep left near the cliff's rim for 0.8 mile until you rejoin the dirt road near a gap in a wire fence *(GPS location N45°42.336' W121°23.991')*. If you're hiking with kids, make this the highest point of your loop. Turn downhill to the right along the road 200 yards. When the road turns right, veer down to the left on the Labyrinth Trail. This lovely path crosses a creek and then switchbacks downstream past viewpoints and a waterfall to the abandoned road at the bottom of Coyote Wall.

For a longer hike, continue uphill from the gap in the wire fence. The old dirt roadbed traces the cliff rim 1.2 miles up through glorious meadows. Turn back at the top of the meadow, although the track does continue through woods 1.6 miles west to Courtney Road or 4 miles east to Catherine Creek (Hike #61).

The Labyrinth Trail follows a creek valley.

61

Catherine Creek

Easy (3 short hikes)
4.1 miles round trip
600 feet elevation gain
Open all year
Use: hikers, bicycles

The first of these three easy hikes follows a paved loop past views of the Columbia Gorge from the Dalles to Hood River. A second hike climbs through Catherine Creek's park-like valley to a natural rock arch. The third walk explores a nearby hillside where mysterious pits in a rockslide are believed to honor the spirits of Indian dead. In the Catherine Creek area, dogs must be on leash.

Because the trails are so short, it's easy to do them all in a day. If you love wildflowers, you might time your visit to catch the peak displays: grass widows in mid March, blue camas in mid April, and yellow balsamroot in early May.

Start by driving Interstate 84 to Hood River Bridge exit 64. Pay the $1 toll to cross the river. Then turn right onto Washington Highway 14 for 5.7 miles. Just before milepost 71 turn left onto paved "Old Hwy. No. 8" around Rowland Lake. After 0.9 mile, when the road climbs a hill, look for a "Road Closed" sign on a spur to the left. This is the trailhead to the Indian pits. To find the trailhead for the first two hikes, continue 0.5 mile along the county road to a large "Catherine Creek" sign on the right. Park at a long gravel pullout on the left by a green gate (*GPS location N45°42.629' W121°21.724'*).

The first of the three short hikes is a paved, wheelchair-accessible loop that begins on the right, beside the large "Catherine Creek" sign. This wide path tours a dry grassland overlooking the white-capped Columbia River. Scattered ponderosa pines and black oaks provide a bit of shade. Look for Columbia ground squirrels in the fields and cottontail rabbits by the blackberry thickets. If you keep right at all trail junctions, you'll pass a viewpoint to the west (across

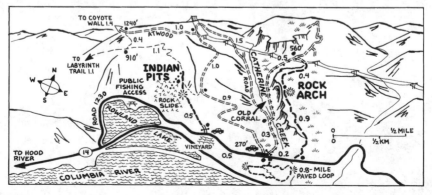

The Catherine Creek trailhead.   Opposite: Catherine Creek's natural rock arch.

the river to Hood River cherry orchards and the top half of Mt. Hood), and a viewpoint to the east (upstream past Memaloose Island to The Dalles), before returning to your car.

For the second hike, walk 50 yards back along the paved county road to a green metal gate on the far side. From here you can explore Catherine Creek's upper canyon on abandoned ranch roads. Take Road 020 to the right across a bedrock flat where white death camas blooms in spring. After 0.3 mile fork to the right across a creek. Next the route passes an old corral at the foot of the rock arch—actually a splinter of rimrock on the canyon wall. Then continue up the old road. Just beyond a crackling powerline fork to the right on what becomes a trail along the rimrock. Blue lupine and white bitterroot bloom here in May. A wooden railing keeps you from venturing too near the arch itself. Beyond the arch continue on a fainter, rockier path down along the canyon rim 0.9 mile to the paved road, just 0.2 mile from your car.

Note that the Catherine Creek valley has shrubby clumps of both poison oak and real oak, so pay attention to the difference. The lobed leaves of poison oak are always in clusters of three. Real oak has single leaves. At times poison oak can also be identified by white berries or shiny leaves.

The third short hike, to the Indian pits, is closed February 1 to June 30 to protect peregrine falcon habitat. Return to your car, drive 0.5 mile back west along county Road 1230. Opposite a vineyard slope, park at a spur on the right marked "Road Closed." Parking is limited here. Walk the steepish track up to the left for 0.3 mile to a viewpoint where you can see across a huge lava rockslide to Rowland Lake. If you look carefully, you'll notice odd walls and pits in the rockslide. To inspect them, continue 100 yards and rock-hop to the left down the rocky slope. The 5- to 15-foot-wide pits are sometimes clustered in groups of 20 or more within meandering rock walls.

Northwest Indians often built small rock-rimmed meditation sites in places where spirits were thought to be powerful, including many mountain peaks. Young men would fast in such locations in the hopes of receiving a spirit vision to guide their adult life. Are the pits here vision quest sites? Perhaps, since they overlook the Columbia River's Memaloose Island. *Memaloose* means "dead" in the language of the Chinook Indians who once lived here, and the island was an important burial site and spiritual center for that powerful rivergoing tribe.

149

62

Cherry Orchard

Moderate
5 miles round trip
1100 feet elevation gain
Open all year

A spectacular trail climbs rimrock bluffs above the Columbia River to sweeping views from an ancient cherry orchard at the dry eastern end of the Columbia Gorge. In spring the arid slopes erupt with wildflowers. Although the trail is open all year, avoid the shadeless heat of August and the icy winds of mid winter.

The stark cliffs on the lower portion of this hike were stripped of soil when 800-foot-deep Ice Age floods scoured out the Columbia Gorge 12,000 years ago. Just above that high-water mark, the orchard site remained fertile enough to attract a farmer during the fruit boom of the early 1900s.

By the late 1900s, when developers were threatening to clutter the Gorge's rim-rock with private homes, one woman began quietly buying up land near Lyle to preserve the scenery. Nancy Russell helped found the Friends of the Columbia Gorge in 1980. In 2009 her estate donated 515 acres to the non-profit group, including all of the Cherry Orchard Trail. Today the scenic path is open to everyone, as long as you sign a liability waiver at a registration box near the trailhead.

To find the trailhead, pay $1 to cross the toll bridge across the Columbia River at Hood River and turn right on Washington Highway 14 for 12 miles to milepost 77. One mile beyond the town of Lyle, and just a few hundred yards past a pair of tunnels, park in a big gravel pullout on the left *(GPS location N45°41.188' W121°15.931')*.

The trail starts at the far end of the pullout and climbs below a cliff through scrub white oak with a lush understory of poison oak. Wear long pants and learn the difference between real oak leaves (which are single) and poison oak

The Columbia Gorge from the Cherry Orchard Trail.   Above: Trailhead sign.

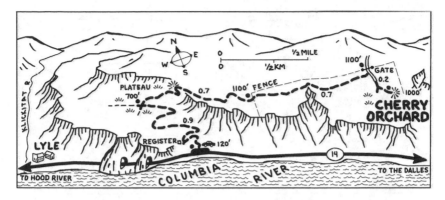

leaves (which grow in triplets). In spring the slopes here also host blue lupine, little yellow fiddleheads, big yellow balsamroot, and white prairie stars.

After 0.9 mile you'll crest a plateau that's filled with spiny flowers. Yellow star thistle is a European alien that thrives in such stark habitats, driving out local plants. In spring you'll see white death camas among the spiny dead stalks of star thistle. In August, star thistle blooms cover the plateau with a yellow haze.

Turn right at a 4-way trail junction in the plateau. Your path now narrows and climbs steeply past astonishing views. After 0.7 mile your climb ends when you sidle through a cattle baffle in an old fenceline.

For the next 0.9 mile the trail ambles through oak copses and little meadows. At times the tread may be faint, but the route is mostly level, and the fenceline to the left keeps you in line.

Yellow star thistle.

When you reach a dirt road by a gate, turn downhill to the right to a meadow.

Only a couple of the ancient cherry trees in this former orchard are still alive, sprouting white blossoms on desperate old limbs. Keep left through the meadow to find an oak cross in memory of an early orchardist *(GPS location N45°41.204' W121°14.799')*. Just beyond is a viewpoint where you can lunch beneath a ponderosa pine. Return as you came.

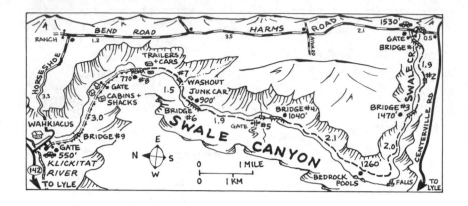

63   Klickitat Rail Trail

Easy (to third bridge)
3.8 miles round trip
60 feet elevation **loss**
Open October through June
Use: hikers, bicycles

Moderate (to bedrock pools)
7.8 miles round trip
270 feet elevation **loss**

Difficult (to Wahkiacus, with shuttle)
12.4 miles one way
980 feet elevation **loss**

After trains stopped running along the Klickitat River north of The Dalles, the non-profit Rails-to-Trails Conservancy acquired 31 miles of the old railbed and turned it over to the Washington State Parks as a long, skinny park, surrounded by private land. Perhaps the most dramatic section of this new path traces remote, roadless Swale Canyon for 12.4 miles, down from a treeless plateau to the settlement of Wahkiacus. Even if you hike only a small portion you'll see spring wildflowers, rimrock cliffs, birds, and old railroad trestles. The route is so sunny that it closes during the summer fire season, when it's too hot to hike anyway.

If you can't arrange a car shuttle, simply hike out-and-back from the upper trailhead. To find this starting point from Interstate 84, take Hood River Bridge exit 64, pay a $1 toll to cross the river, and turn right on Washington Highway 14 for 12.8 miles to Lyle. At the Country Cafe in the middle of town, turn left on Centerville Highway. After 0.4 mile fork to the left to keep on this highway. Then continue 14.5 paved miles and turn left on gravel Harms Road for half a mile to the trailhead on the left, just after a green metal bridge *(GPS location N45°43.416' W121°01.845')*. Dogs must be on leash. Bring a hat for the sun.

Walk past a green gate, cross a 140-foot trestle over Swale Creek, and set off down the gravel railroad grade with Stacker Butte on the horizon ahead. From late March to May the bare hills here turn green and the arid landscape blooms with yellow balsamroot, blue lupine, patches of white phlox, and clumps of yellow desert parsley. If you've never seen Oregon's state bird, the meadowlark, simply trace that melodious warble you're hearing. Swallows and redwing blackbirds are on hand too. Rattlesnakes and gopher snakes live here, but are uncommon.

After 1.3 miles you'll cross a short bridge over a side wash, and in another 0.6 mile you'll cross the third bridge, a curving trestle where the canyon's first ponderosa pines and oaks manage to grow. Turn back here for a short hike. Otherwise continue 2 miles, around a bend in the deepening canyon, to a series of bedrock pools and chutes in the creek to the left. This is a good spot to lunch by the creek, watching ground squirrels and butterflies before turning back.

Of course if you've arranged to leave a shuttle car ahead at Wahkiacus, you don't have to turn back at all. Sally onward down the twisting canyon. Beyond the fourth bridge the valley floor is strewn with boulders from floods, one of which washed out part of the seventh bridge. At the eighth bridge you'll see a few trailers and cars (on private land) that have managed to drive up the trail from Wahkiacus despite signs banning motor vehicles. Then you'll pass half a dozen cabins built in the back-to-the-earth spirit of the 1970s. Push on for the final 2 miles to a locked green gate at the Wahkiacus Trailhead. Then check your collar and cuffs for ticks. If you find any, unscrew them until they let go.

To leave a shuttle car here, turn off Highway 14 beside the Klickitat River bridge at Lyle and take Highway 142 upriver 16.3 miles. Between mileposts 16 and 17, turn right on Horseshoe Bend Road for 200 yards and turn right on Schilling Road for 50 feet to the Wahkiacus Trailhead *(GPS location N45°49.403′ W121°05.906′)*. To drive to the upper trailhead from here, go back to Horseshoe Bend Road, turn right for 3.3 rough uphill miles to a T-shaped junction, turn right on a good gravel road for 1.2 miles to a junction, continue straight on gravel Harms Road for 3.5 miles, jog briefly right on Niva Road, and continue on Harms Road 2.1 miles.

Other Options

A missing Klickitat River trestle interrupts the trail between Wahkiacus and the town of Klickitat, but the 13-mile stretch of railroad grade from there down the river to Lyle is excellent for mountain biking and fair for hiking. For more information and a map, check *www.klickitat-trail.org*.

Trestle at the upper trailhead along Swale Creek.   Opposite: The third trestle.

Mount Hood West

Campgrounds

		Campsites	Water	Flush toilet	Open (mos.)	Rate range
1	**GREEN CANYON.** This quiet, convenient campground in old-growth forest along the Salmon River accesses Hikes #65 and #66.	15			V-IX	$20-22
2	**McNEIL.** Snug against Mt. Hood's west base, this campground has large, sunny campsites in sparse fir/pine woods along the Sandy River.	34			V-IX	$15-17
3	**RILEY HORSE CAMP.** Across from McNeil (see above), this camp is busy on holidays. Res: 877-444-6777 (*www.recreation.gov*).	15			V-IX	$17-19
4	**LOST CREEK.** This barrier-free camp near Ramona Falls' trailhead (Hike #71) has a yurt for $35. Res: 877-444-6777 (*www.recreation.gov*).	16	●		V-IX	$19-37
5	**LOST LAKE.** Secluded sites amid giant trees on a quiet lake with trails, a boardwalk, and rowboat rentals (see Hike #69).	125	●		V-IX	$25-30
6	**TOLLGATE.** Amid cedars along the Sandy River, this camp was built by the CCC in the 1930s. Res: 877-444-6777 (*www.recreation.gov*).	14	●		V-IX	$20
7	**CAMP CREEK.** Large, forested sites on Camp Creek have some highway noise. Res: 877-444-6777 (*www.recreation.gov*).	25	●		V-IX	$18-42
8	**STILL CREEK.** Primitive but lovely, this overlooked camp near Gov't Camp has mountain views. Res: 877-444-6777 (*www.recreation.gov*).	27	●		VI-IX	$20-22
9	**TRILLIUM LAKE.** Crowded in summer, this camp has Mt. Hood views and a "yome" (yurt/dome) for $35. Res: 877-444-6777 (*www.recreation.gov*).	57	●		V-IX	$20-37
10	**TIMOTHY LAKE.** Five nearly adjacent campgrounds (Pine Pt, Cove, Hoodview, Gone Cr, Oak Fork) line this busy lake's south shore (see Hike #78). Res: 877-444-6777 (*www.recreation.gov*).	158	●		V-IX	$17-36
11	**JOE GRAHAM HORSE CAMP.** Corrals near tiny Clackamas Lake access the PCT (*www.recreation.gov*).	14	●		V-IX	$20-22

◁ *Timberline Lodge.*

Cabins, Lookouts & Inns

		Rental units	Private bath	Breakfast	Open (mos.)	Rate range
1	**LOST LAKE RESORT.** 7 rustic cabins sleep 2-10 (woodstoves, no plumbing), 6 lodge rooms. Bring bedding. Hike #74. Information at *www.lostlakeresort.org,* but reservations must be by phone at 541-386-6366.	13	6		V-X	$70-140
2	**THE CABINS CREEKSIDE AT WELCHES.** Cabins have log furniture, vaulted ceilings, kitchens, hot tub. Res: 503-622-4275 (*www.mthoodcabins.com*).	10	●		●	$79-134
3	**SUMMIT MEADOW CABINS.** Cabins have kitchens and bedding; sleep 4-12. Two have hot tubs. Res: 503-272-3494 (*www.summitmeadow.com*).	5	●		●	$180-295
4	**TIMBERLINE LODGE.** Grand 1937 hotel high on Mt. Hood (see Hike #77) has views, pool, hot tub. Res: 800-547-1406 (*www.timberlinelodge.com*).	70	60		●	$105-345
5	**CLEAR LAKE LOOKOUT.** This 14-foot cabin on a 40-foot tower sleeps 4 and has a woodstove and a propane light. Access is by ski or snowshoe in winter. Reservations: 877-444-6777 (*www.recreation.gov*).	1			XI-V	$50

Above right: Trillium Lake Campground.

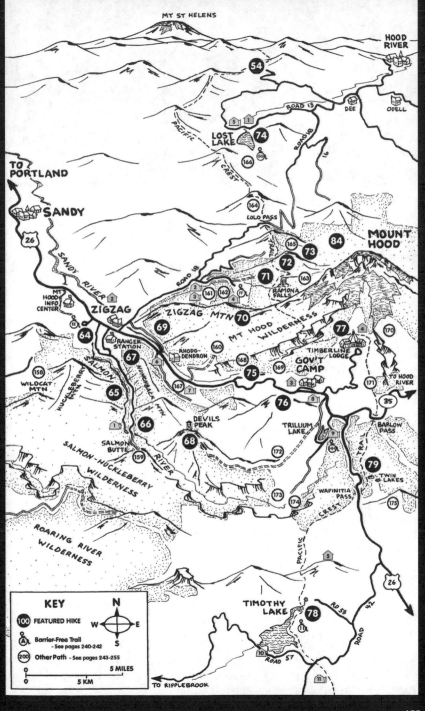

Footbridge across the Salmon River.

64   Wildwood Area

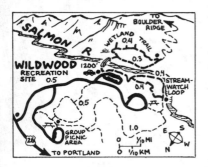

Easy (Wildwood loops)
1.5-mile loop
No elevation gain
Open all year

Difficult (Boulder Ridge Trail)
11.4 miles round trip
3100 feet elevation gain
Open May to mid-November

Difficult (Bonanza Trail)
11.2 miles round trip
3000 feet elevation gain

Two very easy and two very hard hikes begin along the Salmon River west of Zigzag. If you're hiking with children, stick to the two easy, paved loops in the Bureau of Land Management's park-like Wildwood Recreation Site. For a more athletic challenge, tackle the Boulder Ridge or Bonanza trails instead. They both rocket 3000 feet uphill to a rocky ridgecrest atop Huckleberry Mountain, where a view of four snowpeaks awaits.

From Portland, take Highway 26 east toward Mt. Hood. Beyond Sandy 15 miles, and 0.2 mile beyond milepost 39, turn right at a large sign for the Wildwood Recreation Site. The gate here is locked at sunset each day. It's also locked in winter, but hikers can always park here and walk half a mile to the trailhead. If the gate's open, keep left for half a mile and park beside the restrooms in the trailhead parking area.

Both of the short paths are wheelchair-accessible. The paved, 0.8-mile Cascade Streamwatch Trail starts to the right of the restrooms, ambles along the Salmon River, and explores a small side creek before looping back to the parking lot. Along the way you'll pass interpretive signs, a window with an underwater

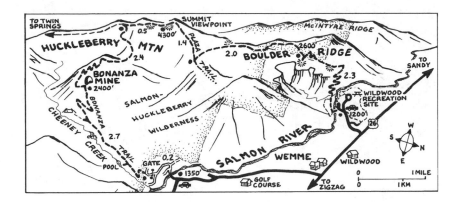

creek view, and a gravel beach suitable for sunbathing.

The next short walk, the Wetland Trail, starts to the left of the parking area's restrooms and crosses a 300-foot bridge over the Salmon River. On the far shore, turn left onto a boardwalk that skirts a slough in an alder forest. Explore four short spurs to the left to find viewpoints of cattails, skunk cabbage, and marsh wildlife. At the end of the boardwalk you can either turn right to return to your car, or you can turn left onto the rugged Boulder Ridge Trail.

If you're ready for a workout, follow the Boulder Ridge Trail. This path switchbacks steeply up through a Douglas fir forest. At the 1.8-mile mark, you'll gain a first glimpse of Mt. Hood. After another grueling half mile, a 20-foot path to the left leads to a cliff edge with an impressive view across Wemme and Zigzag Mountain (Hike #69) to Mt. Hood. This viewpoint makes a good turnaround point for a moderate hike. If you're still going strong, continue 2 miles up Boulder Ridge and turn right on the Plaza Trail for 1.4 miles to the superior view from a rocky crest atop Huckleberry Mountain.

Because it's steep, the Boulder Ridge Trail doesn't see heavy use. The nearby Bonanza Trail offers an even quieter route to the same viewpoint, passing an explorable old mining tunnel along the way. To find the Bonanza Trail, drive Highway 26 east from the Wildwood Recreation Site 1.3 mile to the stoplight at Wemme. Turn right on Welches Road for 1.3 miles, keep left at a fork, continue another 0.7 mile to a junction, and go straight past a "Narrow Bridge" sign. Drive across a bridge, take the second gravel street to the left, and follow East Grove Lane a few hundred yards to a fork. The grassy road straight ahead, closed by a cable, is the start of the trail. But there's room for only two cars to the left of this cable, and parking is vehemently forbidden anywhere else nearby. To avoid being towed, drive back to a small parking space on the far side of the bridge.

Once you've parked and hiked back to the trailhead, walk up the road 200 yards to a sharp right-hand curve and continue straight on a path downhill *(GPS location N45°18.906' W121°57.347')*. This trail is easy for the first 1.6 miles, ambling through dappled alder woods along Cheeney Creek. Then it switchbacks up for 1.1 mile to the rusting ore-cart rails of the Bonanza Mine. A level, 6-foot-tall tunnel beside the trail extends back 100 feet. To continue, follow the Bonanza Trail up another 2.4 miles and turn right on the Plaza Trail along Huckleberry Mountain's ridgecrest. After 0.3 mile you'll pass a saddle with a view, but the best panorama is 0.2 mile beyond.

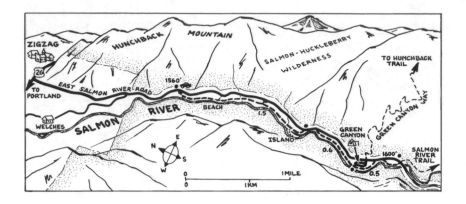

65 Old Salmon River Trail

Easy
5.2 miles round trip
100 feet elevation gain
Open all year
Use: hikers, bicycles

Right: Small beach along the river trail.

One of the most accessible old-growth forests in Oregon towers above this portion of the Salmon River. The popular riverside trail here not only passes 10-foot-thick red cedars, it also leads to small sandy beaches with deep green pools suitable for a chilly summer swim. And since a paved road parallels the route, it's easy to arrange a car shuttle so you can hike the 2.4-mile trail one way.

From Portland, take Highway 26 toward Mount Hood for 42 miles. At Zigzag turn right at a sign for the Salmon River Road and follow this paved route 2.7 miles. Two hundred yards beyond the (vandalized) national forest boundary sign, park at a pullout on the right for the Old Salmon River Trail *(GPS location N45°18.370' W121°56.537')*.

The trail promptly descends to the river—a clear, 40-foot-wide mountain stream. In this ancient forest, huge Douglas firs filter sunlight for an understory of vine maple, sword fern, shamrock-shaped sourgrass, and deep green moss. Look for "nursery logs," fallen giants that provide a fertile platform above the brush for rows of seedling trees to catch light and take root.

Many side paths lead to the water's edge from the heavily used main trail. After 0.5 mile a particularly noticeable cross-path leads to a beach beside a 10-foot-deep pool in the river. Just upstream from this pleasant picnic site the river tumbles over two 4-foot falls.

Continue on the main trail to the 1.3-mile mark. Then watch for another worthwhile side trail to the right. This one crosses a bouldery, mostly dry oxbow slough to a forested island with pebbly river beaches.

Just 250 yards after the side trail to the island, the main trail joins the paved road. Walk along the road's shoulder 200 yards until the riverside trail continues. After another half mile you'll pass the campsites of Green Canyon Campground. Stay on the graveled path past the campground and an adjacent picnic area. Another 0.2 mile beyond, the trail joins the paved road for 200 yards and then ducks back into the woods for 0.2 mile to an upper trailhead parking area at the Salmon River Bridge.

Other Options

If you'd like to extend your hike once you reach the Salmon River Bridge, simply cross the road and continue on the longer, wilder Salmon River Trail described in Hike #66.

66   Salmon River Trail

Easy (to Rolling Riffle Camp)
4.0 miles round trip
200 feet elevation gain
Open all year

Moderate (to canyon viewpoint)
7.2 miles round trip
900 feet elevation gain

Left: Fly fisherman on the Salmon River.

This popular portion of the Salmon River Trail begins with a riverside stroll among huge old-growth trees. After 2 miles, the path leaves the river and climbs to a bluff with a view of the Salmon River's rugged upper canyon. Inaccessible waterfalls roar far below. Backpackers or hardy day hikers can continue on a demanding 15.7-mile loop to the Devils Peak lookout tower.

Start by driving Highway 26 to Zigzag, 42 miles east of Portland. Turn south at a sign for the Salmon River Road and follow this paved route 4.9 miles to a pullout on the left just before a bridge. Start at the "Salmon River Trail" sign on the left and hike upriver through a Douglas fir forest. Large white trilliums bloom here in spring. After 0.4 mile pass a deep, green river pool with bedrock banks. Beyond this point the forest is even grander, with 8-foot-thick, moss-draped firs.

At the 2-mile mark pass a signed "Toilet Area" on the left and Rolling Riffle Camp on the right. The Forest Service asks backpackers to confine camping in this area to the ten riverbank sites. Space is tight on weekends. Campfires are discouraged.

If you're out for an easy day hike, you might want to turn back 0.2 mile farther at a footbridge over a side creek, where the big old-growth trees end and the trail leaves the river. If you'd like a longer hike, however, continue 1.4 miles uphill to a fork in the trail at a "Fragile Area" sign. Veer right for a viewpoint loop across a grassy slope overlooking the Salmon River's huge canyonland. Do not venture off the trail, because the steep, pebble-strewn slopes are deceptively

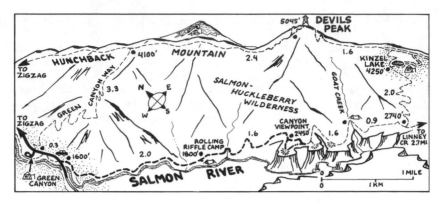

slippery. After 300 yards the narrow path reenters the woods and climbs steeply to rejoin the main trail.

The roar in this canyon is caused by a string of waterfalls. Up the Salmon River Trail another 0.2 mile, a spur to the right leads down to a grassy knoll, where a rugged scramble path to the right descends 0.3 mile to a partly obscured overlook of aptly named Vanishing Falls, Frustration Falls, and Final Falls. This slippery scramble trail is extremely dangerous and is not recommended.

Other Options

If you'd like to tackle the difficult, 15.7-mile loop to Devils Peak, continue up the Salmon River Trail 2.5 miles and turn left on the Kinzel Lake Trail. After climbing 2 miles, ignore a side trail to the right to Kinzel Lake's car campground. Continue uphill on a faint trail to Road 2613 and turn left on the Hunchback Trail to Devils Peak (see Hike #68). Beyond the lookout 2.4 miles take the steep Green Canyon Way left 3.3 miles to the road, 0.3 mile from your car.

For a less strenuous backpacking trip, arrange a car shuttle to the upper end of the Salmon River Trail (see Hike #173) and hike up the wilderness river a total of 14.4 miles.

The Salmon River Canyon.

67   Hunchback Mountain

Moderate (to rimrock viewpoint)
4.2 miles round trip
1700 feet elevation gain
Open late April to mid-November

Difficult (to Great Pyramid)
9 miles round trip
2900 feet elevation gain

Mt. Hood from the Rockpile.

Handy for a bit of exercise, this trail switchbacks from the Zigzag Ranger Station up the long, wooded ridge known as Hunchback Mountain. After climbing steeply for 2.1 miles, the path passes a rimrock viewpoint overlooking the forested valleys of the Salmon-Huckleberry Wilderness. For a better look east to Mt. Hood, continue up and down along the ridgecrest to three other viewpoints.

Start at the Zigzag Ranger Station, 42 miles east of Portland on Highway 26. As you drive into the entrance from the highway, veer left into a large parking area. Park on the far right-hand side where a path leads to a "Hunchback Mountain Trail" message board.

After hiking 50 yards you'll cross a side trail, pass a spring house, and head uphill. The first mile, with eight long switchbacks, is so well graded it's never very steep. Deep moss, lady ferns, sword ferns, and vine maple make the Douglas fir forest here lush and jungly. Traffic noise from the highway slowly fades.

Then the trail suddenly steepens. The second mile, with ten switchbacks, is a grueling climb. Notice the shamrock-shaped leaves of oxalis covering the forest floor. This April wildflower is also known as sourgrass because its leaves have a tart, refreshing citrus flavor when chewed-in small doses, a temporary thirst-quencher while climbing.

The rimrock viewpoint at 2.1 miles makes a good goal. From the rim of a 100-foot cliff, views extend across castle-like crags to the green-fluted canyons of the Salmon River. The top half of Mt. Hood protrudes to the east.

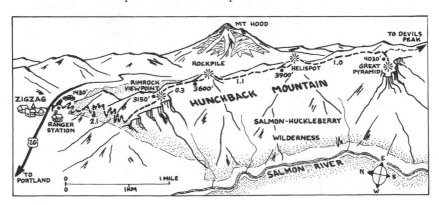

After this viewpoint the poorly graded trail roller-coasters along the ridgecrest. Though views are few from the trail itself, short side trails scramble up to panoramas. At the 2.4-mile mark, you can follow a "Viewpoint Rockpile" sign 100 steep yards to the right to a rocky crest with a full frontal view of Mt. Hood. After another 1.1 mile along the Hunchback Trail, another steep side trail to the right climbs 200 yards to the Helispot summit, where trees now block views. And after yet another mile along the Hunchback Trail, a signed side trail leads to Great Pyramid, a narrow rock promontory jutting out above the Salmon River Valley.

Other Options

The Hunchback Trail continues past Great Pyramid with some steep ups and downs for 3.6 miles to the Devils Peak lookout tower. While this would be a very difficult 16.2-mile round trip from Zigzag, the hike can be shortened by shuttling a car to one of the three trailheads nearer to Devils Peak: Green Canyon Campground, the Cool Creek Trailhead, or the Hunchback Trailhead near Kinzel Lake. These routes are described in Hikes #66 and #68.

68   Devils Peak Lookout

Easy (from Road 2613)
2.4 miles round trip
600 feet elevation gain
Open June to mid-November
Use: hikers, horses

Difficult (via Cool Creek Trail)
8.2 miles round trip
3200 feet elevation gain

The unstaffed lookout tower atop Devils Peak, with a view from Mt. Hood to Mt. Jefferson, is maintained by volunteers as a cozy shelter and lunch spot for hikers. Getting there, however, poses a dilemma. The trail from Road 2613 is short, easy, and scenic-but the drive to the trailhead is a nightmare on a seemingly endless dirt road. The other trailhead is easily accessible—but the hike itself is three times longer and demands five times more climbing.

If you opt for the easy walk (and the hard drive), take Highway 26 to the Trillium Lake turnoff 3 miles east of Government Camp. Follow paved Road 2656 for 1.7 miles—passing the campground entrance—and then keep right on Road 2612 around the lake. After another 1.5 miles turn left onto Road 2613 and follow this narrow, bouldery, rough dirt road for 10 miles to its end at the Hunchback Mountain Trailhead. High-clearance 4-wheel-drive vehicles can navigate these final miles well enough, but passenger cars will find them slow and punishing.

The trail starts beside the foundation of an old garage and traverses a forest full of pink rhododendrons (in June), beargrass blooms (in July), and ripe blue huckleberries (in August). After 0.4 mile emerge from the woods at a ridgecrest with a stunning view of Mt. Hood to the north. Be sure to peer south over the ridgecrest, too, into the Salmon River's wilderness valley. Next the path

switchbacks twice up the side of Devils Peak, passes the steep Cool Creek Trail on the right, and 100 yards later meets a trail on the left to the lookout tower. The tower itself is generally unlocked, with battened windows, a wood stove, two cots, and several resident mice (so don't leave food). Backpackers may stay here for free on a first-come-first-served basis. Leave everything as you found it.

If you prefer to get here on a more rugged hike (but an easier drive), take Highway 26 east of the Zigzag Ranger Station 1.3 miles. Between mileposts 43 and 44, turn south on paved Still Creek Road. After 0.3 mile, at a "No Outlet" sign, fork to the right on Road 12 for 2.6 miles of pavement and an additional 0.4 mile of gravel to a "Cool Creek Trailhead" sign on the right *(GPS location N45°17.840' W121°53.060')*.

Despite its name, the Cool Creek Trail never approaches a creek. Instead it launches up a ridge at a grueling grade. After 0.7 mile the path emerges from the woods to a slope with June-blooming rhododendrons and vistas of Mt. Hood. Then the trail climbs again through woods until the 3.5-mile mark, when it reaches a bare ridgecrest with a view extending all the way to Mt. Adams. After another half mile turn right onto the Hunchback Trail for 100 yards to the lookout path.

Other Options

By arranging a car shuttle, you can descend from Devils Peak on the 8-mile Hunchback Trail to the Zigzag Ranger Station (see Hike #67).

Mt. Hood from the lookout door.   Opposite: The Devils Peak lookout.

West Zigzag Mountain

Easy (to Castle Canyon)
1.8 miles round trip
800 feet elevation gain
Open all year

Difficult (to lookout site)
11 miles round trip
Open May through November
Use: hikers, horses
3100 feet elevation gain

Forests cloak this steep ridge in the westernmost corner of the Mt. Hood Wilderness, but two convenient trails lead to viewpoints above the trees. The first is a short but very steep path to a collection of craggy rock towers. The second is a strenuous conditioning hike—a 3000-foot climb at a steady grade to the clifftop site of a former lookout building.

From Portland, drive Highway 26 toward Mt. Hood 44 miles. For the short hike to Castle Canyon, turn left in the village of Rhododendron, just after milepost 44, onto East Littlebrook Lane. Keep left on a small paved road 0.3 mile, and then turn left on gravel, following a "Barlow Road Route" pointer for 0.4 mile to the trailhead sign on the right. Park on the left-hand shoulder just before the trail.

As you start up the Castle Canyon Trail, you'll switchback through a young Douglas fir forest with a smattering of little vine maple trees that turn brilliant red in autumn. The most common bush here is salal, whose tough blue berries were valued by Northwest Indians. Nineteenth-century botanist David Douglas so admired this evergreen shrub that he popularized its use as an ornamental in England's formal gardens.

After half a mile of stiff climbing you'll pass the first of this canyon's mossy rock outcroppings. Just before the trail peters out at the 0.9-mile mark, contour left to a rocky spine among the towers. Footing is hazardous here, so hang onto children. The barren bluff of the West Zigzag lookout site is visible above to the east while Hunchback Mountain (Hike #67) looms across the Zigzag Valley.

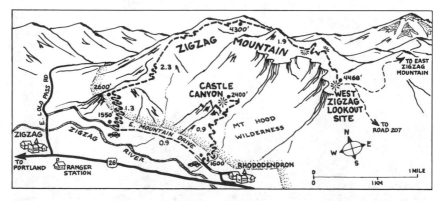

If you'd prefer a tougher climb to the better view at the West Zigzag lookout site, start your hike at a different trailhead instead. To find it, drive back to Highway 26, head west toward Portland 2 miles to the village of Zigzag, and turn north onto East Lolo Pass Road for 0.4 mile. Then turn right onto East Mountain Drive, a potholed gravel lane. After 0.2 mile, keep right at a fork by a telephone pole. In another half mile look for a sign on the left marking the Zigzag Mountain Trail. Park on the shoulder a few hundred feet back.

The Zigzag Mountain Trail climbs relentlessly for its first 3.6 miles, yet it is so well graded that it manages to gain more than 3000 feet without being unbearably steep. On the way up you'll leave the vine maple/salal zone, pass through a level where pink rhododendrons bloom in June, and finally enter a high-altitude fir forest with beargrass and manzanita.

The final 1.9 miles to the lookout site follow the ridgecrest up and down, sometimes skirting cliffs with views east to Mt. Hood or west down the Sandy River toward Portland. Four concrete piers mark the site of the old fire lookout on a dramatic bluff high above the crags of Castle Canyon and the towns of Rhododendron and Zigzag. Flag Mountain looks like the green back of a crocodile sleeping in the Zigzag Valley below, while the tip of Mt. Jefferson peers over the shoulder of Devils Peak (Hike #68).

Cliffs near West Zigzag's lookout site.   Opposite: Salal in bloom.

70   Burnt Lake

Moderate (to Burnt Lake)
6.8 miles round trip
1500 feet elevation gain
Open June through October

Difficult (to East Zigzag)
9.6 miles round trip
2370 feet elevation gain

Dragonflies dip into Burnt Lake's reflection of Mt. Hood, splitting the snowy volcano into ripples. This is one of the cherished sanctums of the Mt. Hood Wilderness, just far enough from the world of roads to keep casual tourists at bay. A well-graded trail to the lake passes a waterfall, wildflowers, and huckleberries. For a longer hike, continue up to East Zigzag, a former fire lookout site with a bird's-eye view of the magic mountain.

To find the trailhead from Portland, take Highway 26 toward Mt. Hood 42 miles to Zigzag. Across from the Zigzag Inn turn left onto East Lolo Pass Road. After 4.2 miles fork right onto paved Road 1825 for 0.7 mile, and then turn right across the Sandy River bridge. Follow Road 1825 another 2.1 miles to the Lost Creek Campground entrance. Then veer left onto a gravel road for 1.4 miles to its end at a parking area.

The trail sets off through a stile designed to enforce a ban on bicyclists and horses. For the next half mile the path traverses second-growth woods with ancient stumps, white bunchberry flowers, and plenty of blue huckleberries (ripe in late August). Then sally into uncut stands of Douglas fir, hemlock, and cedar. Note the 18-inch leaves of spiny devils club among the undergrowth.

After 1.9 miles the path crosses Burnt Lake Creek on stepping stones and passes several gigantic cedar snags. Hollowed by the 19th-century fire that gave

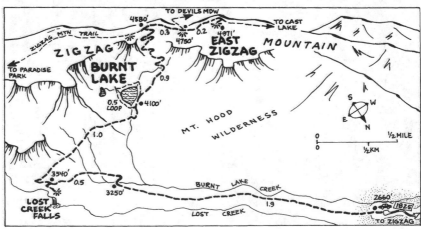

Burnt Lake its name, the blackened 10-foot-wide trunks are large enough for children to stand inside. In another half mile the trail forks. Detour briefly 100 yards down to the left to see Lost Creek Falls, a series of four mossy cascades in a contorted rock gorge. Then continue on the main trail and climb steadily for a mile to Burnt Lake.

If you're stopping at the lake, hike the half-mile path that loops around its shore. Backpackers here are allowed to camp only at designated sites; if the sites are full, plan to continue to Zigzag Mountain or Cast Lake to tent. Fires are banned within half a mile, so bring a stove. And because sound travels so well across this small lake, keep voices low.

If you're continuing to East Zigzag, keep right past the lake for 0.9 mile up to a junction in a wooded saddle. Turn right on a steep path that traces a ridgecrest toward ever grander vistas of Mt. Hood, distant Mt. Adams, and truncated Mt. St. Helens. Along the way you'll traverse a subalpine rock garden with cushions of lavender phlox, plumes of beargrass, fuzzy cats ears, red paintbrush, and purple larkspur. Continue straight up the ridge half a mile to East Zigzag's summit, where the view opens south past the green swaths of Multorpor Mountain's ski runs to ghostly Mt. Jefferson.

Mt. Hood from Burnt Lake.   Opposite: Burnt Lake from East Zigzag.

Ramona Falls

Moderate (to Ramona Falls)
7.3-mile loop
1000 feet elevation gain
Open late April through October
Use: hikers, horses

Like white lace, 120-foot Ramona Falls drapes across a stair-stepped cliff of columnar basalt. It's understandably one of the most popular hiking goals in the Mount Hood area, even though frequent river floods keep changing the access.

To drive here from Portland, take Highway 26 toward Mt. Hood 42 miles to Zigzag. If you don't have a parking permit for your car, stop at the Zigzag Ranger Station to buy a Northwest Forest Pass.

Then, across from the Zigzag Inn, turn onto East Lolo Pass Road. After 4.1 miles turn right onto paved Road 1825, following a "Campgrounds" pointer for 0.7 mile. Then turn right across the Sandy River bridge. Continue 1.7 miles on what is still Road 1825, and finally fork left onto Road 100 for 0.4 mile to a large gravel parking area at road's end.

The trail starts at the right-hand side of the parking area, ambling through a mossy forest of small alders and hemlocks beside the Sandy River's bouldery outwash plain. The pioneers who named this river thought its milky color was caused by sand. In fact the stream carries glacial silt, rock that has been powdered by the grinding weight of Mt. Hood's glaciers.

After a mile the path crosses the Sandy River on a temporary bridge. Forest Service crews remove the bridge each year in mid-October and replace it each spring, usually in early May, when the snow is gone.

Half a mile beyond the bridge you'll reach a trail junction with signs marking the start of the loop. The shortest route to the falls is the horse trail to the

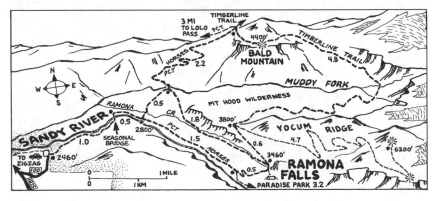

right, but it's much less scenic, so leave it as a possible return route. Instead go left. This path crosses a creek and traverses a lodgepole pine forest to the wild Muddy Fork of the Sandy River. Here, turn right on a path that soon follows the mossy bank of Ramona Creek—a delightful woodsy stream that leads up to the base of the falls. If you're backpacking, note that camping and fires are banned within 500 feet of Ramona Falls. A side path leads to an approved camping area just south of the falls.

To return on a loop, turn right at the falls and keep right on a horse trail.

Other Options

A much more difficult, 13.2-mile return loop from Ramona Falls climbs to a spectacular viewpoint on Bald Mountain. For this route, turn left at Ramona Falls and follow the Timberline Trail around Yocum Ridge 3 miles to Muddy Fork, a milky, glacial outwash river. The bridgeless crossing is scary in June and on summer afternoons, when snowmelt swells this two-branched torrent. Horses are banned on this trail because it often has washouts and rough sections on steep slopes.

After negotiating both branches of Muddy Fork, the Timberline Trail climbs steadily to a cliff-edged meadow on Bald Mountain, where Mt. Hood dominates a sweeping view. Half a mile beyond the viewpoint turn sharply left at a 4-way trail junction, following signs for the Pacific Crest Trail. This path descends in seven long switchbacks to a 60-foot bridge over the Muddy Fork. Cross the bridge and keep right to complete the loop back to your car.

Ramona Falls.   Opposite: Mt. Hood from the temporary Sandy River bridge.

72   McNeil Point

Easy (around Bald Mountain)
2.2-mile loop
400 feet elevation gain
Open June to early November

Moderate (to ponds below McNeil Point)
6.8 miles round trip
Open mid-July through October
1640 feet elevation gain

Difficult (to McNeil Point shelter)
9.6 miles round trip
2220 feet elevation gain

Wildflowers, tumbling brooks, and craggy mountain vistas lend alpine splendor to this ridge on Mt. Hood's northwest shoulder. An easy loop circles Bald Mountain to a picture-postcard view of Mt. Hood. But for real alpine drama, climb the Timberline Trail to a pond reflecting massive McNeil Point — or better yet, continue up a new route to McNeil Point itself, where you'll find a stone shelter on a ridge.

Turn north off Highway 26 across from the Zigzag Inn (42 miles east of Portland) onto East Lolo Pass Road. After 4.2 miles fork right onto paved Road 1825. After 0.7 mile, just before a bridge, go straight on unsigned, one-lane paved Road 1828. Continue 5.6 miles and fork to the right on gravel Road 118 for 1.5 miles to the Top Spur Trailhead, with parking on the left *(GPS location N45°24.446' W121°47.147')*.

The Top Spur Trail starts in a patch of blue huckleberries (ripe in August), and climbs through a forest of hemlock and Douglas fir. Look for bunchberry, carpeting the ground with white blooms in June and red berries in fall.

 After 0.5 mile turn right on the Pacific Crest Trail for 60 yards to a big, 4-way trail junction that can be confusing. *Go uphill to the right* on the Timberline Trail. Don't go left, and don't take the Pacific Crest Trail to the far right. The correct path emerges from the woods after 0.3 mile onto the steep, meadowed face of Bald Mountain, with views ahead to Mt. Hood and west to the distant Willamette

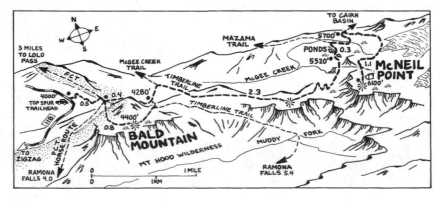

Mt. Hood and McNeil Point from a timberline tarn.   Opposite: McNeil Point's shelter.

Valley. Stay on the trail to avoid trampling the fragile flowers.

After 0.4 mile through these meadows, watch carefully for the unsigned loop trail around Bald Mountain. When the trail reenters the woods after the second, smaller meadow, continue 150 steps to a fork in a draw *(GPS location N45°24.163' W121°46.242')*. If you reach a stock gate to block horses you've gone too far.

Take an unmarked left-hand fork over a ridge 100 yards to an unsigned junction with another section of the Timberline Trail. For the easy loop, turn left here to return to the car. If you'd like a longer hike, turn right.

If you turn right on this portion of the Timberline Trail (heading *clockwise* around Mt. Hood this time), you'll climb up a ridgecrest with wind-dwarfed firs, summer-blooming beargrass, and mountain views. After 1.9 miles the trail switchbacks four times up a steep wildflower meadow. Then you'll pass a cascading, mossy creek and a trail fork at a (sometimes dry) pond amidst a dazzling display of early August wildflowers: red paintbrush, blue lupine, and beargrass *(GPS location N45°24.091' W121°43.970')*. Here sharp eyes can spot the McNeil Point shelter high on the ridge above.

If you're backpacking, be sure to camp in existing campsites and not on the fragile meadows. Bring a stove, as campfires are discouraged anywhere near timberline and are banned within 500 feet of the McNeil Point shelter.

If you're heading for McNeil Point (or if black flies are a problem at this tarn), keep right at junctions, following the Timberline Trail another 0.3 mile. Then turn right at a "McNeil Point" pointer *(GPS location N45°24.167' W121°43.705')* and follow a trail up a ridgecrest. The path traverses to the right across a rockslide or snowfield and climbs 1.1 mile to the 10-foot-square stone shelter *(GPS location N45°23.727' W121°43.926')*, built in the 1930s by the Civilian Conservation Corps and later named to honor Portland newspaperman Fred McNeil (1893-1958). Return as you came.

73   Cairn Basin & Owl Point

Easy (to Owl Point)
4.8 miles round trip
650 feet elevation gain
Open mid-July through October

Moderate (to Cairn Basin)
7.9-mile loop
1700 feet elevation gain

Left: Mt. Hood from the trail to Owl Point.

Since a 2011 wildfire burned through the forests high on Mt. Hood's scenic north face, the Vista Ridge Trail now offers two interesting options: either climb through the burn to the spectacular alpine wildflower vales at Cairn Basin, or avoid the burn altogether, hiking away from the mountain to views at Owl Point.

From Portland, drive Highway 26 toward Mt. Hood 42 miles to Zigzag. Across from the Zigzag Inn, turn left onto East Lolo Pass Road 18. After 4.2 miles fork left and continue on Road 18 another 6.3 miles to Lolo Pass. Here turn right on gravel McGee Creek Road 18 for 10.5 miles. Pavement resumes along the way. At a sign for the Vista Ridge Trail, turn right on Road 16 for 5.4 miles to a broad intersection. Turn sharply right on gravel Road 1650 for 3.6 miles, keeping left to its end at the trailhead *(GPS location N45°26.583' W121°43.775')*.

The trail begins along an old cat road but soon dives into a lichen-draped forest of hemlock and Douglas fir. After 0.4 mile you'll reach a T-shaped trail junction atop Vista Ridge. You'll also reach the edge of the burn, with silver snags to the right and green trees to the left.

If you opt for the easier hike through unburned woods to Owl Point, turn left. Blue huckleberry bushes line the route with fruit in August. The path climbs a mile along the ridgecrest before you get your first viewpoint of Mt. Hood, on a 20-foot spur to a clifftop to the right. Then continue 0.7 mile, up and down, to a signed trail junction in a saddle. Turn left for 200 yards, and then take a spur to the right 200 yards to the rockfield atop Owl Point *(GPS location N45°27.432' W121°43.091')*. The view sweeps from the Hood River Valley to Laurance Lake

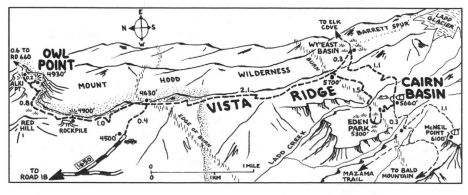

DOLLAR LAKE (Hike #84) narrowly escaped a 2011 fire
that scorched trails on Mt. Hood's north slope.

LOOKOUT MOUNTAIN (Hike #86) offers perhaps the best view of Mt. Hood from the east.

THE MAZAMAS, a Portland outdoor club, organized atop Mount Hood in 1893, when 155 men and 38 women convened on the summit.

CLIMBING MOUNT HOOD

Mount Hood is one of the most climbed snowpeaks in the world. It has been scaled by a man with no legs, a woman in high heels, and even a gibbon named Kandy.

Still, the climb remains technical and dangerous. Rockfalls and sudden blizzard whiteouts cause fatalities almost every year. An ice ax and crampons are essential. Climbers must fill out a wilderness permit. They should also register at Timberline Lodge and carry their human waste out in plastic bags.

The trek up from Timberline Lodge usually takes seven hours to the top and four to return. Plan to start before dawn to avoid the afternoon's soft snow.

The most popular climbing route ascends from Timberline Lodge to Crater Rock (at far left), traverses to the right on an icy knife-edge ridge called the Hogback, and leads around a dangerous glacial crevasse to the top.

THE BARLOW TRAIL

Samuel Barlow and his wife Susannah set off from Illinois with their extended family on March 30, 1845, joining 3000 others who took covered wagons on the trail to Oregon that year. When they reached the Columbia River they found an unexpected bottleneck.

Wagons were crowded on the riverbank six miles west of The Dalles, where the trail ended at the Columbia Gorge. The rapids ahead had already wrecked countless jerrybuilt rafts.

Sam noticed a low point on the horizon south of Mount Hood and announced, "God never made a mountain without a way over it or under it, and I'm going to try." He led eleven wagons up toward the mountain, and another 17 followed a few days later. When they reached the Cascades' forests the group arduously chopped, sawed, and burned trees, trying to clear a path. They finally left their wagons and hiked on to Oregon City on foot.

The next year Barlow built a crude road to rescue the stranded wagons and began charging other traverlers a toll—even though his route was so rough that wagons had to be lowered down Laurel Hill's rocky chutes on ropes (see Hike #75).

174

BAGBY HOT SPRINGS (Hike #95) offers free soaks in cedar tubs, but expect to wait an hour or two in summer.

LOOKOUT MOUNTAIN (Hike #86) offers a close-up view of Mt. Hood's snowy east face.

TABLE ROCK (Hike #89) is a lava mesa ringed with columnar basalt cliffs.

OLALLIE LAKE (Hike #98) reflects Mt. Jefferson on a misty summer morning.

175

WILDFLOWERS OF THE LOWLANDS

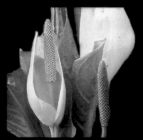

SKUNK CABBAGE (*Lysichiton americanum*). Pollinated by flies, this swamp bloom smells putrid.

QUEEN ANNE'S LACE (*Daucus carota*). This ancestor of the garden carrot blooms in valley fields.

BACHELOR BUTTON (*Centaurea cyanus*). One of many showy blue composite flowers with this name.

BLEEDING HEART (*Dicentra formosa*). Look near woodland creeks for these pink hearts.

BALSAMROOT (*Balsamorhiza spp.*). In April and May, this bloom turns entire hillsides yellow.

FRINGECUP (*Tellima grandiflora*). Often overlooked, this trailside woodland stalk is cute up close.

SALMONBERRY (*Rubus spectabilis*). This slightly stickery rainforest shrub has edible berries in July.

WILD ONION (*Allium acuminatum*). This onion fills Dog Mountain's meadows with tangy aroma in June.

NOOTKA ROSE (*Rosa nutkana*). This elegant wild rose loves valley hedgerows and open oak woods.

MONKSHOOD (*Aconitum columbianum*) blooms on head-high stalks in damp subalpine meadows.

CAMAS (*Camassia quamash*). The roots of this valley wetland flower were an important Indian food.

SALSIFY (*Tragopogon dubius*). This dry June roadside flower turns to a giant dandelion-like seed puffball.

WILDFLOWERS OF THE FORESTS

STAR-FLOWERED SOLOMONSEAL *(Maianthemum stellatum)*. These delicate stars decorate deep forests.

OREGON GRAPE *(Berberis aquifolium)*. Oregon's state flower has holly-like leaves and blue berries.

SOURGRASSS *(Oxalis oregana)*. The shamrock-shaped leaves carpet forests and taste tart when chewed.

CANDYFLOWER *(Claytonia sibirica)*. Common by woodland creeks and trails, candyflower is edible.

TRILLIUM *(Trillium ovatum)*. This spectacular woodland lily blooms in April, a herald of spring.

FAIRY SLIPPER *(Calypso bulbosa)*. This 6-inch-tall orchid haunts the mossy floor of old-growth forests.

TWINFLOWER *(Linnaea borealis)*. This double bloom grows in the far North around the globe.

LARGE SOLOMONSEAL *(Maianthemum racemosum)*. White plumes lean across forest paths.

FAIRY BELLS *(Prosartes hookeri)*. This lily of moist woodlands later develops pairs of orange berries.

ANEMONE *(Anemone oregana)*. Sometimes white, these 5-petaled blooms carpet forests in spring.

PRINCE'S PINE *(Chimaphila umbellata)*. Also known as pipsissewa, this blooms in shade.

RHODODENDRON *(Rhododendron macrophyllum)* blooms in May and can grow 20 feet tall.

WILDFLOWERS OF THE MEADOWS

FIREWEED *(Epilobium angusti-folium)*. After a fire, this plant crowds slopes with tall pink spires.

STONECROP *(Sedum oreganum)*. This plant survives in bare, rocky ground by storing water in fat leaves.

SHOOTING STAR *(Dodecatheon jeffreyi)*. Early in summer, shooting stars carpet wet fields and slopes.

WILD IRIS *(Iris tenax)*. Also called an Oregon flag, this June bloom varies from blue to yellowish white.

ASTER *(Aster spp.)*. This daisy relative blooms in high meadows late in summer.

DEATH CAMAS *(Zigadenus spp.)*. Dangerously similar to edible camas, this bloom's root is poison.

PEARLY EVERLASTING *(Anaphalis margaritacea)*. Try this roadside bloom in dried floral arrangements.

COLUMBINE *(Aquilegia formosa)*. In wet woodlands, this bloom has nectar lobes for hummingbirds.

LARKSPUR *(Delphinium spp.)*. Stalks of larkspur stand up to two feet tall in high meadows.

FOXGLOVE *(Digitalis purpurea)*. Showy 5-foot foxglove stalks spangle sunny summer meadows.

MARSH MARIGOLD *(Caltha biflora)*. This early bloomer likes high marshes full of snowmelt.

TIGER LILY *(Lilium columbianum)*. This showy July flower can pack a dozen blooms on one plant.

WILDFLOWERS OF TIMBERLINE

BUNCHBERRY *(Cornus canadensis)*. A miniature version of the dogwood tree, this 6-leaved plant carpets forests each June with 4-petaled blooms (left). By September the blooms become a colorful cluster of red berries (right).

AVALANCHE LILY *(Erythronium montanum)*. These blooms erupt a week after the snow melts.

LUPINE *(Lupinus spp.)* has fragrant blooms in early summer and pea-pod-shaped fruit in fall.

PAINTBRUSH *(Castilleja spp.)* has showy red-orange sepals, but the actual flowers are green tubes.

PHLOX *(Phlox diffusa)*. Like a colorful cushion, phlox hugs arid rock outcrops with a mat of blooms.

PENSTEMON *(Penstemon spp.)*. Look for these red, purple, or blue trumpets in high, rocky areas.

WESTERN PASQUE FLOWER *(Anemone occidentalis)*. This high alpine flower is named for Easter because it blooms so early, but by August it develops dishmop-shaped seedheads (right) that win it the name "Hippie on a Stick."

CATS EAR *(Calochortus subalpinus)*. On rocky knolls, this fuzzy lily makes a May splash.

CASCADE LILY *(Lilium washingtonianum)* has spectacular, waist-high, palm-sized blooms.

BEARGRASS *(Xerophyllum tenax)* resembles a giant bunchgrass until it blooms with a tall, lilied plume.

CATS EAR *(Calochortus subalpinus)*. On rocky knolls, this fuzzy lily makes a May splash.

179

LITTLE CRATER LAKE (Hike #78) is as blue as its National
Park cousin because of deep artesian springs.

and Mt. Hood. Listen for the *meep!* of pikas, the rock rabbits that live here.

After checking out Owl Point, go back 200 yards to the main trail and detour 200 yards to the right to Alki Point, a rockslide with a better view to the north. Here you'll see Mt. Adams, flat-topped Mt. St. Helens, and distant Mt. Rainier in between. Then return along Vista Ridge as you came.

These viewpoints are nice, but only those who dare to hike through the burn will earn the alpine wonders of Cairn Basin. If you'd prefer this harder, more spectacular hike, turn right when you first reach the trail atop Vista Ridge. This route passes a Wilderness permit registration box, with reminders that backpackers cannot camp or build fires in alpine meadows.

For the next 2 miles you'll climb through a forest of burned snags with views and green seedlings. Just after leaving the fire zone you'll reach a trail junction on a meadowed ridge with views of four mountains: Hood, Adams, St. Helens, and Rainier. The alpine wildflowers — best in early August — include red paintbrush, pink heather, blue lupine, and entire hillsides of delicate white avalanche lilies.

Turn left at this junction for 0.3 mile to a basin called Wy'East — after Mt. Hood's legendary Indian name. Turn right in Wy'East Basin's lupine-filled meadow following a sign for Cairn Basin. This path crosses a ridge and switchbacks down to a bridgeless crossing of Ladd Creek. Look up and down this sometimes raging stream for the safest place to cross. On the far shore the path leads into the forested but badly trammeled Cairn Basin area. A 10-foot-square stone shelter stands on the left *(GPS location N45°24.234' W121°43.380')*, while a path to the right leads to a designated camping area.

The main trail is lined by rocks to show the route through old campsites in the trees. At a trail junction beside a wildflower-lined creeklet, veer right and switchback down 0.3 mile to Eden Park's meadowy bowl. Just beyond Eden Park, recross bridgeless Ladd Creek as best you can. On the far shore the path scrambles upstream a bit before climbing back to the Vista Ridge Trail and the route back to the car.

Mt. Hood from Cairn Basin.

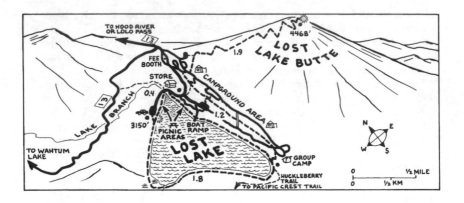

74   Lest Lake

Easy (around the lake)
3.4-mile loop
100 feet elevation gain
Open mid-May through October

Moderate (to Lost Lake Butte)
3.8 miles round trip
1300 feet elevation gain

An old-growth forest circles Lost Lake, the classic setting for picture post-cards of Mt. Hood. For an easy loop, try the 3.4-mile lakeshore trail. If this isn't enough exercise, climb a neighboring volcanic butte to a former lookout site with a broader panorama.

Lost Lake was known to the Hood River Indians as E-e-kwahl-a-mat-yam-ishkt, or "Heart of the Mountains." When an expedition of white men had trouble finding the legendary lake in 1880 they declared they were not lost; the lake was. Today the lake is quite definitely found. Forest Service projects have restored the overused lakeshore, added a half-mile-long boardwalk through an old-growth cedar grove, and expanded the campground. A concessionaire charges a $7-per-car fee.

To find the lake from Portland, take Highway 26 for 42 miles, turn left at the Zigzag store onto East Lolo Pass Road 18 and follow this paved route 10.5 miles to Lolo Pass. Here turn right onto gravel McGee Creek Road 18 for 7.9 miles of gravel and another 7 miles of pavement. Then turn left onto Road 13 for 6 miles to the Lost Lake entry station booth.

To find the lake from Interstate 84, take West Hood River exit 62, drive into town 1.1 mile, turn right on 13th Street, and follow signs for Odell 5 miles. After crossing a bridge, fork to the right past Tucker Park for 6.3 miles. Then fork to the right to Dee and follow signs 13.8 miles to Lost Lake. Travelers from Portland will

Mt. Hood from Lost Lake.   Opposite: Bigfoot sculpture on the general store porch.

find this route 10 miles longer than the route via Lolo Pass, but entirely paved.

Drive past the Lost Lake entry booth and follow signs to the right to the rustic general store. Continue right around the lake to a picnic area parking lot at road's end. The lakeshore trail begins at the far end of the parking lot, where the view of Mt. Hood is at its finest. Numbered posts along the trail correspond to numbers in a nature trail booklet available at the store for a quarter.

The broad lakeshore path sets out through a forest of big hemlocks and cedars. Count on seeing striped Townsend's chipmunks, orange-bellied Douglas squirrels, gray jays, and pointy-hooded Stellar's jays, all of which are accustomed to gleaning crumbs from the nearby picnic area. Small white wildflowers dot the forest floor in early summer: queen's cup, bunchberry, and vanilla leaf. After 0.6 mile a boardwalk crosses the lake's marshy inlet creek, where huge-leaved skunk cabbage puts out yellow blooms.

At the 1.8-mile mark, the unmarked Huckleberry Trail joins from the right. A hundred yards later veer to the right on the Old Growth Trail. This graveled path switchbacks twice to a campground road. Follow the road 150 feet to find the continuation of the trail—a remarkable half-mile boardwalk through a grove of 8-foot-thick cedars. Decked pullouts have benches and interpretive signs. Beyond the end of the boardwalk 0.3 mile turn left, make your way down through the campground, and follow the lakeshore path onward to your car.

You can climb Lost Lake Butte either at the end of the lakeshore loop or as a separate trip. The butte's trail begins at the entrance to Campground Loop B and climbs steadily through woods thick with rhododendrons and beargrass. The old lookout tower has been reduced to a pile of boards, but the view is intact: huge Mt. Hood to the south, a glimpse of Lost Lake to the west, Adams and Rainier to the north, and the brown Columbia River Plateau far to the east.

75   Laurel Hill

Easy (to 2 viewpoints)
2.4 miles round trip
400 feet elevation gain
Open March to mid-December

Moderate (Pioneer Bridle Trail)
8.2 miles round trip
900 feet elevation gain
Use: hikers, horses, bicycles

For a walk through history, explore the trails on this forested ridge near Government Camp. A one-mile tour visits a pioneer wagon chute on the old Barlow Road. A 1.4-mile loop follows an abandoned portion of the 1921-vintage Mt. Hood highway to Little Zigzag Falls. For a longer hike across Laurel Hill, take the Pioneer Bridle Trail, a portion of the Barlow Trail that was converted to a hiking path by Civilian Conservation Corps workers in 1935.

Sam Barlow laid out his wagon road from The Dalles to Sandy in 1845 to spare Oregon Trail pioneers the dangers of rafting the Columbia River. Most travelers ended up cursing Laurel Hill, where Barlow's brushy route plunged so steeply into the Zigzag River Valley that wagons had to be unhitched and winched down backwards. Ironically, the rhododendrons that now delight hikers with pink blooms in early summer only infuriated the pioneers, who typically passed here in bloomless October and mistook the tough-limbed brush for laurel.

For a quick look at Laurel Hill's infamous wagon chute, drive Highway 26 east from Portland toward Mt. Hood. Just before milepost 51, park at an "Oregon History" signboard on the right. A trail leads up stone steps 200 feet to an abandoned section of the old Mt. Hood loop highway. Turn right 100 feet to the bottom of the rocky chute. Just beyond, turn left and keep left on a switchbacking trail up through the woods 0.4 mile to the top of the chute, where Barlow Trail wagon ruts are still visible. Then return to your car.

A slightly longer loop from the same roadside pullout visits more of the historic roadway and a lovely waterfall as well. To find this path, walk 200 feet downhill along the shoulder of Highway 26 and *carefully* cross the busy highway. At the end of a guardrail, head into the forest on a path with a small broken wood sign on a tree, "Route of . . . Road."

After 0.1 mile, at a T-shaped junction, turn right on the Pioneer Bridle Trail. When this path ducks through a tunnel, turn left onto another abandoned section of the old Mt. Hood loop highway. In just 200 yards you'll reach the Little Zigzag Falls trailhead. Turn right on this streamside path for 0.3 mile to its end at the falls' 30-foot fan. Then return to the abandoned highway and follow it back the way you came. To complete the loop, continue on the old road straight past the tunnel to the shoulder of Highway 26, a few steps from your car.

For a more substantial trip across Laurel Hill, hike a 4.1-mile section of the Pioneer Bridle Trail. This route is open to bicycles and horses too. If you can arrange a shuttle, plan on doing this section of trail one way. To leave a shuttle

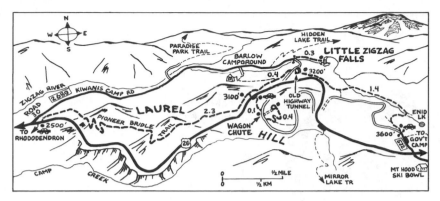

car (or bicycle) at the upper trailhead, drive Highway 26 to between mileposts 52 and 53, a mile west of Government Camp. Opposite the western entrance to Mt. Hood Ski Bowl, turn north off the highway onto Road 522 at a "Glacier View Sno-park" sign. After 0.2 mile, park at a gate. Trail signs here are confusing, but the Pioneer Bridle Trail is the forest path just to the right of the paved road ahead, past a tree with two blue diamonds.

To start your hike at the lower trailhead, drive Highway 26 to between mileposts 48 and 49. Just 200 yards east of the intersection with Road 39, park on the north side of the highway by a "Pioneer Bridle Trail" sign. When you reach the middle of the 4.1-mile trail, you might want to detour on hiker-only side paths to see the wagon chute and Little Zigzag Falls.

Roadside history sign at Laurel Hill.   Opposite: Trail tunnel beneath old highway.

Mirror Lake

Easy (to Mirror Lake)
3.2 miles round trip
700 feet elevation gain
Open mid-May to mid-November

Moderate (to summit viewpoint)
6.4 miles round trip
1500 feet elevation gain

Avoid this popular hike on summer weekends, when the unmarked parking area is jammed and the trail crowded. But on weekdays or in the off-season, the trip is hard to beat. The relatively easy path starts at a waterfall and climbs to a subalpine lake mirroring Mt. Hood. Hikers with weary soles can stop to reflect by the lake while more energetic hikers chug on up through the wildflowers to an even more spectacular viewpoint atop Tom Dick & Harry Mountain.

Drive Highway 26 to between mileposts 51 and 52, about 2 miles west of Government Camp. Park on the highway's south shoulder by a footbridge and (usually) a cluster of other cars *(GPS location N45°18.441' W121°47.482')*. If you're parking overnight, leave nothing in your car here. The footbridge spans Camp Creek just above Yocum Falls, a long, lacy cascade overhung with yellow monkeyflowers. Cross the bridge and enter a deep, cool forest. In early summer expect pink rhododendrons and numerous white woodland wildflowers: 6-leaved bunchberry, wild lily-of-the-valley, and star-flowered solomonseal.

After 0.4 mile traverse a rockslide where you're almost certain to hear the cheeping cry of pikas; with patience, you'll spot one of these little round-eared "rock rabbits." Then switchback up another mile to a trail junction. Keep right around the lakeshore.

Heavy use has brought some restrictions here. Do not enter areas that have been roped off to allow plants to regrow. If you're backpacking, tent well away from the shore. Six sites are designated.

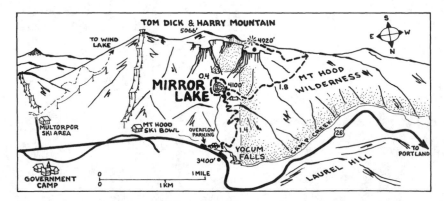

Mirror Lake from Tom Dick & Harry Mountain.   Opposite: Mt. Hood from Mirror Lake.

The first little beach you pass is the best for swimming. The lake bottom is muddy, but the water warms by late summer. Another 100 yards past the beach the trail forks. Keep left if you'd like to circle the lake (and discover some quieter picnic spots). Turn right if you're headed to the viewpoint atop Tom Dick & Harry Mountain.

The viewpoint path traverses a slope cleared of trees by winter avalanches. In summer the hillside sports alpine wildflowers, masses of huckleberries (ripe in late August), and views of the Zigzag Valley. After climbing 0.8 mile, turn sharply left at a monstrous 6-foot rock cairn. The trail grows fainter and rockier on this wooded ridge, and after 0.7 mile ends altogether at a summit rockpile. Continue 100 yards up to a 3-sided rock windbreak atop the shaley summit. Purple penstemons and a shaggy brown marmot live here. Views extend south across the green ridges of the Salmon-Huckleberry Wilderness to Mt. Jefferson, and north across Mirror Lake to Government Camp and Mt. Hood.

Tom Dick & Harry Mountain was named for its three distinct summits. The trail ends at the westernmost of the tops. The other two are off-limits to protect wildlife.

77 Timberline Lodge Trails

Easy (to Zigzag Canyon)
4.4 miles round trip
500 feet elevation gain
Open mid-July through October
Use: hikers, horses

Moderate (to Silcox Hut)
2.2-mile loop
1100 feet elevation gain

Difficult (to Paradise Park)
12.2-mile loop
2300 feet elevation gain

Mt. Hood's Timberline Lodge began as a Depression-era make-work program, but by the time President Roosevelt dedicated this elegantly rustic hotel in 1937 it had become a grand expression of Northwest art. Surprisingly, few visitors venture very far into the scenic alpine landscape that lured hotel builders here in the first place. Three particularly tempting goals await hikers: the Silcox Hut, Zigzag Canyon, and Paradise Park. To reach the trailhead from Portland, drive Highway 26 toward Mt. Hood 54 miles. On the far side of Government Camp, turn left for 6 miles up to the lodge's huge parking lot.

The Silcox Hut served as the upper terminus for Timberline's original Magic Mile ski lift from 1939 to 1962. Reopened as a chalet in 1992, it now offers overnight bunks for groups and a limited cafe in the European alpine tradition. To hike there, walk past the right-hand side of Timberline Lodge and follow a paved walkway uphill 200 yards. Turn right on a big rock-lined path—the Pacific Crest Trail—across a snow gully for 100 feet. Then turn uphill onto the Mountaineer Trail, a braided path through wind-gnarled firs and August-blooming blue lupine. After 0.6 mile, join a dirt road for the remainder of the climb to the hut. To return on a loop, contour 100 yards across a snowfield from the Silcox Hut to the new Magic Mile chairlift and follow a service road back down to the lodge. Tenderfeet should note that the lift is open to non-skiing passengers 9am to 3pm from June 1 to Labor Day for about $15.

For a more wilderness-oriented hike, take the Pacific Crest Trail to Zigzag

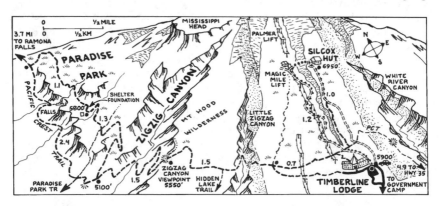

Mt. Hood from Paradise Park.   Opposite: The Silcox Hut.

Canyon or Paradise Park. Start by walking past the right-hand side of Timberline Lodge on a wide, paved walkway uphill. After 200 yards turn left on the Pacific Crest Trail amidst lupine and cushion-shaped clumps of white phlox. This path ducks under a chairlift and contours through gorgeous wildflower meadows with views south to Mt. Jefferson and the Three Sisters. At the 1-mile mark the path dips into a 200-foot-deep gully to cross the Little Zigzag River on stepping stones (a possible turnaround point for hikers with small children). Continue another easy 1.2 miles to an overlook of Zigzag Canyon, a 700-foot-deep chasm gouged into Mt. Hood's cindery flank by the glacier-fed Zigzag River.

If you're headed for Paradise Park, keep left at this point, continuing 1.5 miles on the PCT, which switchbacks down through the forest to cross the huge gorge. The Zigzag River is usually small enough here that you can hop across on rocks. At a trail junction on the far side of the canyon, turn right onto the Paradise Loop Trail and climb another mile to meadows stuffed with August wildflowers: fuzzy cats ears, red paintbrush, blue lupine, and white bistort—a rank little fuzzball also known as "dirty socks." If you're backpacking, tent on bare sand or fir needle duff, and *not* in the fragile meadows. Fires are banned.

To complete the loop, keep straight on the Paradise Loop Trail until it crosses a big creek and reaches a bare area—the site of a stone shelter smashed by a falling tree in 1994 and painstakingly removed. From the shelter site, head slightly uphill (north) to find a path traversing left below a cliffy bluff. This path leads 1.1 mile through heather fields before descending to the PCT. Then turn left for 2.4 miles to return to Zigzag Canyon and the route back.

Other Options

For a shorter walk than any of these, follow the PCT east from Timberline Lodge and descend half a mile to an overlook of the White River Canyon.

For a 3- to 5-day backpack, tackle the entire 39.3-mile Timberline Trail around Mt. Hood (see Hike #170). The route starts out along the PCT to Paradise Park.

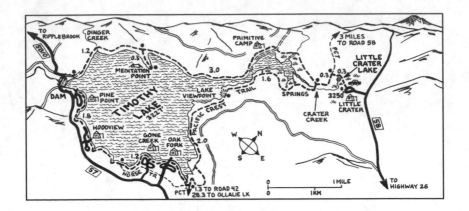

78   Timothy Lake

Easy (to Timothy Lake viewpoint)
4.4 miles round trip
100 feet elevation gain
Open May through November

Difficult (around Timothy Lake)
12-mile loop
200 feet elevation gain
Use: hikers, horses

This hike starts at sapphire Little Crater Lake and follows the Pacific Crest Trail to the forested shore of Timothy Lake, one of the Cascades' larger and more scenic reservoirs. Hikers interested in a longer loop can continue all the way around Timothy Lake, passing four campgrounds, several beaches, and views of Mt. Hood and Mt. Jefferson.

Little Crater Lake may only be 100 feet across, but it's as blue and as geologically unusual as its bigger National Park cousin. For centuries an artesian spring has been welling up in a wildflower meadow 15 miles south of Mt. Hood. The cold, gushing water has gradually worn away an underlying layer of soft siltstone, leaving a 45-foot-deep funnel of astonishingly clear blue water.

From Portland, drive Highway 26 past Mt. Hood to a turnoff 3.4 miles east of Wapinitia Pass (between mileposts 65 and 66). At a sign for Timothy Lake, turn onto paved Skyline Road 42 for 4 miles. Then turn right onto paved Abbott Road 58 for 1.4 miles to Little Crater Campground. Park at the far end of the campground loop by a trail sign.

The short paved path to the lake crosses a meadow with blue gentians and a view of Mt. Hood. Go right around the little lake, cross a fence on a stile, enter an old-growth forest of big Douglas firs, and reach the Pacific Crest Trail. Turn left onto this wide trail for 0.3 mile to a junction marking the start of the Timothy Lake loop. Keep left on the PCT.

Little Crater Lake.   Opposite: Mt. Hood from Timothy Lake.

After this junction the PCT promptly crosses swift, 50-foot-wide Crater Creek on a scenic footbridge—a possible turnaround point for hikers with small children. For the next mile, occasional springs gush out beside the trail. Several side trails to the right lead into lakeshore meadows dotted with stumps and grazing cows. Beyond Crater Creek 1.6 miles the trail climbs through woods to a "Timothy Lake" sign and your first view across the main body of the lake. This makes a good stopping point, particularly if you bushwhack 100 yards down to a scenic peninsula.

If you'd like to hike all the way around the lake, continue 2 miles on the PCT and turn right on the Timothy Lake Trail. Follow this path across the lake's main inlet (the Oak Grove Fork Clackamas River) and then keep right, sticking to the lakeshore. In the next 3 miles you'll pass a number of car campgrounds, boat ramps, and bathing beaches.

Cross the dam on the road. Then continue on the lakeshore path 1.2 miles before detouring to the right to explore Meditation Point, a peninsula with a boater campground. Then continue 3 miles around the lake to complete the loop.

Other Options

You can also drive to Timothy Lake from the Clackamas River side. Take Highway 224 east of Estacada 25.6 miles to the bridge at Ripplebrook (milepost 50), turn left onto paved Road 57, and follow signs to Timothy Lake. In this case, it's quicker to start your hike at the dam. Equestrians should also start the lake loop here.

Mount Hood East

Campgrounds

	Campsites	Water	Flush toilet	Open (mos.)	Rate range
1 KINNIKINNICK. This walk-in camp is on a sparsely forested peninsula of Laurance Lake, a reservoir close to Mt. Hood but without views.	20			VI-IX	$12
2 TILLY JANE. Very high on Hood's shoulder at Cooper Spur (see Hike #83), this dry camp has mountain hemlocks and a bumpy access road.	14			VI-IX	$10
3 SHERWOOD. This camp is wedged between the roaring whitewater of the East Fork Hood River and equally noisy Highway 35 (see Hike #82).	14			V-IX	$12
4 NOTTINGHAM. Young trees and meadows line East Fork Hood River at this new, quiet campground. Like Sherwood, it's free in winter.	23			V-IX	$12
5 KNEBAL SPRINGS. At a sometimes-dry spring on the edge of The Dalles watershed, this camp accesses an 8.5-mile trail loop (Hike #182).	8			V-X	$11
6 EIGHTMILE. This quiet camp is at a mountain stream on a paved road directly below the rentable Fivemile Butte Lookout.	21			V-XI	$11
7 FIFTEENMILE. This primitive campsite on a mountain stream serves as a trailhead for Oval Lake (Hike #87) and a 10.2-mile loop (Hike #183).	3			VI-X	$10
8 BONNEY MEADOW. A very rough access road stops crowds to this meadow with views and a loop trail to Boulder Lake (Hike #177).	6			VI-X	$11
9 FROG LAKE. This campground, on a shallow lake just off Highway 26, accesses the Pacific Crest Trails and a loop to Twin Lakes and Frog Lakes Butte (Hike #175). Res: 877-444-6777 (www.recreation.gov).	33	●		VI-IX	$20
10 BEAR SPRINGS. A dusty camp on the bank of Indian Creek at the border of the Warm Springs Indian Reservation.	21	●		V-IX	$13
11 ROCK CREEK RESERVOIR. This small reservoir on the dry side of the mountains has views of Mt. Hood from a picnic area, but not from the campground. Reservations: 877-444-6777 (www.recreation.govm).	33	●		IV-X	$17-18
12 BONNEY CROSSING. In woods beside a rushing stream, these primitive campsites access the Badger Creek Trail (Hike #88).	8			V-X	$11
13 LITTLE BADGER. Beside a creek in the pines of the dry side of the mountains, this camp is near the loop to Ball Point (Hike #185).	3			V-X	$11

◁ *Flag Point Lookout.*

Cabins, Lookouts & Inns

	Rental units	Private bath	Breakfast	Open (mos.)	Rate range
1 FLAG POINT LOOKOUT. Available only in winter when it's accessed by a 6-mile ski trip, this 14-foot cabin perches atop a dizzying 60-foot tower with views (Hike #87). Has propane stove, solar lights, firewood, pulley system for gear. Reservations: 877-444-6777 (www.recreation.gov).	1			XI-V	$50
2 FIVEMILE BUTTE LOOKOUT. This 14-foot-square cabin on a 30-foot tower has solar lights, a propane stove, and a woodstove. Ski 3 miles to access in winter. Reservations: 877-444-6777 (www.recreation.gov).	1		●		$50

Above right: Mt. Hood from Cloud Cap (Hike#83).

79 Twin Lakes

Easy (Wapinitia Pass to Lower Twin)
5.1 miles round trip
700 feet elevation gain
Open June to early November
Use: hikers, horses

Moderate (Barlow Pass to Upper Twin)
7.5-mile loop
1300 feet elevation gain

Children like Lower Twin Lake for lots of reasons. The hike from Wapinitia Pass isn't too long, the water's swimmable, the beach has logs for climbing, campsites are plentiful, and there's a path around the lake for exploring.

If you're hiking without kids, however, consider a slightly longer loop from Barlow Pass to Upper Twin Lake instead. This less crowded route includes a side trip to Palmateer Point for a view of Mt. Hood.

To find the Wapinitia Pass trailhead, drive Highway 26 to milepost 62 (east of Government Camp 8 miles), and turn at the Frog Lake Sno-Park. Park at the far left-hand end of this huge lot. After 50 feet the path from the parking lot meets the Pacific Crest Trail. Turn right on this wide route, climbing gradually from a mountain hemlock forest into woods dominated by firs. Expect ripe huckleberries in late summer.

After 1.4 miles, turn right at a pointer for Lower Twin Lake. This path crests a saddle and descends to a junction near the far end of the lake. Turn right for 100 yards to the shore, with a camping area and a 0.9-mile path circling the lake.

You could continue on to Upper Twin Lake and Palmateer Point from here, but those goals are actually easier to reach if you start at Barlow Pass instead. To find the Barlow Pass trailhead, drive Highway 26 east of Government Camp 3 miles and take Highway 35 toward Hood River for 2 miles to the summit of Barlow Pass. Then turn right on a paved road for 0.3 mile (passing the historic Barlow Road) to a large paved parking area that serves as a sno-park in winter.

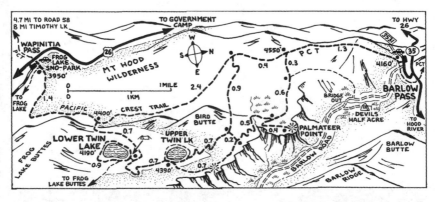

Near the entrance to the paved lot, take a path to the left 50 feet to a picnic table at a junction with the Pacific Crest Trail. Turn right, past a "No Bikes" sign, following the PCT uphill through a forest of mountain hemlock and true fir. The gray-green *Alectoria* lichen that beards the trunks above 9 feet serves as a natural gauge of the average winter snow depth here. Lichen can't grow under snow.

After 1.3 miles ignore a left fork for the Palmateer Trail (the return route of your loop). Continue straight on the PCT another 0.4 mile and then turn left on a trail signed for Upper Twin Lake. This path descends gradually 0.9 mile to a junction in a lodgepole pine flat. Go straight another 0.7 mile, switchbacking over a pass to Upper Twin Lake.

Follow the lakeshore trail left around Upper Twin Lake to a big trail junction at the lake's outlet, with a view across the lake to the tip of Mt. Hood. After enjoying the view, backtrack counter-clockwise around the lake 100 steps to find the poorly marked Palmateer Trail angling up to the right. Although too rough for horses, this is the most scenic return route for a hiking loop. If you keep right at junctions for the next 1.6 miles you'll pass cliffs and canyons to the rocky ridge-end at Palmateer Point, overlooking a dramatic, glacially carved valley that served as the route for the 1845 Barlow Road between The Dalles and Sandy. The meadow visible far below was one of the highest campsites used by covered wagon pioneers on Sam Barlow's rugged trail. Travelers named the meadow the Devil's Half Acre because of its wintry weather early in autumn.

Hike back down from Palmateer Point 0.4 mile, turn right for 0.9 miles, and turn right on the Pacific Crest Trail to return to your car.

Mt. Hood from Palmateer Point.   Opposite: Upper Twin Lake.

Umbrella Falls.   Opposite: Sahalie Falls from the historic highway bridge.

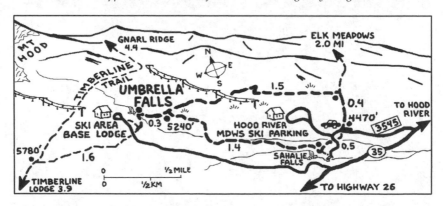

80   Umbrella Falls

Easy
4.4-mile loop
800 feet elevation gain
Open late June through October
Use: hikers, bicycles, horses

With two lovely waterfalls and a forest full of huckleberries, it's easy to forget that this loop hike on Mt. Hood traverses one of the state's largest ski areas. A compromise shifted the condomiums and shops once planned for Hood River Meadows to the already-developed area at Government Camp. A walk to Umbrella and Sahalie Falls shows how much natural beauty was saved.

The trailhead is the same as for the more difficult Hike #81 to Elk Meadows. From Portland, drive Highway 26 past Government Camp and take Highway 35 toward Hood River for 7.6 miles. Beyond the Mt. Hood Meadows turnoff 1.3 miles, turn left at a sign for the Elk Meadows Trailhead. Follow this paved road 0.3 mile to the trailhead parking pullout on the right. Equestrians on this trail may use only processed livestock feed. And although the huckleberries at Hood River Meadows are tempting, they are reserved by treaty for members of the Warm Springs tribes.

Set out on the Elk Meadows Trail to the right, but after 0.4 miles turn left at a sign for Umbrella Falls. This path climbs across several ski runs—narrow meadows with blue lupine and huckleberry bushes. Elk like these treeless swaths so much they've built their own meandering paths. Your route crosses under a chairlift and passes a few small mountain brooks.

At the 1.9-mile mark you'll reach a junction in a small wildflower meadow. The loop route turns left toward Sahalie Falls, but first go straight 0.3 mile to a 50-foot bridge beneath Umbrella Falls. This is a great lunch spot, and you really won't notice how close you are to a ski lodge parking area unless you scramble to the top of the waterfall's 60-foot fan.

After admiring Umbrella Falls, return 0.3 mile to the meadow junction and turn downhill for 1.4 miles to a sign for Sahalie Falls. The sign points you down a steep spur trail to the right 200 feet, where there's a disappointing view of the falls through the trees. But if you continue down on a steep scramble trail 150 feet you'll reach an abandoned concrete highway bridge with a terrific view of the waterfall. Part of the scenic Mt. Hood loop highway from the 1920s, the bridge is now unsafe for cars, but fine for hikers. Traffic noise from the modern highway, just downstream, is drowned by the rush of falling water.

Rather than scramble back up from Sahalie Falls the way you came, you might turn left on the old paved highway for 0.3 mile to where the trail crosses the road. Then turn right on the trail, crossing a creek on a footbridge back to your car.

Elk Meadows

Moderate (to Elk Meadows)
6 miles round trip
1230 feet elevation gain
Open late June through October
Use: hikers, horses

Difficult (to Gnarl Ridge)
9.4 miles round trip
2230 feet elevation gain
Open mid-July through October

Two of Mt. Hood's most scenic hiking goals are tucked away on the mountain's southeast flank: a rustic shelter amidst Elk Meadows' wildflowers, and Gnarl Ridge's breathtaking cliff-edge viewpoint amid wind-dwarfed pines. Visit either destination, or take a slightly longer loop and visit both. The trailhead is the same as for Hike #80 to Umbrella Falls, so if the weather looks iffy or you're feeling cautious, you can opt for that easier loop at the last minute.

From Portland, drive Highway 26 past Government Camp and take Highway 35 toward Hood River for 7.6 miles. Beyond the Mt. Hood Meadows turnoff 1.3 miles, turn left at a sign for the Elk Meadows Trailhead. Follow this paved road 0.3 mile to the trailhead parking pullout on the right. Equestrians on this trail may use only processed livestock feed.

The Elk Meadows Trail starts on the right, setting off through a fir forest with

Mt Hood from the Elk Meadows shelter.   Above: Lamberson Butte on Gnarl Ridge.

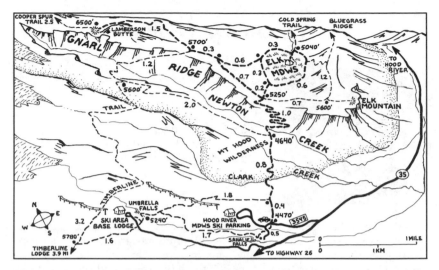

blue lupine blooms in July and lots of ripe blue huckleberries in late July and early August. Keep straight on the main trail, ignoring side paths to Umbrella Falls and the Newton Creek Trail. After 1.2 nearly level miles you'll have to cross raging Newton Creek on logs. This can be tricky in the high water of summer afternoons.

The path now launches up a wooded ridge in eight long switchbacks, finally reaching a 4-way trail junction at a saddle. If you want the shortest route to Gnarl Ridge, turn left here and stick to the ridgecrest for 2.5 uphill miles.

But if you're headed for Elk Meadows, go straight. After 0.2 mile, turn right on the Elk Meadows Perimeter Trail, a 1.2-mile circuit designed to keep hikers from tramping through the fragile meadows in the middle. If you're backpacking, note that although tents are banned in the meadows (and in tree islands within the meadows), the perimeter trail passes several acceptable campsites in the woods. After 0.6 mile the perimeter trail turns left at a junction beside a creek. Forty yards later reach an unmarked fork. Keep left here to find a three-sided shelter with a picture-postcard view across the meadows to Mt. Hood *(GPS location N45°20.631' W121°36.359')*.

To return to your car, simply follow the perimeter trail the rest of the way around the meadows. If you still have the energy to climb to Gnarl Ridge, however, hike 0.3 mile from the shelter along the perimeter trail and turn right at a sign, "To Gnarl Ridge." This route climbs 0.9 mile to the Timberline Trail. Follow the "Cloud Cap" pointer to the right and climb 1.5 miles into an alpine landscape where views extend from Mt. Adams to the Three Sisters. Finally pass the remains of a stone shelter on the left and reach a colossal cliff edge overlooking Newton Creek's 800-foot-deep chasm. Cowering whitebark pines form a gnarled mat along the rim. Turn back here — or, if you're feeling sprightly, scramble up Lamberson Butte, a rocky outcrop 400 yards to the south.

Other Options

If you've hiked to Gnarl Ridge, it's only 1.2 miles farther to return on a dramatic loop across Newton Creek's canyon. Just stay on the Timberline Trail as it descends to Newton Creek (which may have no bridge, so use caution). Then climb briefly to the Newton Creek Trail junction and turn left.

82 Tamanawas Falls

Easy
3.8 miles round trip
500 feet elevation gain
Open late April through November

The Northwest Indians believed everyone has a *tamanawas*—a friendly guardian spirit. Tamanawas Falls seems as though it might be Mt. Hood's guardian, an inspiring 100-foot curtain of white water in a green canyon at the mountain's eastern base. The path to the falls is a delight, with scenic footbridges and lots of access to mossy-banked Cold Spring Creek.

Drive Highway 35 around Mt. Hood to the well-marked Tamanawas Falls Trailhead near milepost 72, about 0.2 mile north of Sherwood Campground. Park by a message board at the north end of the pullout. Walk 200 feet to the East Fork Hood River, a bouldery torrent milky with the silt of Hood's glaciers. Cross on an impressive footbridge and turn right on the East Fork Trail.

The mountain hemlock forest here is carpeted with twinflower, a tiny double-belled white wildflower with shiny little leaves. This delicate flower's Latin name is *Linnaea borealis* because it was a favorite of Linnaeas, the 18th-century Swedish botanist who invented the system of identifying plants with two Latin names.

After 0.6 mile on the East Fork Trail, turn left on the Tamanawas Falls Trail, crossing another footbridge and following Cold Spring Creek upstream a mile. When the trail turns uphill to the right, keep left on the 0.3-mile path to the Tamanawas Falls viewpoint. The trail ends here, but sure-footed adventurers can hop across rockslide boulders for 200 yards to explore the misty overhang behind the falls.

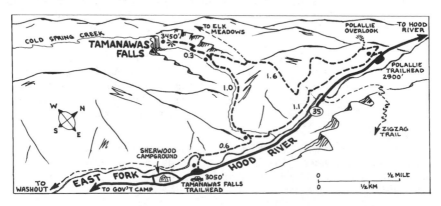

Other Options

Most hikers return from Tamanawas Falls as they came, but if you'd like to return on a longer loop, hike back 0.3 mile, turn left, and take the Tamanawas Tie Trail up to a ridgetop junction. Turn right, following the Polallie Campground pointer, and descend gradually for a mile. At this point there's a 150-yard side trail to the Polallie Overlook, but it may be blocked by windfall trees, and the clifftop view of brushy Polallie Creek is impressive only if you know the creek's history. In 1980 an 80-foot-deep flash flood roared past here, destroying an old growth forest and 6 miles of Highway 35. (To see the flood's origin, a raw canyon headwall 4 miles upstream, take Hike #83 to Cooper Spur.) To complete the loop, continue 200 yards on the main trail and turn right onto the East Fork Trail.

Tamanawas Falls.   Opposite: Footbridge across the East Fork Hood River.

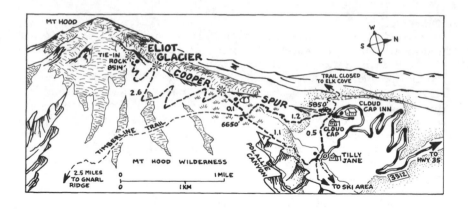

83   Cooper Spur

Moderate (to shelter)
3-mile loop
1000 feet elevation gain
Open mid-July to mid-October

Difficult (to Tie-In Rock)
8.2-mile loop
2800 feet elevation gain

The highest hiking trail on Mt. Hood switchbacks up Cooper Spur's cindery shoulder to Tie-In Rock, where mountain climbers traditionally rope up. From this vertiginous perch, peaks from Mt. Rainier to the Three Sisters dot the horizon. The massive Eliot Glacier writhes below, a splintered river of ice. And if the thought of a 2800-foot ascent leaves you winded, Cooper Spur has a much easier hiking option: a 3-mile loop to a historic stone shelter at timberline.

Drive Highway 35 around Mt. Hood to the Cooper Spur Ski Area turnoff between mileposts 73 and 74. Head west on Cooper Spur Road for 2.3 miles to Cooper Spur Junction, turn left onto Cloud Cap Road for 1.4 paved miles, ignore the ski area entrance on the left, and continue straight (following a "Tilly Jane" pointer) on a slow, bumpy, one-lane gravel road for 8.1 miles. At a T-shaped junction, turn right toward Cloud Cap 0.5 mile to a restroom marking the trailhead on the right (*GPS location N45°24.166' W121°39.264'*).

From the restroom, walk across the primitive campground 200 feet to a message board and go steeply uphill to the left on the Timberline Trail. This path sets out through a fir forest where blue lupine bloom in mid-summer and blue huckleberries ripen in late summer. After 0.2 mile fork left, following the Timberline Trail up into a bouldery gully at the head of Tilly Jane Creek. The only plants able to grow here are alpine partridge foot and sand verbena. Large rock cairns mark the path up through the sand. Then the path climbs through a patch of twisted whitebark pines to a trail crossing in a broad field of blue lupine.

Turn right at this junction, taking the Cooper Spur Trail up 200 yards to a 10-foot-square stone shelter built in the 1930s by the Civilian Conservation Corps. The view here extends from Mt. Adams and the Hood River Valley to the brown scablands of the Columbia River Plateau. A spur trail continues 200 yards to a viewpoint of the Eliot Glacier, a good turnaround spot.

If you're interested in the tougher 8.2-mile hike, continue up past the shelter on a remarkably well-graded trail with occasional overlooks of Eliot Glacier. After 2.6 switchbacking miles reach a crest with four low stone windbreaks and a rock commemorating a 1910 Japanese climbing party. This makes a good stopping point, or you can continue 500 yards along the ridge to Tie-In Rock, a big boulder. But unless you have climbing equipment *do not* venture onto the deceptively dangerous snowfields beyond.

To complete the loop, hike down from the Cooper Spur shelter and go straight at the Timberline Trail junction, following the pointer toward Tilly Jane Campground. This path descends along the rim of Polallie Canyon, a quarter-mile-wide bowl created in December 1980 when rains launched a colossal landslide and flash flood. After 1.1 mile reach a trail junction near a windowless plank cookhouse built by the American Legion in 1924. Turn left, passing the historic Tilly Jane Guard Station and climbing gradually half a mile to your car.

Mt. Hood from the Cooper Spur shelter.   Opposite: Eliot Glacier's headwall.

84 Elk Cove & Pinnacle Ridge

Difficult (to Elk Cove)
9.2 miles round trip
2250 feet elevation gain
Open mid-July through October

Difficult (to Dollar Lake)
9 miles round trip
2350 feet elevation gain

Arguably the prettiest and quietest timberline meadows at Mt. Hood are on its north flank — on the opposite side of the mountain from the tourist crowds at Timberline Lodge. This hidden Eden became even quieter after a glacial flood closed the Timberline Trail near Cloud Cap and a wildfire scorched the forests.

Only two paths climb to this shoulder of Mt. Hood, and both traverse several miles of black snags. Consider it the price of admission. If you're backpacking, you can combine both trails in a grand loop and still have time to explore the glorious, unburnt meadows at timberline.

Start by following signs to the Mt. Hood Railway station in Parkdale. If you're coming from Hood River, take Highway 35 south 13 miles, turn right near milepost 83 for 2 miles to a flashing light, and turn right for half a mile to Parkdale. If you're coming from Government Camp, take Highway 35 to milepost 80 and turn left on Baseline Road 2.8 miles.

When you get to Parkdale turn left beside the railroad station onto Clear Creek Road for 2.7 miles and fork to the right on Laurance Lake Drive for 4.2 mostly paved, narrow miles to Kinnikinnick Campground at Laurance Lake. Then turn uphill to the left on gravel Road 2840 for 1.1 mile to a fork.

To the left at this fork is the parking area for the Elk Cove Trail, which climbs to Elk Cove. If you fork to the right for 1.8 miles, however, the road ends at a parking area for the Pinnacle Ridge Trail, which climbs to the Dollar Lake area. The two trails are about the same length, but the Elk Cove Trail is better graded.

If you start your hike at the Elk Cove Trailhead you'll cross a creek on a foot-

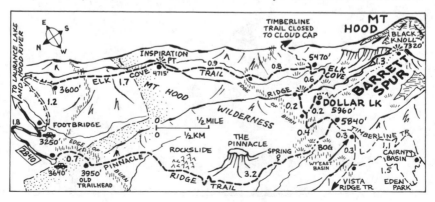

bridge and follow an abandoned roadbed 1.2 miles uphill. Then turn left on the actual Elk Cove Trail, which climbs a ridge into the snags of the 2011 fire. After another 1.7 miles you'll pass Inspiration Point, a rock outcrop with a view up the canyon to Mt. Hood. After another 0.9 mile you'll cross a creek and leave the burn. A final 0.8 mile brings you to the Timberline Trail at Elk Cove's meadows. Fields of blue lupine and mountain brooks spill down from the glacier-clad crest of Mt. Hood. Camping is banned in the meadow and its tree islands, but there are approved sites in the woods before you reach the Timberline Trail junction.

The Pinnacle Ridge Trail may be a rougher route to these timberline marvels, but it's quieter and takes you more directly to Dollar Lake. Since the 2011 fire, Road 2840 now ends in a parking lot, and the new Pinnacle Ridge Trail parallels the abandoned road for 0.7 mile. Then you enter the burn. You'll cross a 5-foot-wide creek, traverse a rockslide, and skirt the Pinnacle, a rock knoll. At the 2.8-mile mark you'll cross a spring, and then climb to a steep, boggy slope where the trail seems to disappear. Slog 100 feet to the far upper side of the boggy slope to find the trail where it reenters the woods. Then coninue up through increasingly gorgeous meadows for 0.8 mile to the Timberline Trail *(GPS location N45°24.743′ W121°42.557′)*. Turn left.

The unofficial path to Dollar Lake is easy to miss. The best plan is to hike left on the Timberline Trail 0.6 mile until it turns sharply to the right at a ridge end. Continue 100 feet to a breathtaking view of Elk Cove and Mt. Hood. Then turn around and backtrack on the Timberline Trail 0.2 mile, watching closely for the Dollar Lake trail. After 400 steps, when you reach a minor gully on the left with view of the tip of Mt. Hood, turn uphill on a little path that heads straight toward the mountain amid lupine, paintbrush, and Christmas-tree-sized hemlocks. In 0.2 mile you'll reach the 60-foot-wide lakelet *(GPS location N45°24.675′ W121°42.242′)*.

Adventurers eager for grander views should look for a trail on the opposite side of Dollar Lake. This faint path switchbacks up onto Barrett Spur and follows its crest 1.3 miles amid lupine and *krummholz* (storm-bent alpine trees) to a black knoll at the head of Elk Cove's canyon.

Mt. Hood from Dollar Lake after the 2011 fire.   Opposite: Inspiration Point.

85 Bald Butte

Difficult
8.4 miles round trip
2630 feet elevation gain
Open mid-March through November
Use: hikers, horses, bicycles

When the Hood River orchards blossom beneath snowy Mt. Hood, there's no better place to enjoy the springtime panorama than from the wildflower fields on Bald Butte's summit. Just don't tackle the long climb to this former fire lookout site in August, when heat shimmers from the exposed slope where the route passes beneath giant, crackling powerlines.

From Interstate 84 at Hood River take exit #64 and follow Highway 35 for 14.8 miles toward Government Camp. Just 1 mile past the Hood River Ranger Station turn left on Smullen Road for 0.3 mile. Immediately before the first curve turn left onto an unmarked gravel road to a turnaround with confusing spur roads. Park here.

Start on a small footbridge over a ditch with a sign for the Oak Ridge Trail. The path begins in a young clearcut with scrub oaks, blue bachelor buttons, and small Douglas firs. After 0.4 mile the path crosses a gravel road and launches uphill in a series of 25 tight switchbacks. For the first 0.3 mile you'll climb through a dry forest of Douglas fir and long-needled ponderosa pine. The views begin when the path emerges onto a grassy ridgecrest of Oregon white oaks and cheery, sunflower-like balsamroot wildflowers. Mt. Hood gleams above the Upper Hood River Valley's crazy quilt of fruit orchards.

At the 1.4-mile mark the path passes an open wood gate and ducks into a cooler, higher elevation fir forest with white wildflowers. Look for the large triple leaves of vanilla leaf and the arching fronds of large solomonseal. This upper, shadier part of the trail has 9 more switchbacks.

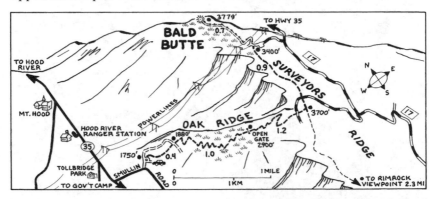

Mt. Hood from Bald Butte.   Opposite: Bald Butte's summit road.

After climbing a total of 2.6 miles, cross a gravel road on top of Surveyors Ridge and 100 yards later turn left onto the Surveyors Ridge Trail. This path follows the broad crest of the fault-block mountain that walls in the Upper Hood River Valley. As you hike north you'll cross a gravel road and an old clearcut before descending slightly to a dirt road in a grassy pass below four sets of enormous powerlines.

Continue straight on the dirt road, climbing under the powerlines. Another 0.7 mile along the up-and-down road brings you to Bald Butte's summit meadows, ablaze with yellow balsamroot in May *(GPS location N45°32.180' W121°31.964')*. From the foundation pier of the old lookout tower the view includes three Washington snowpeaks and even the tip of Mt. Jefferson through a pass on Mt. Hood's left flank.

Other Options

If you turn south along the Surveyors Ridge Trail instead of north you'll reach another former fire lookout site at Rimrock Viewpoint, atop a sheer rock cliff. The goal is 0.7 mile farther than Bald Butte and lacks the flowers, but the view is as good and doesn't require hiking a jeep track under powerlines.

86   Lookout Mountain

Easy (from High Prairie)
2.5-mile loop
570 feet elevation gain
Open July through October
Use: hikers, horses

Difficult (from Highway 35)
10 miles round trip
2980 feet elevation gain

This summit overlooks every Cascade peak from the Three Sisters to Mt. Rainier and offers a rare panorama of the Columbia River Plateau and the Badger Creek Wilderness. Certainly the view of Mt. Hood is hard to beat.

Two very different routes climb to Lookout Mountain. The loop from High Prairie is easy enough for hikers with children. Although the climb from Highway 35 via Gumjuwac Saddle is long and tough, it starts at a convenient trailhead and offers views of its own.

For the easy loop, drive Highway 35 around the east side of Mt. Hood to the turnoff for Dufur Mill Road 44 (just north of Nottinham Campground, between mileposts 70 and 71). Turn east on this paved road for 3.7 miles. Beyond the Surveyors Ridge Trailhead a tenth of a mile, turn right onto gravel High Prairie Road 4410. After 4.7 miles on this washboard route—always keeping uphill—reach a T-shaped intersection. Turn left on High Prairie Road for 0.1 mile to the end of gravel and park in a large gravel parking lot on the left *(GPS location N45°21.154' W121°31.870')*.

Walk uphill across the road and take the wide High Prairie Trail 30 feet to a junction. The main trail (an old road) continues straight, but the prettiest route to Lookout Mountain is really the "loop trail" to the right. So turn right on this path, ambling through meadows with purple aster, blue penstemon, and bistort—the little white fuzzballs also known as "dirty socks." Also look for the foot-long, boat-shaped leaves of hellebore, an odd plant with a stalk of green flowers. Indians believed the plant's poisonous root could ward off evil spirits.

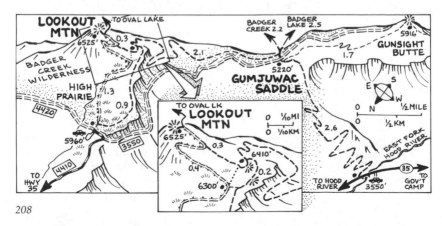

Soon you'll start glimpsing Mt. Hood through the trees. At the 0.7-mile mark ignore a side trail from the left that connects with the main road/trail. Then climb past a scenic rock pinnacle for 0.2 mile, turn left on the Divide Trail from Gumjuwac Saddle, and keep uphill 0.3 mile to the summit. To return on a loop, simply follow the old road downhill 1.3 miles to your car.

For the longer hike with a handier, paved trailhead, drive Highway 35 around the east side of Mt. Hood to a bridge across the East Fork Hood River between mileposts 68 and 69. Look for the small trailhead message board at the north end of the bridge, where parking is tight. The path switchbacks up 2.6 miles at a stiff grade to a big junction at Gumjuwac Saddle (named for Gum Shoe Jack, a rubber-booted shepherd). Cross the dirt road and keep left on the Divide Trail for 2.4 increasingly scenic miles to Lookout Mountain's summit.

Other Options

If you've already hiked to Lookout Mountain via Gumjuwac Saddle and would like to try a different viewpoint, turn right on the Divide Trail at Gumjuwac Saddle for 1.7 miles up to Gunsight Butte. This route traverses rock gardens of red paintbrush and purple penstemon to a shaley butte with a front-row view of Mt. Hood.

Mt. Hood from Lookout Mountain.   Opposite: Mt. Jefferson from Lookout Mountain.

Oval Lake.   Below: The Flag Point lookout.

87   Fret Creek & Oval Lake

Moderate (to Oval Lake and Palisade Point)
4.8 miles round trip
1180 feet elevation gain
Open mid-July through October
Use: hikers, horses

A pleasant forest trail from a paved road climbs along this creek to Oval Lake. And although the little lake doesn't have much of a view, an extra half mile takes you to Palisade Point, a crag atop a 300-foot cliff overhanging the Badger Creek Valley, where you can see Mt. Adams, the plains of Eastern Oregon, and the top third of Mt. Hood.

Drive Highway 35 around the east side of Mt. Hood to the turnoff for Dufur Mill Road 44 (just north of Nottingham Campground, between mileposts 70 and 71). Turn east on this paved road for 5.2 miles to a junction. Following "Flag Point" signs, turn right to stay on Road 44 for 3.1 miles, turn right on one-lane, paved Road 4420 for 2.2 miles, and continue straight on paved Road 2730 for another 2.1 miles. Beyond Fifteenmile Campground 300 yards, park in a pullout on the left by a trail messageboard made of logs *(GPS location N45°20.979′ W121°28.313′)*.

The Fret Creek Trail starts on the opposite side of the road with a short scramble up into the woods. The mountain hemlock forest here has blue huckleberries in August, but they're sparse. After climbing assiduously for 0.4 mile the path relaxes and crosses Fret Creek at a bridge where kids could play. Look for lupine, white valerian, and woodland wildflowers here. After bridging the creek two more times the trail steepens to a junction at the 1.9-mile mark with an "Oval Lake" sign.

At this point detour left on a side trail 50 yards down to admire the lake.

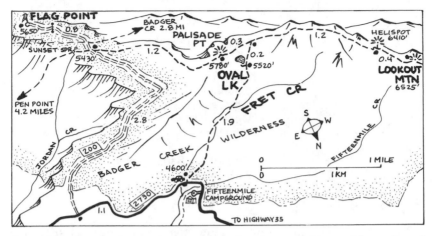

Ringed by forest, it's too shallow for swimming or fishing, with reeds and moss-like water plants, but it has a view of Palisade Point's rock wall. To see the view from the wall, return to the main trail, continue uphill 0.2 mile, and turn left on the Divide Trail for 0.3 mile through huckleberry fields that do put out fruit in August. At a crest, take a side trail 80 feet to the right, scrambling out a rock outcrop to the vertiginous crag of Palisade Point *(GPS location N45°19.847' W121°29.844')*. Soak in the view and return as you came.

Other Options

If you keep right at junctions from Oval Lake you'll reach the even better viewpoint atop Lookout Mountain in 1.8 miles (see Hike #86).

If you continue east beyond Palisade Point you'll follow a ridge trail up and down 1.2 miles to Road 200. Then walk 0.8 mile to the right along this pleasant, primitive dirt track to the Flag Point Lookout. Staffed in summer, but available for rent in winter and spring for $50 (see page 192), the cabin on this 60-foot tower has views from Mt. Hood and Mt. Adams to Central Oregon.

Palisade Point has a view of the Badger Creek Wilderness.

88　Badger Creek

Easy (to creekside boulders)
5.8 miles round trip
400 feet elevation gain
Open all year
Use: hikers, horses

Difficult (to Badger Lake)
21.8 miles round trip
2300 feet elevation gain
Open May to early November

Badger Creek's wilderness canyon climbs from the sagebrush flats of Central Oregon to the alpine forests of Mt. Hood. In the middle it crosses a strange, mixed zone known as a pine-oak grassland. A short hike along Badger Creek visits this botanically fascinating middle zone, rich with wildflowers from both the high desert and the mountains. If you continue on a longer trek or backpacking trip you can climb to the creek's headwaters at a high mountain lake.

To drive here from Portland, take Highway 26 past Mt. Hood. Shortly after milepost 68 turn left onto paved Road 43 at a sign for Wamic. After 6 miles turn right onto paved Road 48 and continue 15.2 miles. Then turn left onto Road 4810, following signs toward Bonney Crossing Campground from here on. After just 0.2 mile, be sure to follow Road 4810's unmarked right-hand turn to avoid ending up at Rock Creek Reservoir. Then take Road 4810 another 1.9 miles, veer right onto paved Road 4811 for 1.2 miles, and turn right onto narrow, roughish gravel Road 2710 for 1.8 miles. The trail starts on the left, just beyond Bonney Crossing Campground and a bridge, but parking is tight here, so park in a large lot along the campground entrance road and walk 200 feet to the trailhead.

If you're driving here from The Dalles, take Highway 197 south 34 miles to Tygh Valley and turn right. Follow signs for Wamic, then for Rock Creek

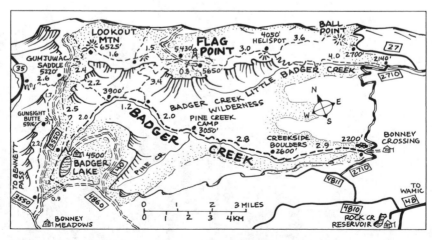

Trailside sign for the Badger Creek Wilderness.   Opposite: Badger Lake.

Reservoir, and finally for Bonney Crossing Campground.

The wildflower show along the lower portion of the trail is at its best from April to June. In dry, grassy areas look for sunflower-like balsamroot, little purple larkspur, erratic-petaled white prairie star, blue lupine, and wild strawberry. In moister conifer woods expect trilliums, twinflower, and solomonseal. If you didn't know orchids grow in Oregon, look beside the trail register at the 0.2-mile mark. You may find the little pink hoods of fairy slipper orchid or the even rarer mountain lady slipper orchid. Of course, don't pick any flowers.

Many of the snags along this trail were killed by spruce budworms. Infestations like this are a normal part of forest health, allowing the strong, surviving trees to stock the forest with insect-resistant seedlings.

Although the creek is never far away, one of the nicest access points comes after 2.6 miles, when the creek squeezes between a pair of 10-foot boulders, creating a pool and a tiny pebble beach. Hikers with children can turn back here, or perhaps continue 0.3 mile past a scenic cliff to another pair of creekside boulders and a 5-foot waterfall.

For a longer trip, continue another 2.8 miles to an old campsite on a riverbend opposite the cascading confluence of Pine Creek. Here the music of the creeks is particularly sweet, beneath a canopy of ancient red cedar and grand fir. Because this old campsite is too close to the creek and the trail for modern low-impact tenting, backpackers should choose more remote flat spots on the far side of the creek.

Backpackers and equestrians can continue 5.2 miles past Pine Creek to Badger Lake, where there are several loop possibilities to the viewpoints at Gunsight Butte and Lookout Mountain.

Clackamas Foothills

Campgrounds

		Campsites	Water	Flush toilet	Open (mos.)	Rate range
1	**LAZY BEND.** The first Forest Service camp on the Clackamas River has secluded, wooded sites. Reservations: 877-444-6777 (*www.recreation.gov*).	22	●	●	IV-X	$21
2	**CENTRAL CLACKAMAS RIVER CAMPGROUNDS.** Four popular riverside camps cluster within a mile along Highway 224 near a green bridge at milepost 39: Carter Bridge, Lockaby, Armstrong, and Fish Creek. Reservations: 877-444-6777 (*www.recreation.gov*).	81	●		V-IX	$16-20
3	**ROARING RIVER.** Giant cedars guard the confluence of Roaring River and the Clackamas at this camp. Res.: 877-444-6777 (*www.recreation.gov*).	14	●		V-IX	$18
4	**INDIAN HENRY.** A quiet riverside camp at the end of the Clackamas River Trail (Hike #91). Reservations: 877-444-6777 (*www.recreation.gov*).	86	●		V-IX	$17
5	**RIPPLEBROOK AREA CAMPGROUNDS.** Riverbank car camps near the Ripplebrook Ranger Station include Ripplebrook, Rainbow, and Riverside. See Hike #93. Reservations: 877-444-6777 (*www.recreation.gov*).	47			V-IX	$18
6	**LAKE HARRIET.** On a small reservoir of the Oak Grove Fork of the Clackamas River, near Ripplebrook.	13	●		IV-X	$16
7	**HIDEAWAY LAKE.** Secluded sites by this small deep lake in a forested bowl access trail to Shellrock and Rock Lakes (Hike #93). Free in winter.	9			VI-X	$16
8	**RAAB.** This camp among rhododendrons is on the bank of the Collawash River. Reservations: 877-444-6777 (*www.recreation.gov*).	26			V-IX	$14
9	**KINGFISHER.** Close to the new Bagby Campground (see Hike #93), this otherwise pleasant creekside site is plagued by loud parties and panhandlers. Reservations: 877-444-6777 (*www.recreation.gov*).	24	●		V-X	$20
10	**PAUL DENNIS.** This Olallie Lake camp has the area's best view of Mt. Jefferson. See Hike #98.	17			V-IX	$15-25
11	**CAMP TEN.** This quiet Olallie lakeshore pullout has a view of Olallie Butte. Expect mosquitoes, of course, when the fish are biting in July.	10			VI-IX	$10
12	**PENINSULA.** Partly burned in 2001, this Olallie Lake camp has a boat ramp; motors are banned (see Hike #98).	35			VI-IX	$10-18
13	**BREITENBUSH LAKE.** This PCT camp requires a high-clearance vehicle (see Hike #100).	20			V-IX	free

◁ *The rentable Olallie Lake Guard Station.*

Cabins, Lookouts & Inns

		Rental units	Private bath	Breakfast	Open (mos.)	Rate range
1	**CLACKAMAS LAKE RANGER'S CABIN.** 3-bedroom cabin from 1930s sleeps 8 (min. stay 2 days, $9 res. fee). Res.: 877-444-6777 (*www.recreation.gov*).	3			V-X	$140-160
2	**OLALLIE LAKE RESORT.** Reopened in 2010, this old-timey resort rents 10 rustic cabins ($35-130) with propane lights, and 2 yurts ($80-100) in the nearby campground. Res: *www.olallielakeresort.com*. No telephone.	12			VI-X	$65-100

Above right: Mt. Jefferson from Bull of the Woods (Hike #96).

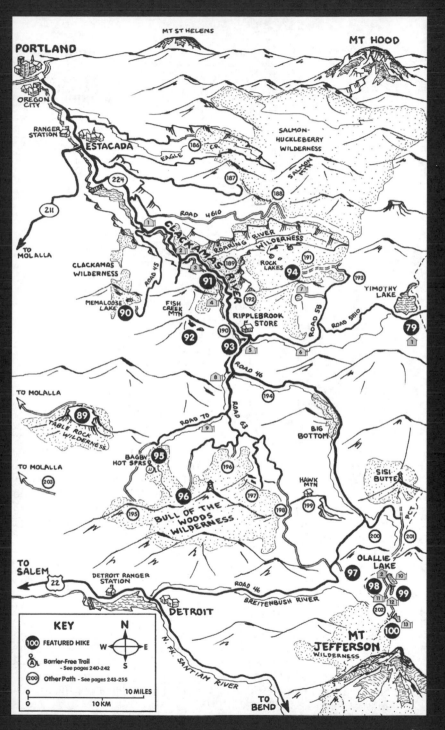

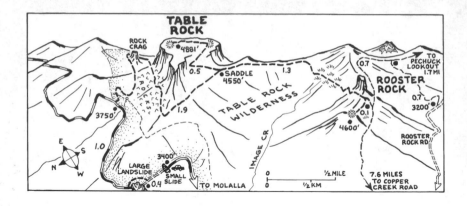

89   Table Rock

Moderate (to Table Rock)
7.6 miles round trip
1500 feet elevation gain
Open June to mid-November
Use: hikers, horses

Difficult (to Rooster Rock)
10.4 miles round trip
2600 feet elevation gain

    This fortress-shaped plateau, centerpiece of a pocket Wilderness near Molalla, offers a formidable panorama of ten Cascade snowpeaks and the Coast Range. The trail skirts a 1996 landslide and ducks below huge columnar basalt cliffs before switchbacking up the plateau's relatively gentle western slope. Rhododendrons flag the route pink in early summer, while gentians dot it with blue in late summer. For a longer hike, continue on a slightly rougher path to Rooster Rock's picturesque crag.

    Start by driving to Molalla, either by heading south from Interstate 205 at Oregon City or by heading east from Interstate 5 at Woodburn. From Molalla drive 0.6 mile toward Estacada on Highway 211, turn right onto South Mathias Road for 0.3 mile, turn left on South Feyrer Park Road for 1.6 miles, and then turn right onto South Dickey Prairie Road. Follow this road past several jogs for a total of 5.2 miles to a poorly marked junction with South Molalla Forest Road 6-3E-6. Signs are often missing from here on, so watch your odometer carefully. Turn right across the Molalla River, follow the paved road 12.5 miles to a fork, veer left onto gravel Middle Fork Road for 2.6 gravel miles, turn right for 1.9 more miles on Road 7-3E-7, and then keep left at a junction. A final 2.3 miles brings you to the trailhead, where a small landslide blocks the road to cars *(GPS location N44°58.559' W122°19.250')*.

Park at the small landslide and hike ahead on the abandoned road, now regrown with alder. After 0.4 mile the road ahead crumbles into a chasm left by a much larger landslide. Both of these slides were launched by the roadcut itself. The second slide grew so large because it was in an old clearcut, with no tree roots to hold the soil. To detour around the large slide, turn right on a new trail that scrambles 150 yards through the trees. Then continue a mile up the road to the old trailhead, where the path heads into an old-growth forest on the right.

After another 100 yards you'll reach a confusing junction. Don't turn right on a wide trail; it's actually an old cat road. Instead go straight, climbing at a steady grade through lichen-draped hemlocks and firs. After a mile you'll traverse below Table Rock's dramatic north cliff—a cutaway view of seven basalt lava flows, 16 to 25 million years old. Here the trail scrambles across the jagged rocks of a rockslide where snow patches linger into July. Listen for the peeping cry of the rabbit-like pikas that store dried plants under the boulders for winter.

After 1.9 miles turn left at a campsite in a ridgecrest saddle and switchback steeply up to the summit. Lined up to the east are Cascade peaks from Mt. Rainier to the Three Sisters. Beyond the quilt of Willamette Valley farmfields to the west, the Coast Range silhouette stretches from the Tualatin Hills to Marys Peak.

To continue to Rooster Rock, return to the saddle junction and go straight, following the rough ridgecrest up and down. The path drops to a thimbleberry meadow before climbing steeply to an open saddle. Turn right and hike 100 yards up to a rocky knoll with a view across Rooster Rock to the High Cascades.

Columnar basalt on Table Rock's face.   *Opposite: Mt. Jefferson from Rooster Rock.*

The trail to Memaloose Lake.   Opposite: Memaloose Lake reflection.

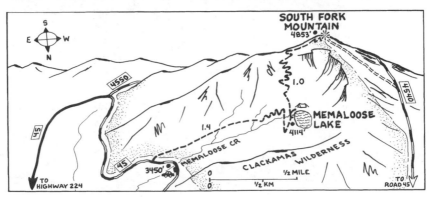

90 Memaloose Lake

Easy (to Memaloose Lake)
2.8 miles round trip
700 feet elevation gain
Open mid-June to early November
Use: hikers, horses, bicycles

Moderate (to South Fork Mountain)
4.8 miles round trip
1400 feet elevation gain

This popular path is only 20 miles from Estacada, yet has the feel of the High Cascades. Hike 1.4 miles through a grand old-growth forest to a mountain lake in the woodsy cirque of a long-vanished glacier. If you like, continue up to the former lookout site atop South Fork Mountain for a view from the Three Sisters to Mt. Rainier. Maximum group size in the Clackamas Wilderness is 12.

From Interstate 205 near Oregon City, take exit 12 and follow signs 18 miles to Estacada. Go straight through town and continue 9.2 miles on Highway 224. Between mileposts 33 and 34, turn right across a green bridge onto Memaloose Road 45. Drive 11.2 paved miles on this road and then keep right on gravel for another mile to a well-marked pullout on the left, just before Memaloose Creek. If the pullout is full, drive another 100 yards to a larger pullout and walk back to the trailhead *(GPS location N45°05.068' W122°13.283')*.

The route of the hike lies within a small island of wilderness, but the valley's steep walls make it seem as though the big woods extend forever. White wildflowers bloom here in May, and for the rest of summer their delicate green leaves remain to blanket the forest floor. Look for vanilla leaf's three large triangular leaves. Oxalis resembles a shamrock, bunchberry has leaves in clusters of six, and star-flowered solomonseal's leaflets are arched fronds.

The path crosses a couple of creeklets overhung with elegant lady ferns before switchbacking up to a picnic table at the shallow lake. When you reach the shore, turn left and cross the outlet creek's bed. On your right you'll find a forested flat with several campsites. Directly in front of you is the unmarked (and unmaintained) path to South Fork Mountain.

If you're interested in a quick climb, follow this path as it switchbacks up into a higher elevation forest with huckleberries, beargrass, and rhododendrons. The trail crests a ridge and follows it up to the old lookout site. A bit of searching will locate all four foundations, inscribed with a 1931 date.

To be sure, an ungated dirt road occasionally brings cars to this summit. But this does not diminish the view. To the right of Mt. Jefferson look for pointy Three-Fingered Jack, Broken Top, and all Three Sisters. To the left of Mt. Hood look for Mt. Adams, Mt. Rainier, and Mt. St. Helens.

91 Clackamas River Trail

Easy (to first beach)
1 mile round trip
100 feet elevation gain
Open all year

Moderate (to Pup Creek Falls)
7.6 miles round trip
1050 feet elevation gain

Moderate (entire trail, with shuttle)
7.8 miles one way
1300 feet elevation gain

This all-year trail through the Clackamas River's canyon features hidden beaches, mossy forests, and whitewater viewpoints. A highway unobtrusively follows the river's far shore, making it easy to arrange a car shuttle and hike the 7.8-mile trail one way. If you can't find a second car to shuttle, try a short walk to the trail's first beach or a moderate hike to Pup Creek Falls.

From Interstate 205 near Oregon City, take exit 12 and follow signs 18 miles east to Estacada. Go straight through town, continuing 14.4 miles on Highway 224. Beyond milepost 39, and just after crossing the second of two green bridges, turn right onto Fish Creek Road 54. Follow this paved road 0.2 mile, cross the Clackamas River on yet another green bridge, and park at a big lot on the right. A concessionaire may charge a special $5 parking fee here in summer.

The trail starts at the far end of the parking lot and crosses the road. (To leave a shuttle car at the upper trailhead you'll have to drive another 7 miles up Highway 224 to a final green bridge, go straight at a sign for Indian Henry Campground, follow Road 4620 for 0.6 mile, and park on the right, opposite the campground entrance.)

When you start out from the lower trailhead on Fish Creek Road, you'll notice that the first 2 miles of the trail were overswept by a forest fire, a normal part of the forest ecology here. Like a good groundskeeper, the 2003 blaze burned underbrush but left most of the trees green. Among the regrown plants look for April-blooming oxalis, a white wildflower with shamrock-shaped leaves that

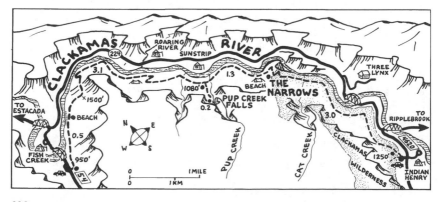

The Clackamas River from the first beach.   Opposite: Pup Creek Falls.

have such a tart flavor they're also called sourgrass. Spring also brings trilliums and yellow wood violets to these woods.

After half a mile the trail accesses a lovely stretch of riverbank. The little beach here is suitable for wading, and the mossy bedrock invites summer sunbathing. In October, battered 3-foot-long salmon lay eggs in the pebbly shallows here, and males battle to fertilize the redd.

Beyond the beach the trail spends a mile climbing through the forest to avoid riverside cliffs. Then the path leaves the burn area and continues up and down along the shore. At the 3.6-mile mark *(GPS location N45°08.927′ W122°06.223′)*, in a powerline clearing just before the trail descends to Pup Creek, turn right at a "Falls" pointer on a 300-yard side trail to a view of 3-tiered, 100-foot Pup Creek Falls, plunging from a basalt cliff colored by green moss and yellow lichen. This makes a good turnaround point.

If you continue on the main trail, you'll reach another side path in 0.9 mile that leads left across a plank to a campsite by a whitewater riffle — the last beach access of the hike. Next the trail climbs a bluff with a view of The Narrows, a 20-foot-wide river gorge. Continue down the far side of the bluff and take a side trail to the left to see this chasm close up. In the final 2.9 miles to Indian Henry Campground, the trail ducks beneath a cliff's overhang, passes a side creek's thin waterfall, and contours through an old-growth forest of 5-foot-thick cedars.

92   Fish Creek Mountain

Difficult
8.4 miles round trip
2400 feet elevation gain
Open June to early November
Use: hikers, horses, bicycles

This ridgecrest trail high above the Clackamas River climbs to a panormic summit and a quiet mountain lake. Storms marooned the path in 1996 by washing out access roads in the Fish Creek Valley. The Forest Service decided to decommission the roads permanently, turning the entire valley into a haven for its namesake wildlife: fish. Now volunteers have helped open an alternate trailhead, so you can once again hike to Fish Creek Mountain.

From Interstate 205 near Oregon City, take exit 12 and follow signs east 18 miles to Estacada. Go straight through town, continuing 21.4 miles on Highway 224. Just before the third green bridge across the Clackamas River, go straight on paved Road 4620, following a sign for Indian Henry Campground. After half a mile, ignore the campground entrance and instead go straight on what now becomes a one-lane paved road. After another 4.6 miles, at a fork where pavement ends, veer uphill to the right. After 2.2 miles on gravel, ignore a red gravel fork to the left. Then continue a final 0.4 mile to the trailhead *(GPS location N45°03.037' W122°07.221')*.

The parking area is actually a 50-foot segment of a washed-out road that once forked to the left here, but is now blocked by dirt berms. The trail begins between the forks in the road. After climbing 0.2 mile through young woods you'll enter an old-growth forest with Douglas fir, red cedar, and western hemlock as much as five feet in diameter. Look for tiny twinflower and white vanilla leaf blooms here.

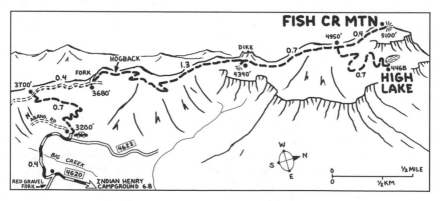

At the 0.7-mile mark you'll crest a ridge and meet another decommissioned road that's been churned up with little hummocks *(GPS location N45°02.895′ W122°07.543′)*. Follow this somewhat brushy roadbed to the right 0.4 mile amid alders, rhododendrons, and tiger lilies. Long pants are recommended. At a fork in the overgrown road, go straight up a bare dirt ridge between forks for 50 feet to find the tread of the original Fish Creek Mountain trail.

This path climbs a forested ridgecrest where rhododendrons bloom in June and blue huckleberries ripen in August. Some of the anthills along the trail have been dismantled by bears hungry for larvae. After 1.3 miles you'll pass a volcanic dike, a rock outcrop atop the ridge. The dike formed millions of years ago when lava squeezed into a crack in the ground. Detour 50 feet to the right to a clifftop viewpoint of distant Mt. Jefferson. Then continue 0.7 mile to a junction with the trail down to High Lake *(GPS location N45°04.465′ W122°07.457)*.

First continue straight another 0.4 mile along the roller-coastering ridgecrest to the summit of Fish Creek Mountain, where four concrete piers remain from the fire lookout built here in 1933. The view of Mt. Jefferson is still good, but trees now block the vista north. To see Mt. Hood, keep an eye out over your shoulder as you hike back down from the summit 0.4 mile to the trail junction.

Then turn left down the 0.7-mile trail to High Lake, a 400-foot pool in a cirque left by a small Ice Age glacier. A rockslide from Fish Creek Mountain backs the lake's western shore, but there are campsites on the eastern side. On a hot day, the 20-foot-deep lake is just fine for a swim before heading home.

High Lake.   Opposite: Mt. Jefferson from the summit of Fish Creek Mountain.

The Clackamas River.   Below: Gravel bar rocks.   Opposite: Red cedar roots.

93   Riverside Trail

Easy (to Rainbow Campground)
5.2 miles round trip
500 feet elevation gain
Open all year
Use: hikers, bicycles

An old-growth forest flanks this popular portion of the Clackamas River. Explore it on a riverside trail that visits secluded beaches and clifftop viewpoints. A private concessionaire operates the campgrounds on either end of the trail—and may charge $6 for parking—so plan to start at the Riverside Trailhead along Road 46 (or find a safe place to park just outside the campground gates).

From Interstate 205 near Oregon City, take exit 12 and follow signs east 18 miles to Estacada. Go straight through town, continuing 26 miles on Highway 224 to the bridge at Ripplebrook. Then fork right onto Road 46 for 1.8 miles to a small Riverside Trailhead sign and pull into a parking lot on the right *(GPS location N45°03.357' W122°02.914')*.

The path sets off toward the river amid big Douglas fir and hemlock. The forest understory includes vine maple and Oregon grape, whose clustered yellow blooms are Oregon's state flower. After 100 yards, turn right on the Riverside Trail to a blufftop viewpoint of the curving stream below. Continue north along the trail, switchbacking down through a magnificent grove of ancient 5-foot-thick Douglas fir to a footbridge over Mag Creek.

Half a mile beyond Mag Creek the trail dips to a lovely river beach, just before a second footbridge. If you're hiking with kids, you might make this beach your destination. The riverbend of sand and cobbles, palisaded by giant firs, is a perfect spot to skip rocks, read a book, or sunbathe.

If you continue beyond the beach on the main trail, you'll cross the Tag Creek bridge and climb over a hill 0.8 mile to another interesting river access, just before the trail's third footbridge. Turn left on a side path here to discover a small sandy cove beside a chilly but swimmable 50-foot pool, protected from the river's swift current by a large rock. Beyond this turnoff, the Riverside Trail skirts tall clifftops overlooking the Clackamas River. Then the path follows the smaller Oak Grove Fork to trail's end at Rainbow Campground.

Other Options

If you're not yet tired after returning to your car, continue south on the other portion of the Riverside Trail. This 1.4-mile segment follows within a stone's throw of Road 46 for a half mile. Then the path curves out around a pretty riverbend with a large beach before ending at the Riverside Campground loop.

Although mountain bikes are discouraged on the Riverside Trail because of heavy use by hikers, you might bring a bicycle to use as a shuttle. Here's the plan: Stash a bike at Riverside Campground, drive back to the Riverside Trailhead, hike 1.4 miles along the trail to your bike, ride 3 miles downhill on paved Road 46 to Rainbow Campground, and then hike the river trail 2.6 miles back to your car.

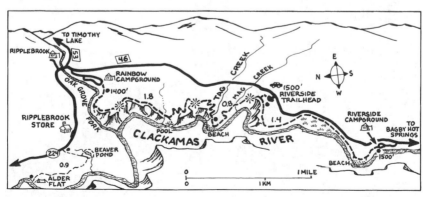

94

Shellrock & Rock Lakes

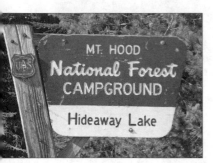

Easy (Shellrock Lake)
1.8 miles round trip
130 feet elevation gain
Open May to mid-November
Use: hikers, horses, bicycles

Easy (Hideaway Lake)
2-mile loop
50 feet elevation gain

Moderate (Rock and Serene Lakes)
7.7-mile loop
1500 feet elevation gain
Open mid-June to early November

The half dozen mountain lakes hidden here remain surprisingly uncrowded—perhaps because the bumpy dirt road to the old trailhead at Frazier Turnaround is so nerve-wracking. But now there's a new trailhead on a good gravel road, opening up a couple of easy paths to the area's lower lakes. All of the lakes are souvenirs of the last Ice Age, when glaciers gouged high, bowl-shaped valleys into the tableland between the Clackamas and Roaring Rivers.

From Interstate 205 near Oregon City, take exit 12 and follow signs east 18 miles to Estacada. Go straight through town, continuing 26 miles on Highway 224 to the far side of Ripplebrook. At a bridge by milepost 50, fork left onto paved Road 57 (toward Timothy Lake) for 7.4 miles. Then, following pointers for Hideaway Lake, turn left on paved Road 58 for 3 miles and fork to the left on gravel Road 5830 for 5 miles. Ignore the Hideaway Lake Campground entrance on the left and continue 0.3 mile to the Shellrock Lake Trailhead on the right (*GPS location N45°07.626' W121°58.233'*).

The easy trail to Shellrock Lake starts out in a young stand of subalpine fir. In June expect the blooms of pink rhododendrons, white beargrass plumes, and red fireweed. In August, expect blue huckleberries. After half a mile the path

Shellrock Lake.   Above: Hideaway Lake Campground entrance sign.

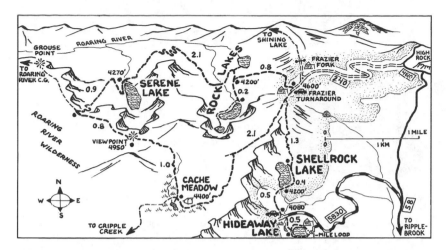

enters old-growth hemlock woods and turns to the right along Shellrock Lake's shore, passing lots of nice lunch spots. A good turnaround point is where the trail angles uphill past a "Frazier Turnaround" arrow at the far end of the lake.

When you get back to the car you'll have hiked less than 2 miles, so why not add a loop around Hideaway Lake? Simply walk 100 feet left on the gravel road from your car. The trail here skirts a marshy meadow through the woods for 0.5 mile to a T-shaped junction with the 1-mile lakeshore loop. A campground briefly confuses this loop, but just stick to the shore.

If you're tackling the longer loop to the Rock Lakes and Serene Lake, you might want to save 4.4 trail miles by driving the awful road up to the old Frazier Turnaround trailhead. To find it from Ripplebrook, take paved Road 57 toward Timothy Lake for 7.4 miles and turn left at the pointer for Hideaway Lake on paved Road 58. But then stick to Road 58 for 7.9 miles, ignoring spurs to Hideaway, Pyramid, and Anvil Lakes. At a T-shaped junction turn left on (possibly unmarked) paved Road 4610 for 1.3 miles, and then go straight across a gravel flat onto dirt Road 240. Follow this rocky, slow track 4.2 miles, keep left at Frazier Fork, and continue 0.2 mile to road's end at the primitive Frazier Turnaround Campground *(GPS location N45°08.910′ W121°58.167′)*.

Start down to the right on the Serene Lake Trail for 0.8 mile and turn left for a few hundred yards to a campsite at Middle Rock Lake. Explorers can veer right across the lake's outlet creek, follow a faint path to the far end of the lake, and hike up a slope to discover Upper Rock Lake. To find the third lake in this valley, return to the main trail, continue downhill 500 feet, and follow a pointer 500 feet to the right to Lower Rock Lake.

Then continue on the main trail 2 miles to large, green, very deep Serene Lake. A fork to the left ends at the lake's bouldery east shore, while the main trail continues to a forested campsite on the west side. Here the trail turns uphill and climbs for most of a mile to a trail junction on the edge of a high, forested plateau. Go left. In 0.8 mile you'll pass a viewpoint of Serene Lake, Mt. Hood, and three Washington snowpeaks.

Next the trail descends a mile to a 4-way junction at Cache Meadow, with its lakelet and flowers. Turn left past the a former shelter site 0.3 mile, fork left on Trail 517, climb a mile to an old roadbed, and follow it right a mile to your car.

227

95

Bagby Hot Springs

Easy
3 miles round trip
200 feet elevation gain
Open all year

Cedar logs have been hollowed to create 8-foot-long bathtubs at this rustic, free hot springs. Even if you don't plan to soak, the trail here is a delight, leading through a towering old-growth forest along a fork of the Collawash River. Just don't expect solitude. On weekends and all through summer the trail is heavily used and there's a long waiting line at the bath house.

Parking and hiking are free, but a private concessionaire charges $5 per person to use the hot springs. Kids under 13 are free. The required wristbands can be bought at the store in Ripplebrook or from a uniformed employee at the trailhead. This system has reduced the trailhead's notorious vandalism problem. The concessionaire also operates a car campground at the trailhead with $16 tent sites.

From Interstate 205 near Oregon City, take exit 12 and follow signs east 18 miles to Estacada. Go straight through town, continuing 26 miles on Highway 224 to the bridge at Ripplebrook. Then, following signs for Bagby Hot Springs, keep straight on paved Road 46 for 3.6 miles, turn right onto paved Road 63 for 3.5 miles, and turn right onto paved Road 70 for 6 miles to the trailhead parking lot on the left *(GPS location N44°57.129' W122°09.931')*. Pets must be on leash.

The trail crosses a footbridge over Nohorn Creek and launches into a magnificent ancient forest of big Douglas firs and red cedars. In April and May look here for yellow clusters of Oregon grape blossoms and a variety of white blossoms: vanilla leaf, 3-petaled trillium, and bunchberry. In autumn, vine maple leaves become red pinwheels.

Trail sign at entrance to hot springs area.   *Above: Tub carved from a cedar log.*

Hot tubs in a shed beside the old bathhouse.

At the 1-mile mark pass an overlook of a 10-foot slide falls in the Hot Springs Fork. In another 0.2 mile cross the green-pooled river on a long bridge and climb to a signboard at the hot springs. The log cabin behind the signboard is the original Forest Service guard station. To the left is the bath house, with long benches outside for the waiting line. The old bath house burned in 1979 when nighttime bathers carelessly used candles for light. A non-profit group rebuilt the structure to include five private rooms and an annex with four additional tubs.

To fill a tub, unplug a bunghole in the hot water trough. To adjust the temperature, use one of the plastic buckets to dip cold water from a vat outside. Remember the area's rules: no unleashed dogs, no music, no baths longer than 1 hour, and no soap—it pollutes the creek and harms the tubs. Swimsuits are rare.

If you keep right at the log cabin, you'll follow the Bagby Trail through a meadowed picnic area. After 0.2 mile, a side trail to the right descends to eight riverside campsites. Shortly thereafter the Bagby Trail passes Shower Creek Falls—a thin, 50-foot cascade that some people use for a quick cold shower after their hot bath.

Other Options

If you continue up the Bagby Trail you'll enter the Bull of the Woods Wilderness, leave the river, and cross eight small side creeks. After hiking 6 miles from the hot springs (and gaining 1800 feet), you can take a spur trail to the right, climbing 0.2 mile to a campsite at forest-rimmed Silver King Lake.

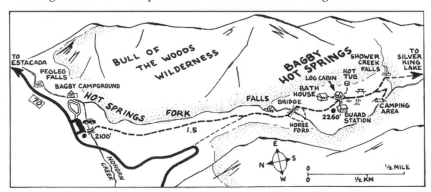

229

96　　Pansy Lake　

Easy (to Pansy Lake)
2.4 miles round trip
500 feet elevation gain
Open mid-May to mid-November
Use: hikers, horses

Moderate (to Bull of the Woods)
7.1-mile loop
2000 feet elevation gain
Open July through October

The romp to this popular mountain lake is easy enough for children, but there's adventure here for hardier hikers as well. A scenic loop continues up to a historic lookout tower in the heart of the Bull of the Woods Wilderness.

This area is part of a 16- to 25-million-year-old volcanic mountain range predating the more famous High Cascade peaks. Erosion has carved up this older range, exposing quartz veins with ore that attracted prospectors in the late 1800s. One of these early visitors was Robert Bagby, who blazed a trail from Bagby Hot Springs (Hike #95) to a cabin he built by this lake. Because of the color of the copper ore he found here, he named his claim the Pansy Blossom Mine—and the lake became known as Pansy Lake. Some say the name "Bull of the Woods" refers to a big elk bagged by Bagby, but others note the phrase was common in Oregon's ox-logging days as a title for a tough crew boss.

From Interstate 205 near Oregon City, take exit 12 and follow signs east 18 miles to Estacada. Go straight through town, continuing 26 miles on Highway 224 to the bridge at Ripplebrook. Keep straight on paved Road 46 for 3.6 miles and then turn right onto Road 63. Follow this paved road straight for 5.6 miles. At a sign for the Pansy Basin Trail turn right onto Road 6340 for 7.8 miles. Then fork right onto Road 6341 for 3.5 mostly paved miles. Park at a large pullout on the right just before an "end maintenance" road sign (*GPS location N44°53.964' W122°06.994'*).

The trail starts at a message board on the opposite side of the road in a magnificent

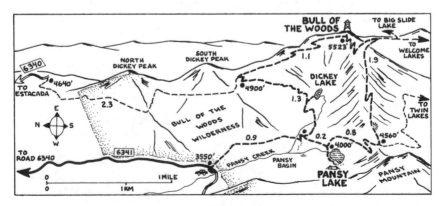

stand of 5-foot-thick Douglas firs and hemlocks. After climbing gradually for 0.8 mile, cross a charming creek and reach the first of three confusing trail junctions. Go left at this first junction (the abandoned path straight ahead dives down to Pansy Basin's mini-meadow). Continue uphill 140 yards, switchbacking to a second fork in the trail. This time veer right (the left-hand fork, marked "549", is the return route of the Bull of the Woods loop). Now continue 400 yards to the third confusing junction, almost within sight of shallow Pansy Lake. A right-hand turn here leads around the lakeshore to a camping area.

If after enjoying the lakeshore you'd like to continue on the loop up to the lookout tower, return to the junction beside Pansy Lake and take the other fork, following a pointer toward Twin Lakes. This path climbs above Pansy Lake at a steady grade for 0.8 mile to trail junction at a wooded pass. Turn left and traverse 1.9 miles up a hillside with occasional views of Mt. Jefferson. At a marked junction just before a ridgecrest, turn left and switchback up 0.7 mile to the summit. The 1942-vintage lookout tower isn't staffed, but the view is panoramic, encompassing every summit from the Three Sisters to Rainier. Below to the east is Big Slide Lake (see Hike #196).

To complete the loop, continue past the lookout on a path descending the ridge to the north. After 1.1 miles *watch carefully for a small signboard on the left marking a side trail*. Turn here, taking this switchbacking path downhill to the left. After 0.8 mile a short spur to the left leads to pretty, brush-rimmed Dickey Lake. Then continue half a mile down to the Pansy Lake Trail and turn right to return to your car.

Other Options

An easier route to the lookout tower starts near Dickey Peaks. Drive almost to the Pansy Basin Trailhead, but instead keep on Road 6340 to its end, following signs for the Bull of the Woods Trailhead. This 3.4-mile path gains only 900 feet.

South Dickey Peak from Pansy Lake.   Opposite: The Bull of the Woods lookout.

97

Red Lake

Easy (to Red Lake)
3.2 miles round trip
1000 feet elevation gain
Open mid-June to early November
Use: hikers, horses, bicycles

Moderate (to Potato Butte)
7.2 miles round trip
1700 feet elevation gain

Hundreds of lakes dot the forested Olallie Lake plateau north of Mt. Jefferson, but Red Lake is one of the few to offer a glimpse of the big snowy mountain itself. And once you've climbed to Red Lake, it's not much further to visit three other lakes on your way up Potato Butte, an old volcano with a far better view across the plateau to Mt. Jeff. Mosquitoes can be a problem the first half of July.

From Interstate 205 near Oregon City, take exit 12 and follow signs east 18 miles to Estacada. Go straight through town, continuing 26 miles on Highway 224 to the bridge at Ripplebrook. Keep straight on Road 46 for another 26.7 paved miles, following signs for Detroit. Beyond the Olallie Lake turnoff 4.9 miles, at a (possibly missing) sign for the Red Lake Trail, turn left on gravel Road 380 for 0.9 mile and watch closely for a small "Red Lake Trail" sign on the left. Park on the opposite shoulder *(GPS location N44°49.279' W121°52.388')*.

If you're driving here from Salem or Bend, turn off Highway 22 in Detroit and follow paved Breitenbush Road 46 for 18.2 miles to the feebly signed Red Lake Trail turnoff on the right.

The trail briefly crosses a clearcut before climbing steeply through an old-growth forest of western hemlock and Douglas fir trees, some of them 5 feet in diameter. After 0.4 mile the path enters a powerline clearing and joins a dirt road. Turn left on the road for 50 feet and then turn right on a spur road for 200 feet to find the continuation of the trail.

The path reenters the woods and climbs steadily for a mile to a plateau where

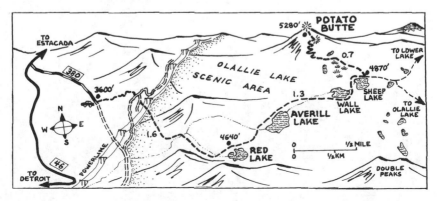

Mt. Jefferson from Potato Butte.   Opposite: Potato Butte from Wall Lake.

huckleberries grow among lodgepole pines. At a big and obvious stump, turn right on a side path to a small beach beside shallow Red Lake. Dragonflies zoom and rough-skinned newts laze in the shallows. Campsites abound.

Having climbed all the way to Red Lake, it's hard not to continue another 1.3 level miles past larger Averill Lake and Wall Lake to Sheep Lake. And once you've reached the far end of Sheep Lake, why not turn left for a climb to a really good viewpoint on Potato Butte? The 0.7-mile trail heads left when it reaches a small meadow (in early summer, a pond) and then switchbacks steeply up a slippery cinder slope to the broad summit with its view of Mt. Hood and Olallie Butte. To see Mt. Jefferson, however, you'll have to hike back down the trail 300 yards and take a spur trail left 50 feet to a slope of boulders. Atop these rocks is the view you really wanted, including most of the lakes you passed on the hike.

Other Options

Backpackers or hardy day hikers can explore the Red Lake Trail further east. It's 1.7 miles from Sheep Lake to Top Lake and the route described in Hike #99.

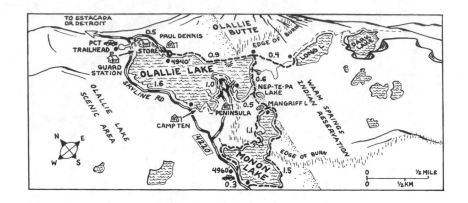

98 Monon Lake

Easy (around Monon Lake)
2.9-mile loop
100 feet elevation gain
Open July to mid-October
Use: hikers, bicycles

Moderate (starting from Olallie Lake)
6.9-mile loop
200 feet elevation gain

As you hike around the many-bayed shore of Monon Lake you'll gain a view of nearby Mt. Jefferson, pass bedrock worn smooth by Ice Age glaciers, and visit an area changed by a 2001 fire. For a longer hike with even better views, start at the old-timey resort on Olallie Lake. Mosquitoes can be a problem in July.

From Interstate 205 near Oregon City, take exit 12 and follow signs east 18 miles to Estacada. Go straight through town, continuing 26 miles on Highway 224 to the bridge at Ripplebrook. Keep straight on paved Road 46 for another 21.4 miles to a large junction with a (possibly missing) sign for Olallie Lake, and turn left onto one-lane Road 4690. (Travelers from the south can reach this junction by taking Breitenbush Road 46 from Highway 22 at Detroit for 23.5 paved miles.) Drive Road 4690 for 6.1 miles of pavement and another 1.9 miles of gravel to a T-shaped junction. Then turn right onto gravel Road 4220 for 5 miles to a junction for the Olallie Lake Resort.

There is no parking for hikers in the resort area to your left—it's reserved for people visiting the rustic store or getting a campsite, yurt, cabin, or rental rowboat. Mile-long Olallie Lake is so pure it's a drinking water source, and as a result, this is the only lake in the area where swimming is banned. Motorboats aren't allowed either, but canoes are common.

To start your hike at Olallie Lake, keep right at the resort junction for 100 yards to a Pacific Crest Trail parking lot. Then walk back across the road to the old guard station (now a rental cabin), take a path along the lakeshore 200 yards to the resort's general store, and follow the shoreline 0.4 mile to the far end of Paul Dennis Campground, where the official lakeshore trail starts at a post behind campsite #14. The view of Mt. Jefferson is especially fine here.

As you hike along Olallie Lake's shore you'll enter the 2001 fire zone, with red fireweed, alder, pine seedlings, and huckleberries thriving among the silver snags. At the far end of the lake ignore a side trail to the left to Long and Dark Lakes—a path open only to those who have purchased a tribal fishing permit at the store. After following the lakeshore another 0.4 mile, turn left for 0.2 mile to a junction with Monon Lake's 2.9-mile shoreline loop trail. Go clockwise around Monon Lake and then return as you came, along Olallie Lake's scenic east shore.

If you'd rather cut to the chase and focus your hike on Monon Lake's 2.9-mile loop, don't park near Olallie Lake at all. Drive straight past the resort turnoff for 1.3 miles, ignore a turnoff for Peninsula Campground on the left, and continue straight on a rougher dirt road 0.4 mile to a pullout on the left for the Monon Lake Trail (*GPS location N44°47.688' W121°47.391'*).

Hike to the left, heading clockwise around Monon Lake. After half a mile you'll enter the burned area, which also has the best views. Note the exposed bedrock, scratched by glaciers 6000 years ago. Keep right around the lake until you hit the dirt road and then turn right for 0.3 mile to your car.

Olallie Butte from Monon Lake.   Opposite: Mt. Jefferson from Olallie Lake.

99   Top Lake

Easy (to Top Lake)
3.1-mile loop
500 feet elevation gain
Open July to mid-October
Use: hikers, horses

Moderate (to Double Peaks)
5.3-mile loop
1100 feet elevation gain

Half a dozen woodsy lakes and a viewpoint of Mt. Jefferson make this loop on the Pacific Crest Trail fun even for children—if you wait until after the July mosquito season ends. Hikers with extra energy can add a short but very steep side trip up Double Peaks for an even better panorama of the lake-dotted Olallie Lake Scenic Area.

If you're driving here from the Portland area, take Interstate 205 near Oregon City to exit 12 and follow signs east 18 miles to Estacada. Go straight through town, continuing 26 miles on Highway 224 to the bridge at Ripplebrook. Keep straight on paved Road 46 for another 21.4 miles to a large junction with a (possibly missing) sign for Olallie Lake, and turn left onto one-lane Road 4690. Drive this road for 6.1 miles of pavement and another 1.9 miles of gravel to a T-shaped junction. Then turn right onto gravel Road 4220 for 5.1 miles to the junction for the Olallie Lake Resort. Keep right for 0.3 mile and look closely for a small wooden sign on the right marking the Red Lake Trail. Park at a pullout on the road's opposite shoulder (*GPS location N44°48.685' W121°47.668'*).

If you're driving here from Salem or Bend, turn off Highway 22 in Detroit, follow Breitenbush Road 46 for 23.5 paved miles, turn right onto Road 4690 for 8.1 miles, and turn right on Road 4220 for 5.4 miles.

The Red Lake Trail ambles through a high-elevation forest of mountain hemlock and lodgepole pine where masses of blue huckleberries ripen in late August. After passing three ponds, keep right at a possibly unmarked trail junction (the

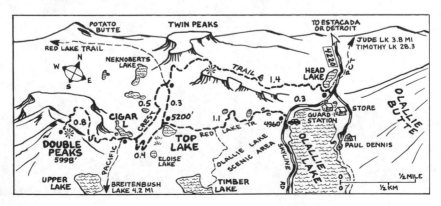

Double Peaks from Top Lake.   Opposite: Mt. Jefferson from Double Peaks.

small left-hand path deadends in 0.7 mile at Timber Lake). Soon the main trail reaches Top Lake, with a pebbly beach and a view ahead to Double Peaks. This is a nice spot to wade, pick berries, or simply watch dragonflies zoom about.

At the far end of Top Lake you'll reach a T-shaped junction. To take the easy loop back, simply turn right and keep right at every junction you find. You'll join the Pacific Crest Trail, pass a rockslide, and descend along a cliff-edged ridge with a view of Mt. Jefferson. Stop here to notice how the clifftop rock has been rounded and scratched by the Ice Age glaciers that buried this whole landscape with moving ice just 6000 years ago. Then continue down the trail to Head Lake, turn right, and walk along the road 0.3 mile to your car.

To take the longer loop to Double Peaks, turn left at the Top Lake junction. This trail switchbacks up to the Pacific Crest Trail, where you turn left for 100 feet to a sign announcing Cigar Lake, a rock-lined, dumbbell-shaped lake. Walk 200 feet past the Cigar Lake sign and leave the PCT, turning right onto a faint side path toward Double Peaks. This path soon forks, but keep left until it starts scrambling steeply up a slope. The path levels off for a few hundred yards along a clifftop rim to the right before a final, very steep ascent between rockslides to Double Peak's ridgecrest. To the right is the first summit, with a view to Mt. Hood and the jumbled peaks of the Bull of the Woods Wilderness. To the left is the taller summit, with an aerial view of the route of your hike.

When you hike back down to Cigar Lake, follow the Pacific Crest Trail to the left for 1.9 miles to continue the loop.

Other Options

Backpackers or hardy day hikers can explore the Red Lake Trail further west across this forested plateau. It's 1.7 miles from Top Lake to Sheep Lake and the route described in Hike #97. Another option is to hike the PCT south to Breitenbush Lake. It's 2.3 miles from Cigar Lake to the Ruddy Hill junction described in Hike #202.

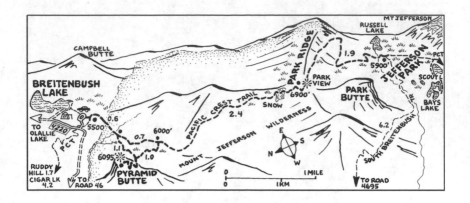

100 Jefferson Park Ridge

Easy (to Pyramid Butte)
4-mile loop
800 feet elevation gain
Open mid-July to mid-October
Use: hikers, horses

Moderate (to Park Ridge)
7.4 miles round trip
1400 feet elevation gain

Difficult (to Jefferson Park)
11.2 miles round trip
2400 feet elevation gain

Mt. Jefferson fills half the sky from the green alpine meadows and sparkling lakes of Jefferson Park. A heavily-used portion of the Pacific Crest Trail climbs across Park Ridge to this patch of paradise. For a less difficult hike, consider setting your goal as the spectacular viewpoint atop Park Ridge itself. An even easier alternative is a short loop on a meadow-lined section of the old Skyline Trail past Pyramid Butte. Be forewarned, however, that the trailhead can be reached only by determined drivers in high-clearance vehicles, and that Jefferson Park is crowded on summer weekends. Group size in Jeff Park is limited to 12 hearts, counting hikers, pets, and stock.

From Interstate 205 near Oregon City, take exit 12 and follow signs east 18 miles to Estacada. Go straight through town, continuing 26 miles on Highway 224 to the bridge at Ripplebrook. Keep straight on paved Road 46 for another 21.4 miles to a large junction with a sign for Olallie Lake, and turn left onto one-lane Road 4690. Drive this road for 6.1 miles of pavement and another 1.9 miles of gravel to a T-shaped junction. Then turn right onto gravel Road 4220 for 10.5 miles. The final 2 miles of this road are *extremely* rough, impassable for most passenger cars. Beyond the Breitenbush Lake Campground entrance 0.3 mile—and immediately after the PCT crossing—turn left to the trailhead's cinder turnaround *(GPS location N44°45.881' W121°47.132')*.

If you're driving here from Salem or Bend, turn off Highway 22 in Detroit,

Mt. Jefferson from Russell Lake.   Opposite: Old sign at the Pyramid Butte junction.

follow Breitenbush Road 46 north for 16.7 miles to a pass with a junction under powerlines, with a "Mt. Hood National Forest" entrance sign. Turn right on gravel Skyline Road 4220 for a mile to an open gate where gravel turns to dirt. The final 5.4 miles of this road to the Mt. Jefferson Wilderness parking area can be impassably muddy and rutted in wet or snowy conditions.

From the trailhead's cinder turnaround, start at the hiker-symbol sign on the right. Sign in at a registration box after 100 feet. Then follow the PCT through subalpine woods with lots of lovely openings. Heather and blue lupine bloom here in mid-summer and masses of huckleberries ripen shortly afterwards.

After 0.6 mile the path crosses a footbridge and forks. To the left is the newer, more direct PCT route to Park Ridge and Jefferson Park. If you have the time, or if you're interested in a shorter loop, turn right on the old, unmarked Skyline Trail. This older path meanders past a gushing spring and several meadows to a junction at the base of Pyramid Butte. Here you can either turn right for the steep, switchbacking half-mile climb to a cliff-edge viewpoint atop Pyramid Butte, or you can head left to climb back to the PCT.

If you're continuing up the PCT to Park Ridge you'll gradually climb past timberline. Alpine heather, white partridge foot, purple aster, and red paintbrush give way to a rocky landscape with snowfields. Follow cairns carefully to keep on the trail. Finally reach Park Ridge's windy crest and a breathtaking view ahead to Jefferson Park.

Beyond this point the PCT descends 1.9 miles to the meadows beside swimmable Russell Lake, first and largest of the park's pools. If you're backpacking, tent at designated sites in the woods, away from the fragile meadows. Camping is banned on the peninsulas of Scout and Bays Lakes. Campfires are strongly discouraged and are banned altogether within 100 feet of water or trails.

Other Options

Two other routes reach Jefferson Park. The less crowded South Breitenbush Trail climbs 2800 feet in 6.2 miles. To find the trailhead, drive paved Road 46 south of Ripplebrook for 33.1 miles (or drive north from Detroit 11.5 miles), and take gravel Road 4685 east for 5 miles. The heavily used Whitewater Trail to Jefferson Park climbs 1800 feet in 5.1 miles. To find it, drive Highway 22 east of Detroit 10.3 miles and turn left on gravel Whitewater Road 2243 to its end.

Barrier-Free Trails

People with limited physical abilities need not miss the fun of exploring new trails. Here are 36 paths within a two-hour drive of Portland accessible to everyone. Most of the trails are paved and several include interpretive signs about natural features or history. Some are open to bicycles. Unless otherwise noted, the paths are open year round. For more information, contact the trail's managing agency. For trails in the Portland area, call the Portland Park Bureau's Adaptive and Inclusive Recreation program at 503-823-4328 (voice or TDD).

PORTLAND AREA (map on page 15)

A. Tualatin Hills Nature Park. The 0.7-mile Oak Trail and the 0.8-mile Vine Maple Tr are both paved, with decked viewpoints of creeks and ponds. At Cooper Mtn Nature Park, all trails are barrier free. See Hike #12. 🚲

B. Fanno Creek Greenway. Follow a paved path along Fanno Creek in Beaverton 4 miles. A side path near Hall Blvd leads to visitable Fanno Farm House, built 1859. Take Denney exit of Hwy 217, go W downhill, park by fish-shaped bike rack. Take trail left 0.7 mi to Hall Blvd, cross at light to Albertsons, continue 3.3 mi to Tigard's Woodard Park. A planned extension will continue to the Tualatin River. 🚲

C. Trillium Trail. Two interpretive nature paths loop 0.3 mile through the woods of Tryon Creek State Park. Start as for Hike #9 but stay on the paved path.

D. George Rogers Park. A paved 0.8-mile path along the Willamette River starts at a historic iron smelter. Take Hwy 43 (alias Macadam Ave, alias State St) to Lake Oswego, turn on Ladd, and turn right on Furnace to a footbridge. 🚲

E. Eastbank Esplanade. A paved path extends 1.8 mile north from OMSI along the Willamette River (and sometimes *on* the river, using floats) to the Steel Bridge. Another 3.2-mile section of the path heads south from OMSI to Oaks Bottom (Hike #8) to connect with the Springwater Trail. 🚲

F. Powell Butte. The Mountain View Trail climbs 0.6 mile to a broad, grassy summit with views, where the paved path ends. See Hike #10. 🚲

G. Springwater Trail. This paved 21-mile path follows an old railroad grade from Oaks Bottom through SE Portland along Johnson Creek, past Powell Butte, and through Gresham's City Park to Boring. See Hike #10. 🚲

H. The Grotto. Gardens, viewpoints, and Catholic statuary line a peaceful 0.9-mile path. An elevator accesses an upper loop, but has a $4 fee ($3 seniors, $2.50 kids age 6-11). Drive or take Tri-Met #12 out NE Sandy one block past 82nd.

I. Champoeg Heritage Area. Hike #13 has three barrier-free options: take a paved path from the Visitor Center 0.6 mile through a meadow to a pavilion, take a gravel 0.4-mile nature loop from the campground, or start at the campground and take a paved path 1.5 miles east along the Willamette River. 🚲

J. Willamette Mission Park. Park as for Hike #14. Either take a 1.2-mile paved path east through a filbert grove to the Willamette River ferry landing, or go west on a 3-mile paved loop through riverside woods. 🚲

SOUTHWEST WASHINGTON (map on page 53)

K. Burnt Bridge Creek. Vancouver's Greenway paved path extends 8 miles

Boardwalk on the Trail of Two Forests near Ape Cave.

through creekside meadows. Drive I-5 to Vancouver's 39th Street exit, turn left for 1.5 mi, turn right on Fruit Valley Rd for 1.7 mi, and turn right on Bernie Dr. ۶

L. Lacamas Lake. The 3.1-mi gravel Lacamas Heritage Trail along this quiet lake is barrier-free, visiting a lakeshore gazebo and dock. See Hike #16. ۶

M. Coldwater Ridge. From the Learning & Science Ctr, the 0.3-mile paved Winds of Change loop tours a blast-killed forest with mountain views. See Hike #20.

N. Coldwater Lake. The paved 0.2-mile Birth of a Lake Trail ends at a pier into a lake created by Mt. St. Helens' 1980 eruption. Drive Hwy 504 past the Coldwater Ridge Learning Center 2 miles and turn left. See Hike #20. Open Apr-Oct.

O. Johnston Ridge. For close-up views of Mt. St. Helens' crater, take the paved but steep and challenging 0.4-mile Eruption Trail loop from the popular Johnston Ridge Visitor Center. See Hike #21. Open June-Oct.

P. Trail of Two Forests. This 0.3-mile interp loop tours a lava cast forest in a 1900-year-old flow. Drive as to Hike #23 but park 0.6 mile before Ape Cave.

Q. Lava Canyon. This spectacular path leads to waterfalls in a mudflow-scoured canyon (see Hike #27). The path is paved for the first 0.5 mile, with boardwalks and interpretive signs. Open May-Nov.

R. Meta Lake. In Mt. St. Helen's recovering blast zone, take a paved 0.4-mile path from a scorched miner's car to a lake. Open June-Oct.

S. Lewis River Viewpoints. Three graveled paths lead to waterfall views. Park as for Hike #31 for the 0.2-mile trail to massive Lower Lewis River Falls. Then drive 5.5 miles west on Rd 90 to Big Creek Trailhead for a 0.7-mile path from a 110-foot falls to a river overlook. Then drive 3.8 miles farther west on Road 90 to the turnoff for the 0.2-mile Curly Creek Falls trail.

COLUMBIA GORGE (map on pages 102-103)

T. St. Cloud Trail. A half-mile loop through homestead orchards offers views across the Columbia to Multnomah Falls. Drive 23 miles east of Vancouver (or 14 miles west of Bonneville Dam) on Washington Hwy 14.

U. Sams-Walker Trail. A 1.1-mile loop tours forest, wetlands, and an orchard along the Columbia. Drive 27 miles E of Vancouver (or 10 miles W of Bonneville

Dam) on Hwy 14. At milepost 33, turn south on Skamania Landing Rd 0.2 mile.

V. Beacon Rock Park. A paved 1-mile interpretive trail loops along the Columbia riverbank from the day-use area, and a 0.5-mile path climbs from the old campground to a viewpoint at Little Beacon Rock (see Hike #41). Also, horse trails from the equestrian trailhead are barrier free (see Hike #40).   ڶ

W. Fort Cascades. Near Bonneville Dam, this 1.2-mile loop visits the site of an 1856 Army fort and passes a petroglyph. Drive 3.2 mile west of Bridge of the Gods on Washington Highway 14.

X. Latourell Falls. Park as for Hike #44, but take a 0.3-mile path *downhill* to Lower Latourell Falls and on to a picnic area, where steps block the route.

Y. Wahkeena Falls. Another glorious Columbia Gorge waterfall. Park at the Wahkeena Falls Trailhead for Hike #46, where a 0.2-mile trail climbs to a stone footbridge beneath Wahkeena Falls.

Z. Tooth Rock. Follow the historic Columbia River Hwy (now reopened as a paved trail) a mile to a cliff-edge viewpoint on a viaduct. See Hike #50.   ڶ

AA. Columbia River Highway. Follow a 2.5-mile segment of the historic Columbia River Highway (now reopened as a paved trail) along I-84 from Cascade Locks to Eagle Creek. The trail starts at the on-ramp of exits 41 and 44.

BB. Mosier Twin Tunnels. Follow a 4.7-mile segment of the historic Columbia River Highway to a viewpoint at two restored tunnels. See Hike #57.   ڶ

CC. Catherine Creek. A paved 0.8-mile loop has great views. See Hike #61.

DD. Columbia Gorge Discovery Center. Park at this museum (off Interstate 84 at The Dalles exit 84) and take a paved path past ponds and along the Columbia River for 3 miles, almost to The Dalles' downtown.   ڶ

MOUNT HOOD - WEST (map on page 155)

EE. Wildwood Area. Two paved interpretive loop trails, each ¾ mile long, tour streambank and wetlands along the Salmon River. See Hike #64.   ڶ

FF. Lost Creek Nature Trail. A barrier-free campground and picnic area features a 0.5-mile paved and boardwalk loop to two barrier-free fishing piers at a creek with snags from 1790 Mt. Hood eruption. Drive as to Burnt Lake (Hike #70) but stop at Lost Creek Campground. Open May-Nov.

GG. Lost Lake Old Growth Trail. This 1-mile trail among cedars is half gravel, half boardwalk with decked pullouts. For a 2-mile loop, return via the lakeshore trail (barrier-free from the group camp to the viewpoint). Drive to Lost Lake (Hike #74), but keep left at the lake to the east picnic area parking lot. Open June-Oct.

HH. Trillium Lake. Views of Mt Hood highlight a 1.7-mile gravel loop around the lake. The route passes barrier-free picnic tables, camping sites, and fishing piers. Drive 3 mi east of Govt Camp on Hwy 26, follow signs 1.6 mile to Trillium Lk CG, and park at a picnic area. Open June-Oct.

II. Little Crater and Timothy Lakes. A paved 0.2-mile path leads to Little Crater Lake (see Hike #78), but a fence blocks access to the Pacific Crest Trail. The 10.8-mi loop around Timothy Lake is level and barrier free except for a rough 0.2 mile from Oak Fork CG to the PCT. Open May-Nov.

CLACKAMAS FOOTHILLS (map on page 215)

JJ. Bagby Hot Springs. Steps block the hot springs, but the first 1.2-mile of the lovely entrance path is barrier free, if challenging. See Hike #95.

103 More Hikes

Adventurous hikers can discover plenty of additional trails within a two-hour drive of the Portland/Vancouver area. The list below covers the most interesting, from urban promenades to rugged wilderness paths. Directions are brief, so be extra careful to bring appropriate maps. Estimated mileages are one-way. Most paths are open only in summer and fall, but symbols beside the entries note which hikes are open all year, and which are suitable for kids, horses, bicycles, or backpackers. For more information, check with the trail's administrative agency.

The appropriate ranger district or other offices are abbreviated as follows: (B) — Barlow, (C) — Clackamas, (CG) — Columbia Gorge National Scenic Area, (D) — Washington Department of Natural Resources, (HR) — Hood River, (MA) — Mt Adams, (MS) — Mt St Helens National Monument, (N) — Nature Conservancy, (O) — Oregon State Parks, (P) — Portland Parks and Recreation, (S) — Sauvie Island Wildlife Area, (V) — Vancouver-Clark Parks 360-487-8311, (W) — Wind River, (Z) — Zigzag. Agency phone numbers not listed here are on page 13.

Easy Moderate Difficult

PORTLAND AREA (map on page 15)

101. Wapato Greenway. A grassy 2.4-mile path circles marshy Virginia Lk on Sauvie Island. Expect birds, some cattle. Drive as to Hike #2 but go straight on Sauvie Is Rd 0.5 mile past the Reeder Rd turnoff. (S)

102. Audubon Bird Sanctuary. Three miles of paths loop through 101 acres of woods from the Portland Audubon nature center on Cornell Rd, next to the Upper Macleay trailhead for Hike #5. (503-292-9453)

103. Terwilliger Trail. A paved 3.5-mile promenade parallels Terwilliger Boulevard from Duniway Park (a block from the Marquam Nature Shelter in Hike #7) to Barbur Blvd. (P)

104. Tualatin River Refuge. Drive Hwy 99W past Tigard to milepost 14, tour visitor ctr, hike 1-mi paved trail to river, bird views. (503-625-5944)

Tualatin River Refuge (#104).

105. Crystal Springs Rhododendron Garden. Stroll 1 mi of trails in 8-acre park with bridges, lakes, rhodies. From Powell Blvd, drive south a mile on SE 28th. Expect a $4 entry fee Thurs-Mon from March through May. (P)

106. Elk Rock Island. Explore a Willamette River peninsula on a 1-mi loop with cottonwoods and herons. Drive McLoughlin Blvd S, take River Rd exit 4 blocks, turn R on Sparrow St to corner of 19th Ave. (P)

107. Mary Young Park. State park on the Willamette River has 2.3-mile path around perimeter amid maples and woodland wildflowers. Drive

2.5 mi S of Lake Oswego on Hwy 43 (alias Macadam Ave). (O)

108. Camassia Natural Area. Tall blue camas blooms Apr-May on a trail network among ponds in this 27-acre preserve at the end of Walnut St off Sunset Ave in West Linn. No pets or flower picking. (N)

109. McIver Park. Start at a fish hatchery and end along the Clackamas River on this 4.2-mi wooded loop, muddy in winter due to horse use. From Estacada take Hwy 211 S toward Molalla 1 mi, follow signs to park and then to hatchery. Trail goes around hatchery to right. (O)

110. Sandy River Delta. Stroll 2 miles amid cottonwoods to a Maya Lin bird blind where the Sandy and Columbia Rivers meet. Start on the north side of Interstate 84 at Lewis & Clark Park exit 18. (O)

SOUTHWEST WASHINGTON (map on page 53)

111. Washougal Dike. Start at a 500-ft dock, then hike or bike a Columbia riverfront dike past an industrial area 5.5 mi to Steigerwald Lk refuge. Take Hwy 14 to Washougal and turn R on 15th St. (CG)

112. Silver Star Mountain via Grouse Creek Vista. This 8.3-mile loop on the south side of the mountain gains 2100 ft (see Hike #17 map). Drive Hwy 14 east to milepost 16, turn L at the Washougal exit, go straight 6.9 mi on what becomes Washougal River Rd, turn L at a sign for Bear Prairie, climb 3.2 mi, turn L on Skamania Mines Rd for 2.7 mi, turn L on gravel 1200 Rd, and keep L for 5.7 rocky mi to Grouse Cr Vista. Park here and hike an abandoned road up to Silver Star Mtn. Return on a loop via Sturgeon Rock and the Tarbell Trail. (MS)

113. Tarbell Trail. Woodsy 5-mi path to 92-ft Hidden Falls (see Hike #17) gains 700 ft, loses 500. Drive Hwy 503 N of Battleground 5.6 mi, turn R on Rock Cr Rd for 8.6 mi, turn R on Sunset Falls Rd 1.9 mi, turn R on Dole Valley Rd 2.4 mi, go left 2.1 mi to Tarbell Picnic Area, where a Washington Discover Pass is required for your car. (D)

114. Silver Star Mtn via Bluff Mountain. Open ridge E of mtn (see Hike #17) has views, flowers. The 7.3-mi tr loses 500 ft, gains 1700. Drive Hwy 503 N of Battleground 5.6 mi, turn R on Rock Cr Rd 8.6 mi, turn R on Sunset Falls Rd 7 mi, turn R on pot-holed Rd 41 for 9.4 mi to pass. Walk a barricaded road 2 mi along a crest to the old trailhead. (MS)

115. Siouxon Peak. Easier route to Hike #19 viewpt gains 1300 ft in 2.2 mi. Drive as to Observation Pk (#32) but where Rd 64 forks, veer R to keep on Rd 64 another 4 mi and turn R on Rd 6403 for 2.6 mi. (MS)

116. Mount Mitchell. This meadowed summit boasts a terrific view of Mt. St. Helens, but the private access road to this hike was gated in 2011, so instead of a 3.1-mile route to the summit, hikers now face a difficult 8-mile route from the trailhead for Hike #115. (D)

117. Goat Marsh Lake. 1-mi stroll to lilypad lake reflecting Mt St Helens. Drive as to Hike #22, but go only 0.6 mi on Rd 8123. (MS)

118. Loowit Trail. Backpack around Mt St Helens on this 29.5-mi loop. See Hikes #22, 24-26, and 28. (MS).

119. Butte Camp Trail. Climb 1550 ft in 3.7 mi to Mt. St. Helens timberline mdws and the Loowit Tr, passing a camp beside Butte Camp Dome (see Hike #22 map). Drive as to #24 but go 3.1 mi on Rd 81. (MS)

120. Strawberry Mountain. Gain 1400 ft in 2.5 mi to viewpt of Mt St Helens' blast zone. Drive as to Spirit L (Hike #29), but only go 4.7 mi on Rd 99 to Bear Mdw, hike R on Boundary Tr 0.5 mi, turn R. (MS)

121. Goat Mountain. Follow blast zone rim 5.5 mi to Deadmans L. Gain 1500 ft, lose 800. Drive to #29 but turn R on Rd 26 for 5 mi. (MS)

122. Ghost Lake. From Norway Pass Trailhead (see Hike #29 map) hike E for 1.5 easy mi on Boundary Tr along blast zone edge to lk. (MS)

123. Craggy Peak. Views await on 4.9-mi path to this Dark Divide peak. Gain 1700 ft. Drive as to Hike #29, but go 5.4 mi on Rd 25, veer R on Rd 93 for 18.7 mi, turn L on Rd 9327 for 0.3 mi. (MS)

124. Boundary Trail. Backpack 56 mi from Mt St Helens to Mt Adams, following Trail #1 along the Dark Divide. The route connects with Hikes #21, 29, 122, 30, 123, 126-128. Ends at Council Lake. (MS)

125. Lower Lewis River Trail. Quiet 9.5-mi part of river trail passes 1921 Bolt Camp Shelter, old-growth woods. Plan shuttle on Rd 90 between trailhds, 1.1 and 9.1 mi W of Lewis R Falls (#31) trailhead. (MS)

126. Quartz Creek. Steep up-and-down path through old-growth canyon leads 4.5 mi to creekside camp, continues 6 mi to Boundary Tr. Drive to Lewis R Falls (#31), continue 2.7 mi on Rd 90 to bridge. (MS)

127. Quartz Creek Ridge. A well-graded path climbs 1700 feet in 2.8 miles to a viewpoint, then continues 4 miles to the Summit Prairie lookout site. Drive 5 miles past Lewis River Falls (Hike #31) on Rd 90, turn left on Rd 9025, and then keep right for 5.5 miles. (MS)

128. Council Bluff. Hike old rd from Council Lake to view of Mt Adams, up 900 ft in 1.5 mi. Drive past #31 on Rd 90 for 17 mi, go L on Rd 23 for 3.2 mi, turn L on Rd 2334, keep R to CG. (Randle Ranger Dist)

129. Killen Creek Meadows. Popular 3.1-mi Killen Cr Tr climbs 1500 ft to vast alpine mdws on N side of Mt Adams. Drive past #31 on Rd 90 17 mi, go L on Rd 23 for 4.7 mi, turn R 5.8 mi on Rd 2329. (MA)

130. Lookingglass Lake. A 2012 fire has left black snags and possible trail closures in this area. Hike up the Shorthorn Tr 2.8 mi, go L on the Round-the-Mtn Tr 2.2 mi, and go L for 0.8 mi past Madcat Mdw to a lake reflecting Mt Adams. Route gains 1500 ft, loses 600. Drive as to Hike #38 but park at Morrison Creek Campground. (MA)

131. Horseshoe Meadow. Follow Pacific Cr Tr up 1400 ft in 4.3 mi to Mt Adams timberline. Take Rd 23 N of Trout Lake 14 mi. (MA)

132. Round-the-Mountain Trail. Backpack ¾ of the way around Mt Adams (rivers, Indian Res block final ¼.) on 27-mi route from Bird Cr Mdws (Hike#38) past Hikes #129-131 to Devils Gardens. (MA)

133. Steamboat Mountain. Gain 800 ft in 1.2 mi to cliff-rimmed lookout site. Drive as to Cultus L (#36) but at end of Rd 30 turn *left* on Rd 24 for 3.5 mi, veer L 1 mi on Rd 8854, go L 1.4 mi on Rd 021 to its end. (MA)

134. Sawtooth Mountain. Hike Pacific Cr Tr S through Indian Heaven huckleberry fields, return via craggy pk with view. 5.2-mi loop gains 1200 ft. Drive as to Cultus L (#36) but only go 0.5 mi on Rd 24. (MA)

135. Placid Lake. Stroll 0.6 mi to this lake in the Indian Heaven Wilderness; if you like, continue 0.4 mi and turn R for 0.5 to little Chenamus Lake. Drive as to Cultus Lake (#36) but when pavement ends, stay on Rd 30 for 2.3 mi and turn R at a "Placid Lk" pointer for 1.1 mi of gravel and 200 yds of bumpy dirt (N46°02.926' W121°48.551'). (MA)

136. Indian Racetrack via Falls Creek Trailhead. Rough 2.3-mi tr gains 700 ft to Indian Heaven lakelet, mdw where tribes raced horses until 1928. For view, continue 0.8 mi up to rd, lookout tower on Red Mtn. Drive as to Junction Lk (#35) but go 5 mi on Rd 65 past jct with Rd 60. (MA)

137. Indian Racetrack via PCT. Hike Pacific Cr Tr 3 mi north, turn left 0.5 mi to Indian Racetrack mdw, lakelet. For 7.5-mi loop, turn L to Red Mtn lookout, then descend rugged Rd 6048 to Rd 60 and car. Drive as to Junction Lake (#35) but only go 2 mi on Rd 60. (MA)

138. Nestor Peak. Gain 2000 ft in 4.1 mi to a shed with a view of Mt Hood and the Gorge. Cross Hood R toll br, go L 1.5 mi on Hwy 14, go R 2.2 mi on Hwy 141A, go L 2 mi on Hwy 141, turn L 3 mi to Buck Cr Trhd No. 1. Follow trail that crosses Rd M1000 and follows N1300 for 1.9 mi to end, go L on tr on top. For loop, return on roads N1500 and N1000. (D)

139. Big Huckleberry Mtn. Follow the Pacific Cr Tr 3.1 mi (gaining 1420 ft) to a viewpt of Mt. Adams, Col Gorge. Drive as to Hike #35 but take Rd 65 past Panther Cr CG only 2 mi, turn R on Rd 68 for 4.5 mi. (MA)

140. Grassy Knoll. Climb 1200 ft in 2.2 mi to this viewpoint half-

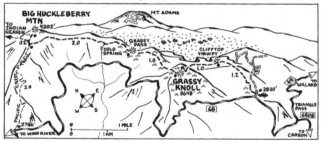

way between Mt. Adams and Mt. Hood. From Hwy 14, turn N through Carson on Hwy 30 for 4.2 mi, turn R on Bear Cr Rd 6808 (gated in winter) for 3.6 paved mi and 7.2 mi of gravel to Triangle Pass, turn L on Rd 68 for 2.1 mi, turn R on Rd 511 for 50 ft. (MA)

141. Bunker Hill. This trail to a wooded knob overlooking the Wind River arboretum gains 1400 ft in 1.7 mi. Drive 8.5 mi north of Carson on Rd 30, turn left 1.5 mi to the ranger station, then turn right on Rd 43 for 0.6 mi, and finally turn right to the Pacific Crest Trail. (W)

142. Dry Creek Trail. Follow path along large cr through old-growth woods 4 mi. For 13-mi loop, continue up Big Hollow Tr to Observation Pk, gaining 3000 ft. Park at Trapper Creek's equestrian trailhead on Rd 5401, where a NW Forest Pass is req'd (see Hike #32 map). (W)

143. Soda Peaks Lake. This back-door route (see also Hike #32 map)

Easy Moderate Difficult

gains 700 ft to craggy Soda Pks, descends 400 ft to lake on 2.2-mi path. Drive 8.5 mi N of Carson on Rd 30, turn L on Hemlock Rd for 0.3 mi, turn R on Szydlo Rd 54 for 13 mi to the marked trailhead. (W)

144. Three Corner Rock. Follow the Pacific Crest Trail to a former lookout site with views of 5 snowpeaks and glimpses of the Columbia Gorge. Drive N across the Bridge of the Gods, turn R on Hwy 14 for 1.5 mi, turn L on Rock Cr Dr for 0.3 mi, turn L on Foster Cr Rd for 0.9 mi, turn L on Red Bluff Rd 0.3 mi, and veer R on gravel Rd CG2000 for 10 mi to its crest at Rock Cr Pass. Then go straight on Rd CG2090 for 0.3 mi to a pass with a pullout. Hike to the R on the PCT for 1.5 mi and turn R for 0.7 mi to the summit. (D)

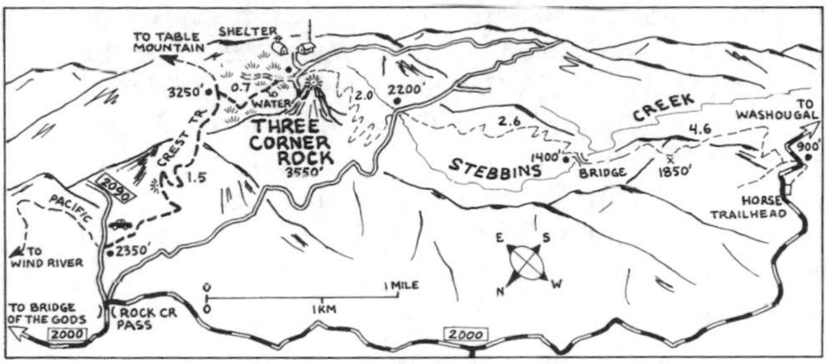

145. Stebbins Creek. Woodsy 9.2-mi trail follows ridges up to Three Corner Rock (Hike #144), gaining 3100 ft and crossing Stebbins Cr twice. Drive Hwy 14 E of Vancouver 17 mi to Washougal, turn L on Washougal River Rd for 22 paved miles, and fork to the R on gravel Rd 2000 for 3.2 mi. Washington Discovery Pass required. (D)

COLUMBIA GORGE (map on pages 102-103)

146. Munra Point. This great, grassy ridge-end viewpoint requires an 1800-ft climb on an unmaintained scramble trail. Park as for Wahclella Falls (Hike #49), take the Gorge Trail 1.5 miles west, turn left 200 yards before Moffett Creek, and climb 1.5 miles. (CG)

147. Rudolph Spur. Rough 11-mi loop gains 3600 ft. Hike up Ruckel Cr Tr (#52), but as soon as tr reaches Benson Plateau turn L past blazes onto faint, unmaintained tr down Rudolph Spur's ridge. Turn L on PCT, go L on Gorge Tr to complete loop. Adventurers only! (CG)

148. Dry Creek Falls. An easy 5.4-mi loop from Cascade Locks follows the Pacific Crest Trail to a little-known waterfall that isn't dry. Park at the Bridge of the Gods, take the PCT south 2.1 mi, and detour R on an old road 0.3 mi to the 50-foot falls. Then return down the old road 2 mi to Cascade Locks and walk L through town to your car. (CG)

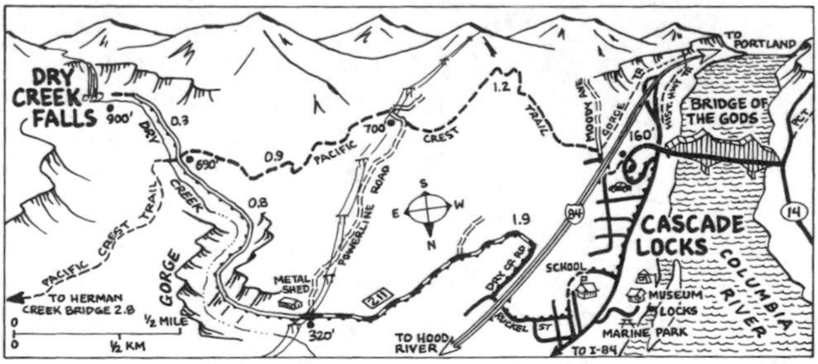

149. Indian Mountain. Trail to stunning viewpt of Mt Hood gains 600 ft in 1 mi from Indian Sprs CG. Drive very rough Rd 1310 from Wahtum Lk (Hike #54) for 3 mi, or hike PCT 3.4 mi from Wahtum Lk. (CG)

150. Carson Hot Springs. Most routes to this natural hot springs on the bank of the Wind River are blocked by private land. The public route is not recommended either, because it requires fording the Wind River. Drive Hwy 14 E of the Bridge of the Gods 8 mi to milepost 49, turn L on Hot Springs Rd 1.2 mile, turn R into the resort's entrance 300 yds, and turn R on a narrow, switchbacking side road 300 yds. Park at the bottom of the hill, walk up the riverbank 0.1 mi, and wade. (CG)

151. Wind Mountain. A rough 1-mile trail gains 1120 ft to one of the Col Gorge's best views, on a knoll near Dog Mtn. Touch nothing, as the summit is sacred to local tribes. From Cascade Locks, cross Bridge of the Gods and turn R on Hwy 14 for 7.7 mi. Between mileposts 50 and 51, turn left on paved Wind Mtn Rd. After 1.1 mi, keep R. In another 0.4 mi turn R on paved Girl Scout Rd for 0.2 mi to a large gravel parking area in a pass. Park here and walk ahead, following a very rough road 200 yards to the steep, unmarked trail on the R. (CG)

152. Wyeth Trail to North Lake. Steep 5.7-mi tr gains 3800 ft to woodsy lake. Continue, keeping R at all jcts, to complete 14.7-mi loop via Green Pt Mtn viewpoint. Take Exit 51 of I-84 to Wyeth CG. (CG)

153. Shellrock Mountain. Take exit 51 of I-84 and park at Wyeth Campground. A trail under powerlines includes a ladder up to the old Col R Hwy. Walk E to find tr up to 1872 wagon rd. Continue E to find tr up to viewpt. Gain 1100 ft in 1.3 mi. (CG)

154. Starvation Creek to Viento Park. Hikable/bikable 1.1-mile section of the historic Columbia River Highway starts at Starvation Cr Falls (Hike #55) and traverses east to the Viento Park exit of I-5. (O)

155. Rainy Lake. Hike past a campable lake and keep left at junctions 1.4 mi to a viewpoint atop Green Pt Mtn, gaining 700 ft. From Hood River take 13th St toward Odell 3.4 mi to a bridge, fork R past Tucker Park 6.3 mi, fork R toward Dee across the river, turn R on Punchbowl Road 1.4 mi, and continue on gravel Rd 2820 for 1.5 mi. (CG)

156. Weldon Wagon Road. A historic roadbed, now a trail, climbs 2.5 mi across wildflower slopes, gaining 1050 ft. From I-84, take the Hood River Bridge across the Columbia and turn left on Hwy 14 for 1.7 mi. Then turn R on Alt Hwy 141 for 2.2 mi and veer left for 4 mi. Just before the bridge in Husum, turn R on gravel Indian Cr Rd for 0.6 mi and fork L for 0.4 mi to a parking pullout on the L. (Klickitat County, 509-773-4616)

157. Hood River Mountain. A 4.1-mi loop gains 600 ft to wildflower mdws overlooking the Hood R Valley, but the trail is on private land, so access may be revoked at any time. From Hood River, take Hwy 35 south 0.6 mi, turn L on East Side Rd for 1.9 mi, and turn L on Old Dalles Dr for 2 mi to a pullout on the R in a pass (*GPS location N45°40.573′ W121°27.718′*). Do not block the county road. The trail climbs 0.9 mile

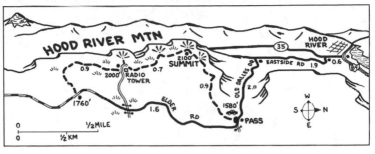

to a summit with a Mt. Hood view and continues 0.7 mile to a radio tower viewpoint. (SDS Lumber Company, 509-493-2155)

MOUNT HOOD - WEST (map on page 155)

158. Wildcat Mountain. Climb a scenic beargrass ridgecrest 4.1 mi to a Mt Hood viewpt, gaining 800 ft. Road access is confused by missing signs. Drive Hwy 26 E of Sandy 2 mi to Shorty's Corner, turn R on Firwood Rd and follow this paved rd through several turns for 3.4 mi to a 4-way jct. Turn L on paved, 2-lane Wildcat Mtn Rd for 8.9 mi to the NF boundary, continue on 1-lane paved Rd 3626 for 9.4 mi to a jct for the old quarry trailhead, and go str uphill for 3.5 mi of pavement and 0.1 mi of gravel. Then turn right on gravel Rd 108 for 0.2 mi to a new trailhead at road's end. Hike straight 0.1 mi to the McIntyre Ridge Tr and turn right. (Z)

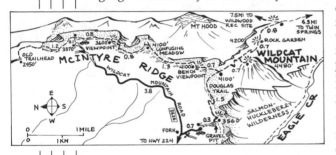

159. Salmon Butte. A road closure has added 1.2 miles to this otherwise popular 4.4-mi trail up through rhodies to a Mt Hood viewpoint. The hike is an athletic challenge, gaining 3170 feet of elevation. Drive as to the Salmon River Tr (Hike #66), but continue 0.5 mi to road's end. (Z)

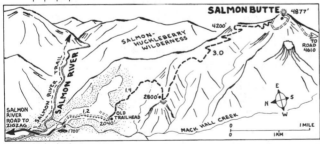

160. East Zigzag Mountain. A rough access road lessens the appeal of this otherwise spectacular hike to a viewpoint and lake on Mt Hood's shoulder. Drive Hwy 26 E of Rhododendron 1.5 mi. Near milepost 46, turn L on paved Rd 27. After 0.6 mi the road becomes a rough, rocky terror. Passenger cars must stop at a switchback after 3.3 mi. Some vehicles continue 1.2 mi to road's end. Hike the Burnt Lk Trail 4 mi up to a ridgecrest jct and turn left for 0.3 mi up to the E Zigzag lookout site. After another 0.7 mi, detour R for 0.6 mi to Cast Lk. Then return

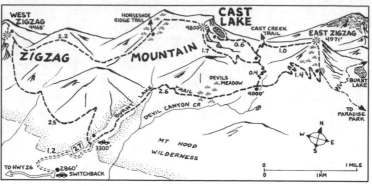

0.6 mi and continue downhill 3 mi to the TH. (Z)

161. Horseshoe Ridge. 5-mi climb to views in beargrass mdw gains 2600 ft, joins Zigzag Mtn Tr (see #160). For 14.5-mi loop, return via Cast L Tr (#162). Drive as to Ramona Falls (#71) but turn R off Rd 1825 on Rd 380 to trailhead at Riley Horse Camp day use area. (Z)

162. Cast Lake. Ascend ridge 2500 ft in 4.3 mi, keep R for 0.9 mi to lake described in Hike #160. Drive as to Ramona Falls (#71) but turn R off Rd 1825 on Rd 380 to Riley Horse Camp day use area. (Z)

163. Yocum Ridge. Very difficult but extremely beautiful, this 8.7-mile route passes Ramona Falls as it climbs 3800 feet to spectacular alpine meadows beside Mt. Hood's Sandy Glacier. From Ramona Falls (see Hike #71), take the Pacific Crest Trail toward Bald Mountain 0.6 mile and turn right up Yocum Ridge 4.7 miles. (Z)

164. Buck Peak. The Pacific Crest Trail follows wooded ridge 7.6 mi N from Lolo Pass to this panoramic lookout site. No camping. (Z)

165. Mazama Trail. Rebuilt by the Mazamas, a Portland outdoor club, this spectacular Mt. Hood trail gains 2500 ft in 4.2 mi up Cathedral Ridge to the Timberline Trail near McNeil Point (see #72 map). From Zigzag, drive Rd 18 for 10.5 mi to Lolo Pass, turn R on gravel McGee Cr Rd 1810 for 5.5 mi, and turn R on Rd 1811 for 2.5 mi. (HR)

166. Huckleberry Mountain Trail. Park just past the group camp at the south end of Lost Lake (see Hike #74), climb 900 ft in 2 mi to the Pacific Cr Tr, and turn R for 3.5 mi to Buck Pk viewpoint. (HR)

167. Flag Mountain. 2.2-mi walk along wooded hill has Mt Hood views, gains 900 ft, ends at rd. Drive Hwy 26 to E edge of Rhododendron, turn S on Rd 20 (2620) for 0.8 mi, turn briefly L on Rd 200. (Z)

168. Paradise Park Trail. Quieter, longer route to famous alpine mdws than from Timberline Lodge (#77) gains 3000 ft in 6.3 mi. Drive 4.1 mi E of Rhododendron on Hwy 26, turn L on Rd 2639 for 1.2 mi. (Z)

169. Hidden Lake. Climb 2 mi to small, viewless lake with rhodies, continue 3 mi to PCT near Zigzag Canyon (see Hike #77). 2800 ft gain. For 13.2-mi loop, return via Paradise Park Tr (#168). Drive 4.1 mi E of Rhododendron on Hwy 26, turn L on Rd 2639 for 2 mi. (Z)

170. Timberline Trail. Classic 39.3-mi backpack route circles Mt Hood from Timberline Lodge (#77). Use maps for Hikes #77, 71-73, 84, 83,

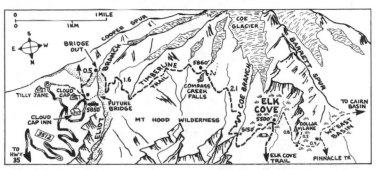

and 81. Allow 3-5 days. Unbridged crossings of Zigzag, Sandy, Muddy Fork, and White Rivers can be dangerous during snowmelt. Water is lower in mornings and after August. Note that a washout at the Eliot Branch has closed the Timberline Trail crossing there (see map), and requires a car shuttle from the the Elk Cove Trailhead (#84) to Cloud Cap (#83). (Z, HR)

171. PCT to Timberline Lodge. Start at Barlow Pass on Hwy 35, gain 2000 ft in 4.9 mi amid flowers, views of White R Canyon. (Z)

172. Veda Lake. 1.2-mi tr to lovely 3-acre lake with huckleberries, Mt Hood view, gains 200 ft, loses 400. Drive as to upper trailhead for Devils Pk Hike #68, but only go 3.5 mi on Rd 2613 to Fir Cr CG. (Z)

173. Upper Salmon River. 5.9-mi loop dips 1200 feet to the Salmon

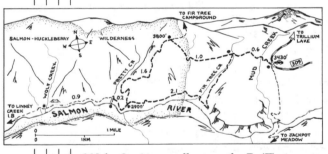

River. Backpackers can continue downstream 11.5-mi to Salmon River Rd (Hike #66). Drive Hwy 26 E of Gov't Camp 3 mi, turn S past Trillium Lk on Rd 2656 for 1.7 mi, turn L to continue on Rd 2656 another 1.8 mi, and go straight onto Rd 309 for 2 mi to a pullout on the R. (Z)

174. Jackpot Meadows Trail. Park as for Hike #173, but descend 1 mi to the Salmon River bridge, and then climb 1.2 mi to Rd 240. The route loses 300 ft, gains 800. Option: Continue 2.5 mi to PCT. (Z)

MOUNT HOOD - EAST (map on page 193)

175. Frog Lake Buttes. Hike to Lower Twin L (see #79), but then follow signs 2.2 mi to Cascade crest panorama at Frog L Butte, also accessible by Rd 290. Follow signs for Frog L to complete 6.3-mi loop. (HR)

176. Barlow Butte. 1.8-mi path to wooded knoll begins at PCT trailhead lot just off Hwy 35 at Barlow Pass. Walk S a few yards, veer L across rd, descend 0.4 mi to mdw, turn L, and climb to Mt Hood viewpoint just past butte's overgrown lookout site. Lose 200 ft, gain 1000. (HR)

177. Boulder Lake via Bonney Meadows. Hike downhill (losing 700 ft) for 1.7 mi to cliff-rimmed lake in ancient forest. Drive Hwy 35 to Bennett

Pass, turn S on miserably rocky Rd 3550 for 4.1 mi, turn R on even rougher Rd 4891 for 1.3 mi, turn L to Bonney Mdws CG. (B)

178. Tilly Jane - Polallie Ridge Loop. Hike up 2.6-mi Tilly Jane Ski Tr with Mt Hood views, flowers to 1924 cookhouse at Tilly Jane CG (see Hike #83), turn L to return 2.9 mi via Polallie Ridge Tr. Gain 2000 ft. Drive as to #83, but only go 1.4 mi on Rd 3512 to tr sign on L. (HR)

179. Zigzag Trail. Switchback up 1200 feet in 1 mile and turn right on the Dog River Trail to a Mt Hood viewpoint. Park at trailhead near milepost 73 on Hwy 35 (see Hike #82 map). (HR)

180. Dog River Trail. Hike 2.1 mi up to a river bridge, then climb a ridge with Mt. Hood views 4.1 mi to paved Rd 44, gaining 2100 ft. Start on Highway 35 near milepost 78. (HR)

181. Surveyors Ridge Trail. Hikable, mostly level 11.7-mi horse/mtn bike path along roaded ridge overlooking Mt Hood includes Bald Butte (Hike #85). To find the southern trailhead, drive Hwy 35 to between mileposts 70 and 71, turn east on Rd 44 for 3.7 mi. (HR)

182. Knebal Spring. 8.5-mile loop climbs wooded ridges, gaining 1800 ft, to a viewpt near Bottle Prairie, crossing some rds and clearcuts. Drive Hwy 35 around Mt. Hood to milepost 70, turn E on paved Rd 44 for 5.3 mi, turn L on paved Rd 1720 for 3 mi to Knebal Spr CG. (B)

183. Fifteenmile Creek. A 10.2-mile loop descends from Fifteenmile Campgd into a forested canyon (losing 1600 ft), and crosses Fifteenmile Creek. The return trail crosses several logging roads. Drive Hwy 35 around Mt. Hood to milepost 70, turn E on paved Rd 44 for 9 mi, turn R on Rd 4420 for 2 mi, and fork L on Rd 2730 for 2 mi. (B)

184. Tygh Creek Trail. Start by creek, climb 1600 ft in 2 mi to wildflowers, views on Pen Point, a knoll in Badger Cr Wilderness. Drive as to Ball Point (Hike #185), but go 1.7 extra miles on Rd 27. (B)

185. Schoolhouse Trail to Ball Point. Climb through pine/oak grass-

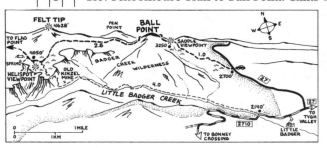

lands with May wildflowers, gaining 1400 ft in 3.6 mi to a pinnacled viewpoint of the Badger Cr Wilderness. Drive to Bonney Crossing (Hike #88), continue north on Rd 2710 another 6.6 mi, turn L on paved Rd 27 for 2.1 mi. (B)

CLACKAMAS FOOTHILLS (map on page 215)

186. Eagle Creek. Often confused with the other Eagle Cr Trail (Hike #51), this little-known path near Estacada follows a creek 6.7 mi through old-growth woods of the Salmon-Huckleberry Wilderness. The unsigned roads to the trailhead have many confusing junctions. Drive Hwy 224 to milepost 19 (4 mi W of Estacada), take Wildcat Mtn Rd 2 mi, continue straight on Eagle Fern Park Rd 2.4 mi, veer R for 1.7 mi, go straight on George Rd 6.3 mi, turn R onto SE Harvey Rd 0.6 mi, turn L for 1.3 mi, fork to the R for 0.1 mi, fork to the R again for 0.6 mi and park. The trail begins as an overgrown road down to the right. (Z) 🥾🐎

187. Old Baldy and Tumala Mtn. Hike to two Salmon-Huckleberry

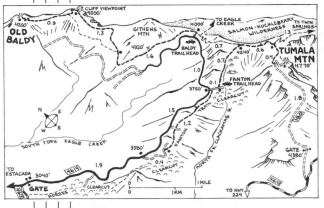

Wilderness viewpoints from a paved backroad. Take Hwy 224 east of Estacada 1.6 miles, turn left on Surface Rd 1.1 mile, and turn right on Tumala Mtn Rd 4614 for 14.4 miles. Just 0.2 mile after the road starts downhill, park in a pullout on the right. Either hike left 3.7 miles to Old Baldy (gaining 1200 feet), or hike to the right 1.7 miles to Tumala Mtn, gaining 930 feet. (C) 🐎

188. Sheepshead Rock. To find this Wilderness viewpt from Estacada,

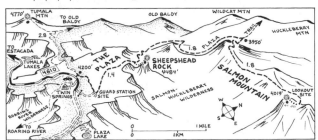

drive Hwy 224 east 6.5 mi, turn left on Rd 4610 for 18.4 gravel miles to primitive Twin Springs CG. Walk back 100 yards, take Plaza Tr 100 feet, and turn right 1.2 mi. Before first switchback, turn right to a clifftop. (C) 🐎

189. Dry Ridge. Steep viewpoint tr from Roaring River CG (on Hwy 224 at milepost 42) switchbacks up 3500 ft in 5.9 mi to Mt Hood view at Grouse Point's beargrass meadow. Connects with Hike #94. (C)

190. Alder Flat. Convenient 0.9-mi path to Clackamas River passes a beaver pond, ends at lovely walk-in campground with 6 picnic tables. Drive 25 mi S of Estacada on Hwy 224 and park on the right, 500 ft before the Ripplebrook store. (C) 🧍🍴🐾

191. Shining Lake. Expect huckleberries, rhodies, and some Mt. Hood views on the 4.3-mi route to this brush-rimmed lake in the Roaring River Wilderness. From Frazier Fork (see Rock Lks Hike #94), hike abandoned road 3.5 mi, descend 600 ft on 0.8-mi tr to R. (C) 🐾🚲🐎

Shining Lake (Hike #191).

192. Cripple Creek Trail. Steep, recently reopened route to Cache

Meadow (see Hike #94 map) gains 2800 ft in 3.6 mi. Drive Hwy 224 east of Estacada 21 mi to Three Lynx and turn L on Rd 200 for a mile to an aqueduct crossing, where a rough trail takes off uphill. (C)

193. Anvil Lake. Level 1.4-mi tr through Blackwolf Mdws to small lake. Drive Hwy 224 through Ripplebrook, turn L on Rd 57 for 7.4 mi, turn L on Rd 58 for 6.2 mi, turn R on Rd 160 for 0.5 mi. (C)

194. Austin Hot Springs. Not recommended because they are on private land, these natural hot pools can only be accessed by wading the cold, wide Clackamas River. From Estacada, drive Hwy 224 east 26 mi to Ripplebrook, continue straight 3.6 mi on Rd 46, and fork left to keep on Rd 46 another 3 mi to riverside pullouts on the right. (C)

195. Whetstone Mountain. Viewpoint of Opal Creek Wilderness and Mt. Jefferson requires a 2.4-mi hike with 1100 ft elevation gain. Drive to Bagby (Hike #95), continue 3 mi on Rd 70, turn left on Rd 7030 for 5.6 mi, turn right on Rd 7020 for 0.7 mi, and turn left on Rd 028. (C)

196. Dickey Creek. Quiet trail to Big Slide Lake in Bull of the Woods

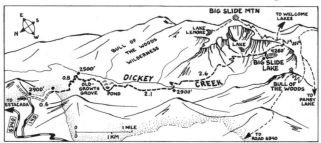

Wilderness loses 500 ft of elevation and then gains 1800 ft in 6.1 mi. Drive Hwy 224 to bridge at Ripplebrook, keep str on Rd 46 for 3.6 mi, turn R on Rd 63 for 5.6 mi, turn R on gravel Rd 6340 for 2.8 mi, turn L on gravel Rd 140 for 0.9 mi. (C)

197. Welcome Lakes. A 5-mi route gains 2000 ft to these small lakes in the Bull of the Woods Wilderness. Drive as to Dickey Cr Hike #196 but go straight on Rd 63 and follow signs to the Elk Lake Trail. (C)

198. Round Lake. Hike gated rd 0.5 mi through old growth to campground, continue on tr 0.5 mi around lake. Drive Hwy 224 south of Estacada 26 mi, go str on Rd 46 for 27.4 mi, turn R on Rd 6350 for 4.8 mi, turn L on Rd 6355 for 0.2 mi, turn L on Rd 150 for 0.8 mi, turn R on Rd 220 for 2 mi, Turn L on Rd 6370 for 3.5 mi. (C)

199. Hawk Mountain. Along the 10-mi Rho Ridge Trail, the route to

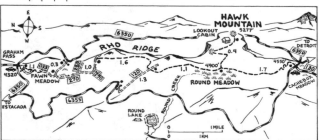

this peak gains 750 feet in 2.1 miles to a cabin with a Mt. Jefferson view. From the crest of paved Rd 46 between Estacada and Detroit, drive 1 mi toward Estacada, turn west on Rd 6350 for 4.8 mi to a 4-way jct, and turn left on Rd 6355 for 0.3 mi to the trailhead, opposite Rd 130. (C)

200. Fish and Si Lakes. Level 1.2-mi path passes Si L to Fish L in dra-

Butte Creek Falls (Hike #203).

matic, forested bowl. Tr continues 1.6 mi across Olallie L Scenic Area to Lower Lake CG. Drive as to Hike #98, but only go 3.4 mi on Rd 4690, turn R on Rd 4691 for 1.5 mi, go R on Rd 120 for 1.2 mi. (C) 🏊🦌🚴🛶

201. Russ and Jude Lakes. Stroll 0.8 mi from Olallie Mdws CG past Brook and Jude Lks to Russ L, view of Olallie Butte. Warm Springs tribal permits req'd for fishing. No camping on Ind Reservation lands. Drive as to Hike #98, but go only 1.4 mi on Rd 4220, veer L to CG. (C) 🥾

202. Ruddy Hill. An easy trail to a lookout site with a front-row view of Mt. Jefferson gains 650 feet in 1.6 miles. Drive to Hike #99, but continue past Olallie Lake on Rd 4220 for 3 miles to Horseshoe Lake. Hike 1 mile up to the Pacific Crest Trail, turn right for 300 yards, and turn left on a very faint path for half a mile to the summit. (C)

203. Butte Creek Falls. These waterfalls in the foothills SE of Molalla spill over the same 15-million-year-old basalt as the more famous Silver Falls. An easy 1-mi loop visits Butte Cr Falls. Nearby Abiqua Falls is on private land and has no developed trail. From exit 10 of I-205 in Oregon City take Hwy 213 south 23 mi. At a flashing yellow light near milepost 23, turn left 2.5 mi to Scotts Mills. Then turn onto Crooked Finger Rd for 11.4 mi and turn left on a large gravel road 1.9 mi, keeping right at junctions, to the Butte Cr Falls Trailhead *(N44°55.277' W122°30.714')*. (Santiam State Forest, 503-945-7200) 🥾🏊

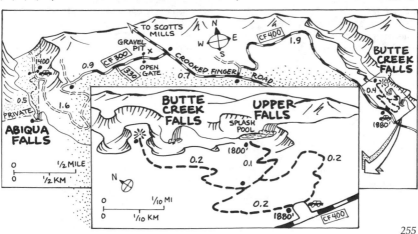

255

Index

100 Hikes in

NORTHWEST OREGON

& SOUTHWEST WASHINGTON

FOURTH EDITION

William L. Sullivan

Navillus Press

Mt. Hood's Paradise Park (Hike #77).

Published by the Navillus Press   *www.oregonhiking.com*
1958 Onyx Street   ISBN 9781939312006
Eugene, Oregon 97403   Printed in USA

Cover: Mt. Hood from Cooper Spur (Hike #83). Inset: Marsh marigold. Spine: Punchbowl Falls. Back cover: Flag Point Lookout. Frontispiece: Moss near Wahkeena Falls
(Hike #46). This page: Coyote Wall (Hike #60).

UPDATES to this book are available at *www.oregonhiking.com*. Corrections and
updates are welcomed and often rewarded. They may be entered online or sent
to the publisher. The author has hiked all 100 of the featured trails, and the trails'
administrative agencies have reviewed the maps and text. Nonetheless, construction,
logging, fires, and storms may cause changes. This book is updated every year.
SAFETY CONSIDERATIONS: Many of the trails in this book pass through Wilderness and remote country where hikers are exposed to unavoidable risks. On any
hike, the weather may change suddenly. The fact that a hike is included in this book,
or that it may be rated as easy, does not necessarily mean it will be safe or easy for
you. Prepare yourself with proper equipment and outdoor skills, and you will be
able to enjoy these hikes with confidence.